The Revisionist Stage salutes the achievements of a revolutionary group of American directors who have galvanized the standard dramatic repertoire by reworking classic theatre into new forms for the contemporary stage. First setting out comprehensive theoretical and practical overviews of the field, Green goes on to present a critical history that features bold directorial ventures by JoAnne Akalaitis, Lee Breuer, Liviu Ciulei, Richard Foreman, Joseph Papp, Lucian Pintilié, Richard Schechner, Peter Sellars, Andrei Serban, Robert Woodruff, and Garland Wright. Green's critique ranges from works grounded in one historical period (Greek and Roman plays) to those authored by one playwright (Shakespeare, Molière, and the operas of Mozart and da Ponte). Specifically discussed are such theatrical events as Serban's *Fragments of a Trilogy*, Breuer's *The Gospel at Colonus* and *Lear*, and Peter Sellars's operatic trilogy.

With singular versatility and insight, Green thus leads the way to a more informed reading of the business of theatrical revision, challenging its claims, celebrating its ingenuities, and conducting a full-scale investigation of a genre remarkable both for its richness and for its ability to arouse spirited public debate.

THE REVISIONIST STAGE

CAMBRIDGE STUDIES IN AMERICAN THEATRE AND DRAMA

General Editor
Don B. Wilmeth, Brown University

Advisory Board
C. W. E. Bigsby, University of East Anglia
Errol Hill, Dartmouth College
C. Lee Jenner, independent critic and dramaturge
Bruce A. McConachie, College of William and Mary
Brenda Murphy, University of Connecticut
Laurence Senelick, Tufts University

Books in the series:
Amy S. Green, *The Revisionist Stage: American Directors Reinvent the Classics*
Samuel Hay, *African American Theatre*
Marc Robinson, *The Other American Drama*

THE REVISIONIST STAGE
AMERICAN DIRECTORS
REINVENT THE CLASSICS

AMY S. GREEN

City University of New York

CAMBRIDGE
UNIVERSITY PRESS

CAMBRIDGE UNIVERSITY PRESS
Cambridge, New York, Melbourne, Madrid, Cape Town, Singapore, São Paulo

Cambridge University Press
The Edinburgh Building, Cambridge CB2 2RU, UK

Published in the United States of America by Cambridge University Press, New York

www.cambridge.org
Information on this title: www.cambridge.org/9780521453431

First published 1994
This digitally printed first paperback version 2006

A catalogue record for this publication is available from the British Library

Library of Congress Cataloguing in Publication data
Green, Amy S.
The revisionist stage : American directors reinvent the classics / Amy S. Green.
p.   cm. – (Cambridge studies in American theatre and drama)
Includes bibliographical references.
ISBN 0-521-45343-7
1. Theatre – Production and direction.   2. Canon (Literature)
I. Title.   II. Series.
IN PROCESS
792′.0233′092273 – dc20   94–15310
CIP

ISBN-13 978-0-521-45343-1 hardback
ISBN-10 0-521-45343-7 hardback

ISBN-13 978-0-521-02892-9 paperback
ISBN-10 0-521-02892-2 paperback

For Steven

CONTENTS

■ ● ■

vii

LIST OF ILLUSTRATIONS

List of Illustrations

PREFACE
■ ❀ ■

The Revisionist Stage: American Directors Reinvent the Classics salutes the vision
and talents of a group of artists who, depending on one's perspective, have
either revitalized or disfigured canonical dramas by adapting them for the
contemporary American stage. The directors' strategies range from the austere to the audacious, and my attempt to cast a net wide enough to encom-
pass their remarkably diverse body of work may be as foolhardy as turning a
classic text on its ear. In fact, no verb exists in the standard theatrical vocabulary to represent what revisionist directors do to, or with, classic plays in
production. It occurs to me that a convenient catchall term will obviate a
string of long and awkward paraphrases of that idea. So, with full awareness
that clever neologisms are the bane of postmodern criticism, I propose to use
"rewright" and "rewrighting" in this discussion. Derived from "playwright,"
the new coinage distinguishes a director's revision from a new author's "re-
writing" of an old play (as Brecht, Anouilh, Stoppard). Its spelling also un-
derscores the idea that these directors craft or shape old scripts into new theatrical events.

   The study begins with a theoretical overview of the practice in the United States since 1968. That is followed by a summary of historical precedents
in Europe and America. Each of the subsequent four chapters focuses, for
purpose of comparison, on productions of plays from a single period or by
a single dramatist. Chapter 3 covers Greek and Roman plays; Chapter 4,
Shakespeare; Chapter 5, Molière; and Chapter 6 takes a detour into opera,
specifically the trilogy of Mozart-da Ponte operas directed by Peter Sellars
in the 1980s. The chosen productions represent a cross-section of the field
rather than an encyclopedic account of all activity. The concluding essay,
Chapter 7, takes a final look at rewrighting in the context of postmodernism.

xi

Preface

I like Goethe's tripartite formula for analyzing works of art. He advises critics to determine what the artist was trying to do before judging how well it was done and whether or not it was worth doing. The routine seems particularly useful here because this directorial approach is inherently idiosyncratic. Interpretive misunderstandings often occur at the first, crucial step. Wherever possible, I allow the directors to articulate their thoughts about their work, either through published statements or personal interviews. In a few cases, a closely involved third party provides the inside story. On the other hand, first-person accounts must be balanced by those of outside observers. Thus, critical reception is also given a prominent hearing. So heated is the rhetoric on all sides of this debate that I often find it irresistible to quote at length.

Mine has been an invigorating journey through these bold and surprising productions. Paramount among the challenges in writing about them has been to avoid being hoodwinked beyond sound judgment by either the directors' theatrical dazzle and persuasive rationales, or by critical explanations that are more engaging than the works they seek to elucidate. At the same time, I have tried to remain open to the possibility that the seemingly outrageous may have unexpected merits. Like the precarious business of reinventing classic plays for the stage, it is a tightrope act that requires a delicate balance of wonder and skepticism.

At various stops along the way, I have been inspired and assisted by the wisdom, insight, and generosity of the following people, whom I would like to thank: JoAnne Akalaitis, Gregory Mosher, Joseph Papp, Richard Schechner, Peter Sellars, Andrei Serban, and Alisa Solomon for personal interviews; Professors Albert Bermel, Marvin Carlson, Daniel Gerould, Stanley Kauffmann, and Gordon Rogoff of the City University of New York Graduate School, for encouragement and guidance; my colleagues at Kingsborough Community College, CUNY; Julius Novick and Gerald Rabkin; the press staffs of the American Repertory Theatre, Arena Stage, the Goodman Theatre, the Guthrie Theatre, La MaMa ETC, Mabou Mines, and the New York Shakespeare Festival for research support; Don B. Wilmeth, for shepherding the manuscript revision with warmth and tact; T. Susan Chang, Michael Gnat, Julie Greenblatt, and Janet Polata at Cambridge University Press; David Berreby, Meg Hertz, Michael Ratomski, and Barbara Drum Sullivan for their friendship; and my loving and supportive family, Frances and Seymour Green, and Steven, Jean-Marc, and Rebecca Ann Gorelick, without whom I'd be lost.

1

REINVENTING CLASSIC THEATRE
≡ ✦ ≡

A classic is classic not because it conforms to
certain structural rules, or fits certain definitions
(of which its author had quite probably never
heard). It is classic because of a certain eternal
and irrepressible freshness.
        EZRA POUND[1]

It is the malleability of a classic that we should
celebrate, not simply its age.
        CHARLES MAROWITZ[2]

Whatever you do on stage must = the public at
the time you stage it.
        PETER SELLARS[3]

CLASSICAL REVIVAL has always meant revision. Ever since
the Romans adapted Greek dramas to their own rougher tastes and
times, dramatic works from previous eras have undergone inevitable
metamorphoses in subsequent centuries. During the Renaissance ancient
scripts were reformulated to conform to neoclassical ideals. Davenant and
Tate regularized Shakespeare for Restoration and eighteenth-century audiences. The actor-managers trimmed the great plays to intensify the focus on
the starring role. Photographs of William Poel's turn-of-the-century "Elizabethan" reconstructions look unmistakably Edwardian to us today.[4] Every
theatrical age remakes the classics in its own image, and with the wisdom of
hindsight these "improvements" tell us much about the *zeitgeist* of the times
in which they were made.

So what of a theatrical moment that remakes *Oedipus at Colonus* as a gospel opera? Relocates a redneck female Lear to rural Georgia? Characterizes
Harpagon's children as near-clones of their miserly father? Sets *Così fan Tutte*
in a diner on Long Island? American directors since the late 1960s have reinvented cherished plays and operas from the past in maverick stagings that

1

defy traditional bounds of directorial license and assert the validity of the American experience. Lee Breuer, Andrei Serban, Peter Sellars, JoAnne Akalaitis, and others have knocked playscripts off their Victorian pedestals into an egalitarian stew of theatrical signs and gestures that may alter, clarify, contradict, criticize, demystify, dislocate, update, or otherwise reimagine the subject text on stage. By abandoning the modernist quest for historical authenticity and the definitive production, these directors have, for better and worse, opened up a seemingly infinite range of theatrical possibilities for classic scripts.

Their work has provoked enough vehement response from both ends of the critical spectrum over the past twenty-five years to have restored the classics (and debate about their production) to the forefront of the American theatrical consciousness. On one hand, there is nothing historically unusual about the way the classics have been treated on American stages since the countercultural revolution of the 1960s: In centuries-old tradition, plays whose central themes resonate with contemporary concerns are adapted to make them more accessible and appealing to contemporary audiences. On the other hand, because contemporary revisionist productions of the classics maintain original texts in radically altered theatrical presentations, they are distinctly different from the literary adaptations that came before. It is this essential contradiction between a familiar, well-established text and its all-new theatrical idiom that marks contemporary classical revival as the unique product of our specific theatrical, cultural, and historical milieu.

DIRECTORS' PERSPECTIVES

While the most radical reinventions have come in the wake of the sixties' countercultural revolution, Americans have been tampering with the classics since the nineteenth century. Many, from the self-centering actor-managers to Augustin Daly and David Belasco, adapted Shakespeare's plays to feature leading actors and cater to popular tastes. With the emergence of the modern American director in the 1920s and 1930s, the staging of classics took a decidedly conceptual turn. Some directors put their marks on established texts by updating or otherwise altering the historical or geographical setting. Orson Welles turned *Julius Caesar* into a meditation on 1930s Italian fascism. Tyrone Guthrie set *Troilus and Cressida* against the battles of World War I. Liviu Ciulei transplanted Molière's *Don Juan* to fin-de-siècle Paris.

A second, more abstract, technique is to strip away all realistic trappings in favor of an abstract metaphorical milieu. Richard Schechner and Andrei Serban each did that when they attempted environmental productions of

Greek and Roman drama in hopes of unleashing the plays' primal emotional powers.

A popular postmodernist approach is to deconstruct the formidable edifice of received meaning by interjecting a spate of anachronistic references. Lucian Pintilié directed a time-warped *Tartuffe* that began in the Garden of Eden and ended at Armageddon. Peter Sellars took a similar tack with *Pericles*, and JoAnne Akalaitis was skewered in the press for hastening the hapless heroine of *Cymbeline* to Milford Haven atop a Victorian velocipede. The aggregate impact of such jumbled images gives new meaning to the old sense of classical "timelessness."

In the 1950s, Guthrie liked to fend off his critics by claiming that he was just "jollying up" the classics to make them less academic and more appealing, but his 1964 memoirs reveal a more serious directorial agenda. "If classics are to be fresh and not preserved in a sort of aspic of uncritical reverence," he wrote, "then there must be constant experiment with their production." Otherwise, he found, actors tend "to feel that they must grope for 'style' which consists of getting into elegant attitudes, tapping snuff boxes, waving fans and lace handkerchiefs and in general carrying-on in a very fancy way," that prevents them from making deeper connections with classic texts.[5]

Besides, Guthrie believed, not even the geniuses who wrote the classics comprehended their infinite complexity. "Were it possible to find out, I would lay any money that Shakespeare had only the vaguest idea of what he was writing when he wrote *Hamlet,* that the major part of the meaning of it eluded him because it proceeded from the subconscious."[6] In the meeting of a text's hidden treasures and a director's insights, Guthrie saw the opportunity to make "personal comments" through the staging of the play. His only rule was that directors not be hampered by their own timidity:

> There is a certain impertinence in relating yourself to a great master and saying, Well now, I've got to interpret you and it's going to be done my way. But Shakespeare ain't here to defend himself. . . . And I think that the conscientious artist has no alternative but to take his courage in both hands, shut his eyes, hold his nose and jump in, and do it the best he knows.

After all, Guthrie insisted, "controversy is far healthier than acquiescence."[7]

By the 1980s, the whole concept of "great masters" had been widely debunked. Literary and performance theorists had affirmed the inability of authors to have more than "the vaguest idea" of what they had written. Poststructuralist criticism had shifted the focus of analysis from internal, sub-

3

conscious impulses to the external, social and historical forces that impinge on the creation of any cultural "product." "Texts" were being "deconstructed," and Barthes had declared the author dead. In the theatre, Artaud-inspired experiments as far back as the 1960s had challenged not only the primacy but the necessity of the playscript in creating performances.

Revisionist directors working in the climate created by critic-theorists like Derrida and Barthes have, if not actually read about deconstruction, absorbed its general outlines through cultural osmosis. They sense that texts are "unstable" and "interactive," and that authors are less reliable sources of meaning (and stage directions) than we once believed. Where once it was assumed that playwrights' intentions could be discerned and "realized" by productions that "served" the play, playwrights' authority, like that of authors in general, is no longer universally considered absolute. Now it is the classic play that serves the production as catalyst, reference point, or fertile ground from which directors and their collaborators may cultivate new theatrical works. In our age of interpretation, directors of progressive and experimental bent take for granted their liberty to remake, rework, "rewright" what venerable playwrights have wrought.

By the early 1990s revisionist productions were in fact the norm. Audiences for the classics are now very much interested in what the director "does to" the play. Productions are advertised and remembered by the director's appellation. We speak of Breuer's *Lear,* Serban's *Miser,* Sellars's *Marriage of Figaro.* Given that circumstance, one could expect to find an environment receptive to such productions, but directors are still frequently forced to defend their rights to exercise interpretive muscle in a dead playwright's absence. In a 1985 interview, Pintilié bristled against those who attacked his work on the basis of violating tradition. "But what is tradition?" the director asked rhetorically:

> What they mean are preconceptions, lack of surprises . . . But no one knows tradition. No one has the right to say "This is what Molière wanted." Yes, I want to express my vision, but only after careful and deep study of the play, after months of exploration. I want it to be un-predictable, even to myself. . . . But even when I express an ostensibly radically different point of view about a play, I believe I remain faithful to it. The worst thing is to kneel before a lot of sacrosanct prejudices. It is best when the obsessions of a modern artist collide with a great work. The miracle of great works is that they can be looked at in new ways every seven years and remain strong and new and surprising.[8]

4

Jonathan Miller claimed even broader directorial license: "I don't believe one has any duty or obligation to an author once he's dead. The play becomes a public object. One should be able to do to it exactly what one wants."[9] In fact, he defines directorial tampering with a classic as a form of tribute. "With the passage of time, Shakespeare's plays have quite properly assumed the status of myths, and it is the honourable fate of all great myths to suffer imaginative distortions at the hands of those to whom they continue to give consolation and nourishment."[10]

Not surprisingly, the absence of the classic playwright is exactly what appeals to adventurous, classically oriented directors. Garland Wright says he denies himself "interpretive fiat" when he directs a brand-new script. The first production should be definitive. It should set the author's intentions for posterity: "The archeology that the director leaves must be the accurate version of what the playwright meant. . . . I leave the interpretive fun for artists who come later." The challenge and the fun of directing a classic play, on the other hand, is that "one is left with the archeological remains of some theatrical event which was specific to its times and social context, and one must *reinvent* it."[11]

Andrei Serban is quite blunt about why he prefers directing the classics: "If you work with a living playwright sitting next to you, there's tension. If you do nothing to his plays, he gets upset: 'Why don't you do something?' If you do something, its always too much. What do I need it for? I prefer dead playwrights!" And what if the playwright somehow showed up at a rehearsal? "Then what he said would be it."[12] But Serban and his colleagues have little cause to fear the sudden arrival and retribution of bygone dramatists. As Guthrie once observed, "the authors of most of the plays that really demand the author's presence at rehearsal are unavoidably prevented from being there by a previous engagement which not even the greatest of mortals can decline."[13]

CRITICAL RESISTANCE

So who, if anyone, is looking out for the interests of dead playwrights? There are, of course, critics who simply cringe at this kind of theatre and are adamant about limiting the margins of directorial play. This is the contingent to whom Herbert Blau refers when he cautions that "Now, when you experiment with the classics, you have to be careful. You risk the chastening assault of a Sunday column in the *New York Times*. Academic scholarship – which was always discomfited by Shakespeare Our Contemporary – feels doubly fortified."[14] Opposing critics often sound like self-appointed guardians of the canon.

Back in the 1950s, Eric Bentley deplored "bright idea" Shakespeare and insisted that any production of the plays be at least 90 percent Bard. With uncharacteristic fuzziness, Bentley warned that Shakespeare should be changed only when a particular play is determined "1. unacceptable; 2. incommunicable; or 3. uninteresting" to a modern audience. Otherwise, he said, he expects to be shown

> the meaning the play had when first written, not any subsequent increment, and certainly not any separate "modern" meaning. The modernities I demand are not those which the director imposes on Shakespeare but those which he finds in Shakespeare. All he can impose is, at best, a modern frame to the picture, and even the modernity of the frame may often be only a more authentic historicity.[15]

In a similar vein, Stanley Kauffmann has complained that "modernization is often egotistical intrusion by a director who feels compelled to have a 'concept' or else is an implicit confession of inability to handle the play in period."[16] Likewise, Gordon Rogoff drips sarcasm when he recognizes "our friend the director with a *concept.*"[17] Moira Hodgson says she recoils whenever she hears that

> some enterprising director has jumped in the deep end with a "controversial new interpretation" of a classic. I feel, to paraphrase Mayakovsky, like reaching for my gun. . . . Does that cast a new light on the work at hand, or is the director simply granting himself the license to turn a classic upside down?[18]

Allan Wallach tosses in this little salvo: "Most of the time, it's only the director who's served by director's theatre. On the strength of a few meretricious embellishments, someone of modest abilities can share credit for a playwright's genius – a kind of gilt by association."[19]

In a 1987 *Saturday Review* article entitled "Directors vs. Playwrights," Richard Gilman argues that conceptual productions reflect directors' arrogant attitude that "the classics are in need of rehabilitation, as though they were wounded, decrepit, abject victims of time." In these new-fangled productions, "anachronism, discordance, idiosyncrasy reign, and a new vision, inferior in its very *au courantism,* is substituted for the old,"[20] Gilman writes, hinting that directors should restrain themselves from doing more than oversee the strict translation of a playwright's instructions to theatrical dimensions. He quotes Jacques Copeau, who said, "Let us hope for a dramatist who replaces or eliminates the director . . . rather than for professional directors who pretend to be dramatists,"[21] and Louis Jouvet, who charged that "the profession of the director suffers from the disease of immodesty."[22]

Of course, Gilman's hypothetical portrait of the servile director is a mirage. He himself concedes that "between any written text and its physical realization on stage is a zone of uncertainty, incompleteness, an area where interpretation is exactly what's necessary."[23] His argument, then, pivots on the breadth of that uncertain zone. The limits of what a director can do, he insists, "are set within the text itself. . . . They have to do with coherence, aesthetic appropriateness, plausibility, and with the imaginative and intellectual vision of a work, its tone, weight, and individuality."[24] But, as we shall see, some of the most revelatory and imaginative productions of these plays in the past twenty-five years soared on daring directorial inventions that deliberately contradict and/or subvert previous notions of the text's "individuality."

The great fallacy of such critical exhortations is the underlying notion that the plays require defending. No matter how seriously we take the deconstructionist challenge to the viability of texts, plays remain intact after the most inspired, invasive, perverse, or just plain silly directorial rewrightings are over. Revisionist productions may erase preconceived notions, but they cannot eradicate the text. Unscathed scripts remain available to be read, analyzed, interpreted, and produced in (or close to) the form in which their authors bequeathed them to future generations. Bad productions reflect badly on the producers, not the proven play. In these types of stagings, it is inevitably the director who takes the blame for a botched job. No classic worthy of its stature could be toppled by a single misguided production, or even a series of them.

Still, so dangerous a business is the contemporary approach to directing canonical dramatic texts that some directors are loath to admit the extent of their own invention. Many deny having done anything "to" the plays at all. Some insist that their versions are what the playwright would have written were he (they're all dead white males in this category) alive today. Some degree of self-imposed naïveté may be at work here, but it would be equally naive to discount the disclaimers as coy excuses by guilt-ridden manhandlers of dramatic masterpieces. A more satisfying explanation is that this style of work is a natural, perhaps even inevitable, phase in the evolution of the art of directing. It does not seem aberrant to its practitioners (or its fans) because it flows so smoothly from its various historical antecedents.

7

HISTORICAL CONTEXTS

Three major twentieth-century developments in the theatre and in the broader cultural community converge in the story of classical revival in America since the late 1960s. First is the evolution of directing. Second is the general discrediting of authors, authority, and language as bearers of meaning or truth. Third is the emergence over the course of the American century of our popular culture to a position of global dominance. Each of these has helped pave the way for American directors to approach classic scripts with an almost audacious confidence and sense of autonomy.

The Rise of the Director

The rise of the professional director to theatrical power and prominence has been nothing less than meteoric in the little more than a hundred years since the Duke of Saxe-Meiningen took command of a troupe of amateur players. At the end of the nineteenth century, directors were welcomed into the theatre as reformers whose purpose was to correct sloppy scenic excess by unifying the elements of production in the service of the playwright's text. In *Theatre Under Deconstruction?*, Stratos Constantinidis describes the mission of the first directors as "logocentric." They perceived themselves as diviners of the author's meaning and facilitators of that message to the audience via the theatrical media of gesture, scenery, lighting, costumes, and, most important, the speaking of the words. In this model of the director's function, "the play-text and the playwright" are understood to be "the origin from which meanings flow to the rest of the theatre artists," and from them to the audience. Playwrights enjoy the "privilege of origin," at the top of a strict hierarchical power structure that positions directors a distant second in command.[25]

If in the early days playwrights maintained theoretical dominion over the play-production system, directors quickly assumed artistic control in the real world of rehearsal and production. Rivalry for ownership and authority over the staged play seems inherent to the process. Collaborations between playwrights and directors have been tempestuous affairs from the beginning. It was not long before ambitious directors sought alternative working arrangements. Within a generation a new strain of initiator-directors, spearheaded by Gordon Craig, asserted their creative autonomy from the playwright. Ironically, notes Constantinidis, Craig's directorial model did not actually break down the hierarchical system of play production. Instead, the "playwright-god" was merely supplanted in his throne by the new "director-guru."[26]

8

Craig's influential descendents in the director's theatre include the likes of Meyerhold, Brecht, Artaud, Grotowski, and Brook, as well as such self-generating director-dramatists as Robert Wilson, Pina Bausch, Richard Foreman, and Martha Clarke. Although the directors of concern to our study of classical reinvention opt to work with established texts, they too belong in this theatrical line. (See Chapter 2 for a more complete history.)

Deconstruction, Performance Theory, and Directing

The theatre's antiliterary prejudice is itself part of the second major cultural influence on contemporary classical production, namely, the late-twentieth-century trend toward the suspicion of text. Unfortunately, much of the prose dedicated to this critical stance is painfully convoluted and obscure, which inadvertently provides good cause for readers to suspect the value of these particular texts. Extracting sense from deconstructionist writing requires patience and determination. Fortunately, a few performance theorists have managed to cull and translate into plain speech some principles and perspectives applicable to the current discourse.

In the most simplistic terms, we can trace the death of the word as near-sacred conveyor of essential truths and reliable meanings to two historical phenomena. The first is Freud's revelation of the unconscious influences over human speech and behavior. His discoveries revolutionized the concept of what a word, phrase, or action "means." Since Freud, everything is open to interpretation. The second factor is the proliferation of distortion, euphemism, and lying in much of the technologically distributed mass communication that has served the century's worst perpetrators of totalitarianism, mass destruction, and economic oppression. Over time, an increasingly literate public grew to distrust authorities and their utterances, and, eventually, language itself. The chain of poststructuralist theory that reflects this skepticism goes back at least to the 1910s, when Saussure showed us that words were mere signifiers, meaningless except by reference to the signified objects, ideas, or actions they represent.

Derrida went further, asserting that words have no fixed referents, only other words in a slippery chain of meaning that never rests on terra firma because our only way of knowing the world is through the words we assign to our sensory experience. Even such elusive meaning changes with context and circumstance. Thus, Derrida posits, all meanings and all texts are unstable and can have no fixed or correct interpretation. Reading becomes an act of *creating with* rather than *receiving* meaning *from* a text. It is in this context that Barthes declared the death of the author as that logocentric being in whom meaning originates and from whom it flows to passive receivers.

Directors who reinvent classic texts on stage are theatrical cousins to those critic-theorists whose "readings" of literature are considered literary works in their own right. Although few of these directors confess to having read much literary criticism, they approach plays as what Barthes calls "methodological fields" for theatrical exploration. As early as 1959, Francis Hodge had chronicled the director's ever-increasing assumption of critical duties: "In the late 19th century [the director] came into the theatre to organize and he stayed to criticize."[27]

As we shall see, the degree of directorial "misreading" or violence toward established texts varies widely. Compare the simplistic transfer of historical setting by which a New York Shakespeare Festival production dropped *The Taming of the Shrew* into the pioneer days of the American West, to the Wooster Group's media-drenched performance pieces. The Group incorporates into its collage-style productions bits and pieces of modern classics, from Chekhov to *Death of a Salesman,* in order to expose their underlying self-contradictions. The *Shrew*'s method, which Robert Brustein calls the "simile" approach (see p. 13), depends primarily on design rather than a profound rereading or critique of the text. The Wooster Group assaults its scripts, their performance and reception histories, and performers' and spectators' familiar, complacent ideas about the plays.[28]

In *Staging Shakespeare,* Ralph Berry defends the inventions of the directors included in his book by asserting that "meanings are not lexical absolutes. Meanings are generated by community and history. . . . It is, then, a complete naïveté to speak of the 'meaning' of a Shakespeare play as an entity that can be defined, established, and placed on record in perpetuity."[29] He rightly labels contemporary directing "an act of criticism."[30] Likewise, Brustein has referred to the "directorial essay."[31]

In his 1983 article for the *Performing Arts Journal,* "The Play of Misreading: Theatre/Text/Deconstruction," Gerald Rabkin cuts through the jargon that encumbers much deconstructionist writing to apply the perspective to just this kind of theatrical production. Deconstructive critics, he explains, surrender the authority to make final pronouncements about texts, and engage instead in open-ended dialogue with them. Deconstruction's goal is perpetual discourse with the elusive text. The critic's function, says Rabkin, is to "unknot the tangle and set the text's elements in motion once more." Reading thus, as we have seen, becomes a creative faculty as privileged as writing, and "the border between art and interpretation is erased."[32]

"Since the director is the main instrument of interpretation in the theatre of our time," writes Rabkin, "the playwright holds no more privilege over the director than literature holds over criticism."[33] Deconstruction refutes the idea that there is such a thing as an original text, one that is not in fact the synthesized by-product of earlier works. Therefore, neither the critic's reading nor the director's production should be considered second-class derivations. Both are new branches on the source script's extended family tree, although, Rabkin concedes, "so ingrained is our assumption that the critic's job is to read *correctly* – and the director's job to interpret the playwright correctly – that such a strategy seems willfully perverse."[34]

"The play's the thing, we used to say," recalls Herbert Blau, "as if we knew what the play was."[35] Contemporary productions are the result of "intertextuality" among the script, its performance history, and the idiosyncratic theatrical expression of the director's (and designers', actors', etc.) responses to the text. Like the *auteur* filmmaker, the stage director has become, to borrow Meyerhold's phrase, the author of an original theatrical event.

The Global Emergence of American Popular Culture

The third major historical development that has shaped recent American stagings of classic drama is the emergence of this country in the twentieth century as the global superpower in politics, military strength, world economy, and culture. Despite the negative consequences of American military and capitalist interventions, we seem, over the course of the American century, to have shed much of our identity as Europe's cultural stepchild. The worldwide dissemination of American popular culture, from movies and television programs to Coke, McDonalds, and Disneyland, attests to this newfound, if dubious, cultural dominance.

The presence of American popular imagery in contemporary stagings of classic plays is, in part, a product of this phenomenon. It is as if American directors, buoyed by our global omnipresence, have rejected once and for all pseudo-European theatrical tradition and mannerisms and asserted that American idioms are worthy of inclusion in classical productions. This has been going on since the 1950s when, for example, Katharine Hepburn starred in a Texan *Much Ado About Nothing* (1957) and the characters from *The Winter's Tale* were dressed as Tarot cards (1958), both at Stratford, Connecticut. In the 1980s, Peter Sellars set *Ajax* in the Pentagon and *Antony and Cleopatra* around the pool of a Holiday Inn. Of course when such transplanted settings constitute the entire conceptual underpinning of a production, this strategy is reductionist. Sellars tends to knead text and trappings into a more profound synthesis. Yet there is a way in which the upstart, entrepreneurial spirit of these productions as a whole seems especially well-suited to the mythic American personality.

FRAMING NEW CRITICAL PERSPECTIVES

Of course, not every directorial essay on a classic text works. Herein lies the essential critical problem in dealing with these productions. If conscious breaks with tradition and assertions of uniquely personal directorial concepts are the hallmarks of these theatre pieces, what criteria can be used to judge their relative merits? How far afield can directors go? Is there a formula for determining how much directorial invention is too much? Do traditional critical standards still apply? Fortunately for the current purpose, critics have not been reticent on the subject.

It is unlikely that any formula could cover the myriad approaches directors have taken to rewrighting dramatic masterpieces for the contemporary stage. It would be similarly unproductive to try to categorize them as a homogeneous lot. "Any attempt to foist a generalization wide enough to cover" them all, wrote cynical, scissor-happy Shakespeare collagist Charles Marowitz, "must produce one of those phoney definitions to which academics are so prone: a kind of new nomenclature which, once devised, is employed to bend a multitude of divergent tendencies into something like an orderly system."[36]

As head of the Yale School of Drama in the 1960s and 1970s, and of the American Repertory Theatre Institute for Advanced Theatre Training in Cambridge, Massachusetts, since 1986, Robert Brustein has insisted that directing and design students work with "production concepts." As artistic director of Yale Rep and the American Repertory Theatre, as well as a working critic, he has been a long-standing, ardent advocate and practitioner of the approach. He wrestled with its critical slipperiness in a 1967 essay that urged American directors to heed Artaud's call for "No More Masterpieces." Brustein wanted American directors to venture into territories unknown beyond grim, prim, pseudo-British monuments to highbrow culture. "Only recently has literature taken on the inviolability of scripture,"[37] he noted as he urged American directors to cast off the shackles of tradition. His only hesitation at opening this theatrical Pandora's box was that he was unable to offer any prescriptions, though he felt responsible to articulate some guidelines.

Just what distinguishes a valid work of conceptual theatre is elusive. The dangers of this line of attack are obvious: everything depends upon the tact, taste, and talent of the director. If new values are not unearthed by a new approach . . . the effort is worthless, and if these new values are merely eccentric or irresponsible, then it is careerism rather than art that has been served.[38]

Charles Marowitz is similarly reluctant to pin the process down to a set of rules. "Describing ways in which a classic can be rethought on stage," he decides, "would be tantamount to giving lessons in original thinking."[39]

In a 1988 survey of developments since 1967, however, Brustein reiterated his position and put forth a rudimentary formula for distinguishing between two general categories of conceptual work, one of which he clearly prefers.[40] "Simile" productions, he writes, are those in which directors redeposit plays wholesale into different historical or geographical contexts. He calls this approach "prosaic," and adds that "directors who are fond of similes assume that because a play's action is *like* something from a later period, its environment can be changed accordingly." Other directors, Brustein says, conceptualize their productions on the basis of a "poetic metaphor." These artists "are more interested in generating provocative theatrical images . . . that are suggestive of the play rather than specific, reverberant rather than concrete."[41] The simile–metaphor analogy is useful, but caution must be taken not to succumb to it as an oversimplified formula for what is "good" or "bad" in revisionist classical production.

Directorial reinvention continues to defy more direct description. Analogies abound: Marowitz insists it must entail a "head-on confrontation with the intellectual substructure of the plays."[42] Grotowski described his own work as a meeting with the text. Jan Kott, whose *Shakespeare Our Contemporary* gave the movement an added boost, uses a more violent metaphor:

Grotowski says that the director meets and does not realize a text. I prefer another notion – that of *collision*. The classics become alive when a collision takes place: the collision of a classical text with a new political and intellectual experience, as well as the collision of the classical text with new theatrical techniques.[43]

Not surprisingly, physician-trained director Jonathan Miller draws his models in *Subsequent Performances* from biology. He compares the script to genetic material that transmits coded instructions to future generations, although the physical manifestations of those instructions will depend greatly on the circumstances of their expression. Once the playtext enters its "afterlife," Miller writes, "the indeterminacy of the text begins to assert itself,"[44] as it moves through its "emergent evolution" from production to production. Miller, too, stumbles in the attempt to define the limits of directorial invention. He suggests that "common sense, tact, and literary sensitivity" should govern their interpretations. A great play, Miller reminds us, is not a "Rorschach inkblot into whose indeterminate outlines the director can project whatever he wants."[45] We know the director has gone too far when "it is difficult to identify any organic continuity between the production in question and its predecessors, and the work appears to be *quoted* rather than *produced.*"[46]

Gerald Rabkin also worries over how to measure the merits of specific directorial "misreadings":

> But how, then, does one avoid excusing weak or banal productions as necessary deconstructive strategies? How does the audience, the critic, discern which directorial "manhandling" is valid, which simplistic reduction or mere caprice? Deconstruction does not assert that anything goes, that all interpretation is equal.[47]

Unfortunately, the criteria he offers are as elusive as anyone else's:

> a strong misreading must be rigorous, tied to a theoretical framework meticulously expressed. It must lead to the dissemination, not closure of the text. It must affirm play and produce pleasure in the reader/audience. Above all, it must be strong, indelible. . . . There is no formula by which strength can be measured. The audience, the critic, and time, the severest critic of all, will attest whether strength has been achieved.[48]

There are good reasons why some people are uncomfortable with directors who press their own theatrical agendas against established dramatic masterpieces. Playwrights and their words, texts, scripts have occupied the topmost seat in the theatrical hierarchy for a very long time. The encroachment of reinterpreting directors whose creative media are primarily physical rather than literary threatens that long-standing, Aristotelian equilibrium. Besides, the status of classical production is considered a good measure of the health of a nation's theatre, and risky, revisionist classics, especially successful ones, upset the status quo. Inferior ones, and there are plenty of them, may not send readers scurrying back to reevaluate standard texts, and they reflect badly on the national theatrical competence.

In any case, the heightened rhetoric that surrounds directorial rewrighting of classic plays reflects the fact that these productions cut to the heart of fundamental questions about the nature of theatre in the twentieth century: What is the relationship between play text and performance? Does a script's age and/or classic stature affect that relationship? What are the director's boundaries? Does the selection of a classic text impose certain obligations, or does the dead playwright's absence from rehearsals give directors carte blanche? What are the practical and implicit dynamics of power in the play-production system? How can the validity of a directorial reworking be determined? Who, if anyone, has the final say?

In *Performing Drama/Dramatizing Performance*, Michael Vanden Heuvel notes that

> the relationship between drama and performance is not as stable as we might have once believed. No longer can we accept a linear, Newtonian model that describes the text and its affects as the absolute reference for measuring theatrical work, and performance as merely an "illustration," "translation," or even "fulfillment" of that text (Carlson 1985, 6). Instead, we are forced to look for new metaphors to describe a more complex relationship, a new language that captures the dynamics between drama and performance.[49]

The most promising way to seek a new vocabulary to deal with these important questions is through close examination of individual productions. The overriding result of America's classical theatre experience in the past four decades, as Brustein puts it, has been a new perspective that holds "that classical theatre [is] a continuum of images and experiences and not simply an event frozen in the past."[50] In the hands of innovative directors, the classics have been made to absorb and/or confront the issues and aesthetics of America's turbulent, fragmented, and cynical century. Through these controversial productions, we have revised our views of the plays and they, in turn, have reflected images of us.

2

HISTORICAL PRECEDENTS IN
EUROPE AND AMERICA
== ● ==

A CURSORY HOP-SKIP-AND-JUMP through the history of innovative directorial approaches to the classics since the turn of the century must inevitably do short shrift to the achievements of many trail-blazing directors, and of the all-important designers who helped make that essential leap from production concept to theatrical entity. In fact, as we shall see, the earliest examples of this movement rely far more heavily on redesign than redirection of action or character. This limited historical narrative will, however, acknowledge influential antecedents to the work of recent American directors and so provide necessary perspective for productions to be examined later in greater depth. Although this chapter is divided into separate European and American sections, significant transatlantic influences will necessitate occasional violations of those discrete categories.

EUROPE

In the absence of the Artist of the Theatre, Gordon Craig was content to stage classics in the austere, abstract style with which he waged war against the nineteenth-century stage. The son of Ellen Terry, Craig was born into a stultifying theatrical tradition, typified by the productions in which his mother costarred with Henry Irving at London's Lyceum Theatre.

> [My mother] loves the theatre, she thinks she is serving humanity and the sacred cause of art, while in my opinion, the theatre of today is hidebound and conventional. When the curtain goes up, and, in a room with three walls and artificial light, those great geniuses, those priests of holy art, show me how people eat, drink, love, walk about, and

16

wear their jackets. . . . We need new forms. New forms are needed, and if we can't have them, then we had better have nothing at all.[1]

The words belong to Treplev, the struggling symbolist playwright and son of a famous actress in Chekhov's *The Seagull,* but it is easy to imagine them in the mouth of Gordon Craig.

Craig believed that it was the director's duty to interpret the dramatist's play, but the author's stage directions "are not to be considered by him. What he must see to is that he makes his action and scene match the verse or the prose, the beauty of it, the sense of it."[2] Where the realistic stage sought verisimilitude, Craig's symbolism sought the unconscious reality of dreams and trance. Craig's interest in classic drama lay not in outward manifestations of intrigue, romance, or worldly greatness, but in the play as a source of transcendent theatrical imagery. Unlike contemporary directors who seek a separate style and idiom for each play, Craig advocated consistent use of the unit set with the specific layout and color scheme modified to the themes of the drama at hand. Still, Craig's reliance on visual imagery and a contemporary aesthetic to illuminate old texts for new audiences have become hallmarks of the revisionist directorial approach.

William Poel's place in this narrative is less obvious. Poel's textual restorations and his attempt to reconstruct the Elizabethan stage for the production of Shakespeare's plays seem at first far too adulatory of the script to relate to the directorial molding under current review. But Jonathan Miller argues persuasively that Poel's clean break with plush nineteenth-century illusionistic staging released the plays "into a dramatic rather than a pictorial space. . . . As soon as the dramatic action was prised away from its literal historical setting, the text acquired an independence that gave subsequent directors a licence to re-set them in any period that struck their fancy."[3] Miller continues: "The ease with which [Shakespeare's plays] could be transferred to a non-historic sixteenth-century limbo suggested that there might be no limit to the way in which these plays could be re-staged in the future."[4] Ironically, by revealing the plays' "essentially literary character," Miller points out, Poel left them "increasingly susceptible to the sort of 'conceptual' interpretations that critics so often deplore."[5] As we shall see, early innovations were more a matter of redesign than textual reinterpretation.

After Poel, Harley Granville-Barker and Max Reinhardt advanced the conceptual agenda through productions that demonstrated their belief that directors have an obligation to put classic plays on stage in fresh and surprising new productions. Granville-Barker's foray into the classics amounted to six plays by Euripides and Shakespeare, the former of which brought the new sensibility to this side of the Atlantic for the first time. The Greek plays, in new translations by Gilbert Murray, were first staged during Granville-Barker's tenure at the Royal Court Theatre between 1904 and 1907. Although Murray's verse seems stilted today, Granville-Barker admired the simplicity of the modern translations, and set out to "make the plays come as naturally to the theatre as possible."[6] He mounted them on an adaptable unit set with painted, conventionalized set pieces to suggest a more specific atmosphere for each of the three plays in the repertory. Costumes for the first Greek production, *The Trojan Women,* were plain draped robes. For *Iphigenia in Tauris* the actors wore stylized variations on contemporary fashions. Lillah McCarthy, Granville-Barker's leading lady, appeared in a long, pleated, white skirt with big, dark polka dots, a simple tunic blouse with wavy, vertical stripes, and a thigh-length overjacket with lines and dots, something like a flapper's toga. The work on *Hippolytus* focused on Granville-Barker's struggle to present the chorus in an appropriately modern manner. His solution, as with most of his work with classic plays, was a tidy, symbolic convention. Each choral passage was preceded and followed by one or two plucks of the harp. The chorus chanted their lines in unison while walking through a few simple choreographed steps.

When the Greek plays toured college stadiums across America in 1915, their first appearance was the inaugural event for Lewisohn Stadium at the City College of New York. For these huge outdoor spaces, Granville-Barker adapted the sets to include a massive, stylized Greek *skene* behind a full-circle orchestra, the floor of which was painted with bold, geometric designs. The effect recalled the grandeur of the fifth century B.C. in a style consonant with the emerging twentieth century A.D. The make-believe quality of Granville-Barker's stage conventions exemplifies a theatricalism common, though not exclusive, to director's theatre. The overt presentational style invites the audience to join in the fiction, as if acknowledging together the imaginative leap required of all participants to bring the past to meaningful life in the present.

Granville-Barker's Shakespeare productions, designed by Norman Wilkinson at the Savoy Theatre in London between 1912 and 1914, used Poel's restored texts but gave each play its own fantastical look and style after which, according to one recent Granville-Barker biographer, "Shakespearian [sic] production [would] never be the same again."[7] The stark modernity of the designs for *The Winter's Tale* confounded contemporary critics. Their umbrage caused Granville-Barker to proclaim that "there is no Shakespearean tradition. We have the text to guide us, half a dozen stage directions, and that is all. I abide by the text and the demands of the text and beyond that I claim freedom."[8] The gauzy, glittery *A Midsummer Night's Dream* included a bower of trees made of strips of gilded fabric hung from a circular rod over the stage. Granville-Barker dropped the traditional Mendelssohn score, commissioned original music by Cecil Sharp, and complemented that with folk tunes. The court scene for the storybook *Twelfth Night* was decorated with trees that resembled huge styrofoam cones with rings cut out of them. Granville-Barker's cosmetic make-over of these plays was widely approved, but the enthusiasm was tempered by a suspicion that Granville-Barker's whimsical treatment of lightweight Shakespearean comedies would not have stood up under the weight of *Hamlet* or *Macbeth*.

Max Reinhardt, in Germany, was a master of the gestalt theatrical concept. Wildly eclectic, a consummate showman, and the progenitor of environmental theatre, Reinhardt insisted that every play demanded a unique theatrical atmosphere. He understood the impact of small, larger, and massive playing spaces and selected among them for his more than 600 productions. When a text defied even these options, Reinhardt pioneered the use of "found" performance spaces. No dogmatist, Reinhardt said he took his inspiration from the "tidal waves of mental images"[9] he experienced while reading plays. "All depends on realizing the specific atmosphere of a play and on making the play live. . . . How to make the play live in our time, that is decisive for us."[10]

His total theatre concepts encompassed the configuration of the playing space, sets, lighting and costume designs, acting style, and whether or not the action would extend into the audience. He staged *The Merchant of Venice* alongside a Venetian canal and *Everyman* in the streets of Salzburg. The Fauststadt, a vertical city, was carved into a mountainside for his annual forays into Goethe's masterpiece. For *The Miracle,* he hired designers (including Norman Bel Geddes for the New York production) to transform the insides of theatres into Gothic cathedral interiors. Reinhardt's lavish *A Midsummer Night's Dream,* in 1905, depicted the two contiguous worlds of the court and the forest on a revolving stage that turned in full view of the audience. His massive *Oedipus Rex,* first staged in Berlin's 3,000-seat Circus Schumann in 1910, required hundreds of extras in the chorus and *hanamichi*-like walkways over the audience's heads for dramatic entrances and exits. The even grander *Oresteia* Reinhardt mounted in his own Grosses Schauspielhaus, in 1919, played to a potential audience of more than 3,300 at a time.

Despite the director's obvious fascination with the physical environment, however, Reinhardt professed his ultimate faith in the actor.

19

There is only one objective for the theatre: the theatre; and I believe in a theatre that belongs to the actor. No longer, as in the previous decades, literary points of view shall be decisive ones. This was the case because literary men dominated the theatre. I am an actor, I feel with the actor and for me the actor is the natural focal point of the theatre. He was that in all great epochs of theatre.[11]

That attitude is confirmed by the statements of actors whom he directed. Even chorus players remember Reinhardt's attention to their individual characterizations. It is possible to dispute whether his top priority was really scenery or acting, but the gist of the preceding quote is that Reinhardt recognized the inherent aesthetic value of the theatre, not as an adjunct literary activity, but as its own valid means of artistic expression.

Extensive tours of his work throughout Europe and the United States, and the original work Reinhardt did during his exile from Nazi Germany, met with pockets of predictable critical scorn, but won its share of supporters as well. The young Robert Edmond Jones, fresh out of Harvard, saw several of Reinhardt's productions during a postgraduation European sabbatical with classmate Kenneth Macgowan. *Continental Stagecraft,* the adulatory chronicle of their tour of European theatre capitals, was published in 1922. Jones, a scenic designer, adopted Reinhardt's conceptual attitude and Craig's unit set in his earliest professional assignments. *Continental Stagecraft* plus Jones's designs in the early 1920s advanced the New Stagecraft movement that elevated American designers from scene painters to scenic artists. Since then, designers have served alongside directors as key members of the core creative team.

"There is something to be said in the theatre in terms of form and color and light that can be said in no other way," Jones would later write.[12] For the 1919–20 Broadway season, Jones erected a massive replica of a segment of the base of the Tower of London for Arthur Hopkins's production of *Richard III,* which starred John Barrymore. Projections were used for scene-to-scene alterations. Macgowan saw in the structure a metaphor for "the empty skull of Richard with the hideous drama within it." The daily critics were less impressed with this first Jones–Hopkins–Barrymore collaboration, and their displeasure continued with the second and third.

Jones created a black-draped, multilevel environment for *Macbeth* in 1921. The expressionistic design also provided bold, metallic set pieces for individual scenes. The play opened with three five-foot-tall tragic masks hanging above three red-robed, bronze-masked witches. Harsh beams of white light poured onto the stage through the slits in the overhead masks. The scenes in

Inverness were marked by golden, expressionist arches. Alexander Woollcott wasn't sure whether they looked like a "giant molar tooth pitched rakishly in space" or "the lodge room of the Ku Klux Klan, Poughkeepsie Chapter."[13] The *Times* critic hated Lionel Barrymore in the title role and felt that the production was overwhelmed by the scenery. "Mr. Jones as Macbeth" was the title of his review. "Perhaps on the seventh or eighth visit . . . one may become so habituated to its new idiom that one can give undivided and even stimulated attention to the tale," he wrote.[14]

John Barrymore played the lead in the Jones–Hopkins *Hamlet* of 1922. This time Woollcott approved of the acting, but was again unhappy with Jones's set. "Trivial and grotesque," he called it, adding that it "encroached upon the playing space and introduced incongruities of locale quite unnecessary." To Woollcott, so heavy was the burden of the design that it reduced the production to "a platform recitation." Jones's beautiful renderings seem to refute Woollcott's assessment, but a drawing cannot represent a performance. A share of the productions' weaknesses might be justly attributed to discrepancies in conception between designer and director. Hopkins's working rule of "complete subservience to the play"[15] seems at cross purposes to Jones's declarative settings. Another sign of the gap between them might be detected in Hopkins's strange statement of admiration for Jones's "unselfishness" in designing so that audiences would not "notice" his designs.[16]

Meanwhile, in the newly declared Soviet Union, Meyerhold strove to marshal the forces of the theatre "to serve the cause of the revolution."[17] He found traditional drama, with its emphasis on the psychological and emotional traumas of middle- and upper-class characters, bereft of topics or treatments that could facilitate that goal. "But," he wrote,

> since all this is merely literature, let it lie undisturbed in the libraries. We shall need scenarios and we shall often utilize even the classics as a basis for our theatrical compositions. We shall tackle the task of adaptation without fear, fully confident of its necessity.[18]

Meyerhold's adaptations were achieved by rearranging texts, performing on abstract, constructivist sets, and acting in the vigorous, athletic style he called biomechanics. The "key idea" he formulated to articulate the motive and motif for each production is the forerunner of the production "concept." So unabashed was Meyerhold in his efforts to remold classics to his own purposes that he identified himself in the program for *The Inspector General,* in 1926, with the notorious label "author of the spectacle." With this tag, writes one of Meyerhold's biographers, he asserted the "tenet that director and actor alike have the duty and right as artists to reinterpret the classics and create contemporary drama as viable art in the theatre."[19] According to another theatre historian, "Meyerhold first of all directors operated on the playtext in the modern sense: he wrote the text anew. . . . [He] knew the text had to be reconstructed in a present."[20]

For contemporary directors, Meyerhold's revolutionary stance toward classic texts is as rich a source of inspiration as his constructivist aesthetics and biomechanical approach to acting. Critics still refer to him as they try to sort out the impact of a strong directorial hand on a classic text. Richard Gilman calls Meyerhold "the man from whom true directorial megalomania might be said to have sprung."[21] Gordon Rogoff, meanwhile, tried to temper the misconception that Meyerhold advocated free-for-all directorial indulgence when he mused that "as for concept, well yes . . . but he didn't mean imposition from the outside – as many contemporary directors do – so much as he meant an incarnation of the playwright's world."[22] For Meyerhold, the classic text was a piece of the past, a historical relic, inappropriate to the urgent purpose of the Soviet stage unless transformed into something totally new and barbed.

Brecht took a similar view of the highly personal and bourgeois focus of classic drama as irrelevant to the audience he liked to call "the children of the scientific age."[23] He deplored the honorifics "universal" and "timeless" as applied to great works of art because they, along with adjectives like "natural," "fated," and "eternal," foster the perception that human and/or social conditions are somehow preordained and thus immutable. Brecht wanted to destroy existing, oppressive social and economic structures by empowering his audiences with the belief that their own actions could change the course of history. "Hunger, cold, hardship. The purpose of our investigation was to make visible the means by which those onerous conditions could be done away with," wrote the German director.[24] He said his work stemmed from "a desire to make the world controllable."[25]

Much of the confusion surrounding the Brechtian terms "epic theatre" and "alienation" subsides when they are understood in relation to his desire to "historicize" the events in drama. By showing dramatic situations to be the results of specific historical contexts, Brecht hoped to demonstrate the impact of the characters' own choices on their destinies and to imply that other alternatives might have resulted in better outcomes. The *Verfremdungseffekt* was his technique for making the familiar strange and the strange familiar in order to help the actors and the audience scrutinize dramatic events from a fresh, historicized perspective, free from automatic acceptance of any circumstance as inevitable or beyond human manipulation. Toward that di-

22

dactic end, and in the service of his high-spirited theatrical style, Brecht resolved "to treat old works of the old theatre as pure subject matter, to ignore
their own style, to make their authors forgotten, and to stamp upon all those
works made for other epochs, the style of our epoch."[26]

While Meyerhold and Brecht were content to remake old plays for their
new theatres, Artaud refused the classics any place in his Theatre of Cruelty.
Artaud's theatre was supposed to purge the individual and the community of
its festering spiritual sores by shocking the senses into new awareness. Such
metaphysical upheaval could brook no polite museum relics on its stages. In
his 1936 essay, "No More Masterpieces," Artaud articulated his revulsion
toward the boulevard obeisance paid to cherished old plays. Ironically, this
essay has since acquired classic status of its own as an early manifesto for the
revisionist approach to the classics in Europe and the United States. "Masterpieces of the past are good for the past," Artaud argues, "they are not
good for us."[27] He concedes that a few of the great dramas (e.g., *Oedipus
Rex*) deal with the primal passions he sought to treat, but "in a manner and
language that have lost all touch with the rude and epileptic rhythm of our
time . . . through adulterated trappings and speech that belongs to extinct
eras." Shakespeare, too, is inadequate, Artaud charges, because he "leaves the
public intact."[28]

> The idolatry of fixed masterpieces is one of the aspects of bourgeois
> conformism. . . . We must get rid of our superstitious valuation of texts
> and *written* poetry. Written poetry is worth reading once, and then
> should be destroyed. Let the dead poets make way for others. Then we
> might even come to see that it is our veneration for what has already
> been created, however beautiful and valid it may be, that petrifies us,
> deadens our responses, and prevents us from making contact with that
> underlying power. . . . Beneath the poetry of the texts there is the ac-
> tual poetry, without form and without text.[29]

For Artaud, all literature is "fixed" and therefore "dead" because it is offered
as a finished product. The theatre, on the other hand, communicates via the
senses in the form of immediate, temporal impulses. Literature, especially
those examples of it that reeked of respect and middle-class culture, simply
did not belong in Artaud's theatre.

> Instead of continuing to rely upon texts considered definitive and sa-
> cred, it is essential to put an end to the subjugation of the theater to
> the text, and to recover the notion of a kind of unique language half-
> way between gesture and thought.[30]

Like Craig, Artaud proposed a theatre without any text at all, created by a single theatre artist. "The old duality between author and director will be dissolved, replaced by a sort of unique Creator upon whom will devolve the double responsibility of the spectacle and the plot," he imagined in the first "Theatre of Cruelty" manifesto.[31] "Thus we shall renounce the theatrical superstition of the text and the dictatorship of the writer."[32] Following his antiliterary lead, those directors who have been inspired by Artaud since the late 1950s, when *The Theatre and its Double* was translated and widely disseminated for the first time, have drawn primarily from the spirit rather than the letter of Artaud's writings, with the notable exceptions of workshops like that directed by Peter Brook in 1964. For the most part, it is Artaud's disdain for stultifying reverence that has inspired later directors to remake classic plays with healthy abandon.

Polish-born Jerzy Grotowski is one of the directors who emerged in the wake of Artaud's book. In the 1960s and 1970s, before he left the theatre to pursue "paratheatrical" activities, Grotowski used classic texts as vehicles for his holy actors. Like Artaud, he believed that the theatre's true power lies in its ability to reach past logical thought into the deepest recesses of the mind and spirit. Images of the great dramas, Grotowski felt, were already deeply embedded in the collective unconscious, where their plots and characters had independent symbolic lives of their own. Live performance could activate and play upon those preconceptions. Grotowski insisted that the survival of the modern theatre depended on its ability to be not just a representation of life, which could be accomplished in cooler dramatic media, but life itself as it unfolds in the live encounter between text, actor, and audience.

For Grotowski, then, the operative word for producing classic texts is "confrontation." "The audience," he says, "can watch the process of confrontation – the story and its motives meeting the stories and motives in our lives." Here there is no point to recreating the past through faithful depiction of a dead author's ideas. "The actor must not illustrate *Hamlet*," according to Grotowski, "he must meet Hamlet."[33] Grotowski demanded that the holy actor sacrifice himself to a scathing internal search for the primal connections between himself and the role, and then to an equally grueling physical quest to translate those discoveries into vocal and facial expressions and gestures. "The problem is always the same: stop the cheating. Find the authentic impulses. The goal is to find a meeting between the actor and the text."[34]

Grotowski's method was to "take the principal elements of the text as context for the creativity of the actor."[35] His radical rewrightings succeeded because he subjected his company and himself to unrelenting standards of discipline and structure. Although he approved of improvisation as a rehearsal technique, and celebrated the role of spontaneity in performance, Grotowski demanded precision in every aspect of the finished production. A good example of the director's theories in practice is the Polish Laboratory Theatre's production of *Akropolis*. In Wyspianski's text, the setting is the Polish Royal Palace, and the characters are figures from a hanging tapestry who come to life to act out biblical allegories related to incidents in Polish history. Grotowski interpreted the palace, and the ancien régime it once housed, as dead relics of the past. He sought a contemporary equivalent setting that would embody a tragic national cemetery. He chose the Auschwitz concentration camp as the locale and recast the characters as inmates, whose task over the course of the performance was to build a crematorium from odd lengths of pipe, the only props or scenery on the stage.

The playing area was an alley amid the divided audience. Grotowski had already abandoned the direct spectator participation he had used in *Faust* for a less contrived arrangement that cast audience members as silent witnesses to the action. In *Akropolis,* they were considered the dead among whom the characters would soon be numbered.

> We did not wish to have a stereotyped production with evil SS men and noble prisoners. We cannot play prisoners, we cannot create such images in the theatre. Any documentary film is stronger. We looked for something else. What is Auschwitz? Is it something we could organize today? A world which functions inside us. Thus there were no SS men, only prisoners who so organized the space that they must oppress each other to survive.[36]

The Lab Theatre's production had none of the text's allegorical whimsy. The revised setting and Grotowski's "poor theatre" aesthetics created a work of pristine purity and wrenching sorrow. The director cut out those parts of the text "with which we can neither agree nor disagree," opening the production to criticism for evading those sections that did not fit the new concept, but Grotowski acknowledged that he relied on text only as a catalyst to the company's experiments. In the Auschwitz setting, the play's Christian values were inverted. "Accepted stereotypes of the sacred are violated, and conventional images of transcendence are discredited."[37] Grotowski was satisfied with the transformations:

> Within the montage one finds certain words that function vis-à-vis our own experiences. The result is that we cannot say whether it is

Wyspianski's *Akropolis*. Yes, it is. But at the same time it is our *Akropolis*.[38]

In Poland and other repressive Eastern European countries, classical production in the twentieth century became a major outlet for social and political criticism. Classic texts allowed directors to make oblique references to current affairs with less risk of censorship or reprisal. This is perhaps the greatest distinction between European and American conceptual theatre. First Amendment guarantees have made it less necessary for American artists to cloak social and political commentary as heavily as their counterparts in more repressive countries, although the denial of grants from the National Endowment for the Arts to certain cutting-edge artists during the Reagan and Bush Administrations threatened to destroy that climate. With the election of President Clinton and the appointment of Jane Alexander to head the NEA, signs are hopeful that things are turning around.

Within the English-speaking theatre, Peter Brook has probably had the greatest direct impact on the American scene. In the late forties, Brook quickly earned a reputation in his native England as an enfant terrible who reset Shakespeare and opera in different or updated historical settings. By the end of the 1960s, he had reinvented Shakespeare for the second half of the century with a handful of highly imaginative productions at the Royal Shakespeare Company, including the Kott-inspired, existentialist *King Lear* (1962) and the white-box, circus-motif *A Midsummer Night's Dream* of 1970 that, according to Jonathan Miller, "altered the play's status as a dramatic event" and made it a different theatrical "object."[39]

In the seventies, he traveled to Asia and Africa to study tribal rituals and experiment in cross-cultural theatrical communication. Since his establishment of the International Centre of Theatre Research in 1970, in an abandoned warehouse in Paris, he has stripped Bizet's *Carmen* of its orchestra and *The Cherry Orchard* of its walls, and trotted around the globe a nine-hour dramatization of *The Mahabharata*. Now called the Centre International de Créations Théâtrales, Brook's company's latest classical offering at the Bouffes du Nord was *The Tempest*, in 1991. Each of these productions was informed by the director's cross-cultural curiosity and penchant for simple, elemental production values (air, water, dirt, and fire were featured prominently in *Carmen*, *The Mahabharata*, and *The Tempest*) as well as the smooth, professional craftsmanship Brook fine-tuned through decades spent in mainstream theatrical outlets.

The essays in Brook's two collections, *The Empty Space*, published in 1968, and *The Shifting Point* (1987) reflect his evolving attitudes toward the staging of classic drama. As a mature director, he denounces the detailed pre-rehearsal plans he once drew up and dictated to his (angry) casts. The empty space of the first book's title refers, of course, to the theatre, which Brook feels should be approached with a completely open mind, free of preconceptions about either the particular text or theatrical conventions in general. The "theatre always asserts itself in the present,"[40] he writes, so it must be remade and reborn all the time. Rehearsals should not be governed by a pre-determined interpretation. Instead, they can be used to explore texts by peeling away dead layers of received meaning, facile first impressions, and hollow theatrical tradition to see what may lie beneath. "Rehearsals should allow the invisible substance of the play to appear fully articulated,"[41] Brook writes in the earlier volume, apparently still convinced that concrete, discernable meanings are embedded in playtexts waiting to be revealed by the right production.

His later writing seems to indicate a somewhat freer sense of directorial play. Instead of a "reductive," one-note "directorial conception,"[42] Brook says in *The Shifting Point,* he starts with

> a deep formless hunch, which is like a smell, a color, a shadow . . .
> a formless hunch that is my relationship with the play. It's my convic-
> tion that this play must be done today, and without that conviction I
> can't do it.[43]

He claims not to impose his ideas on the actors, but to provide their experiments a "sense of direction" and encourage them to respond to the text in as many and as extreme ways as they can. It is out of the abundant fruits of these rehearsals that the director eventually determines what, beyond the play, the production itself is about and selects the elements of the performance.

> If you'd seen us three quarters of the way into the rehearsal period,
> you'd have thought the play was being submerged and destroyed by a
> surplus of what's called directorial invention. . . . All of it was for the
> purpose of having, out of that, such a lot of material that then, gradu-
> ally, things could be shaped. To what criteria? Well, shaped to their
> relation to this formless hunch.[44]

The focus of Brook's work in Paris has been the search for an international form of theatre that communicates across cultural divides. While other companies grapple with the idea of multiculturalism – the simultaneous existence and egalitarian recognition of separate cultures side by side – Brook's experiments aim for a synthetic style that melds diverse performance idioms and the play in a new, organic theatrical form. The international company's pursuit of a theatrical style that conveys reasonably consistent meanings to anyone, regardless of differences in linguistic and/or performance tradition, implies that Brook harbors an old-fashioned faith that "universal meanings" are accessible within classic texts and that he, as director with a hunch, is uniquely able to coax those meanings out and pass them along to the audience via the performers. The setting, costumes, movement, and speech may bear little resemblance to previous productions of the work, but the messages being transmitted supposedly reflect the essence of the script.

> In these last stages, the director cuts away all that's extraneous, all that belongs just to the actor and not to the actor's intuitive connection with the play. . . . [T]he director is in a better position to say then what belongs to the play and what belongs to that superstructure of rubbish that everybody brings with him.
>
> What remains is an organic form. Because the form is not imposed on a play, it is the play illuminated, and the play illuminated is the form. Therefore, when the result seems organic and unified, it's not because a unified conception has been found and has been put on the play from the outset, not at all.[45]

Like the majority of directors who invent new performance modes for old plays, Brook disavows the extent of his own impact. He defines the director's job as being "to take the hints and the hidden strands of the play and wring the most from them, take what was embryonic perhaps, and bring it out."[46] But Brook's self-effacing tone betrays a false modesty. There are no acrobatics "embryonic" in *Midsummer,* nor ponytail whippings in *Marat/ Sade,* nor is there a suggestion in *Carmen* that it should be performed in a dirt pit. These production devices succeeded not because Brook discovered and brought to light clues the playwrights had tucked into the texts, hoping they would someday be detected, but because the director was able to translate his own, personal responses to the original into a unique system of concrete, theatrical gestures. While Brook professes a heavy reliance on textual cues, his reformulation of the theatrical signs through which a play is presented to the audience may be more aggressive toward the text than Brook likes to admit. His own example proves that assertive directors can revitalize classic texts in ways their authors never intended and may not have been able to imagine.

Dozens of other European directors deserve to be included in this narrative. The above are the most prominent and the most widely influential in America. Classical theatre participates in the global marketplace. International cross-fertilization is common. Some of the outstanding European revisionists not mentioned here are Peter Stein in Germany, Giorgio Strehler in Italy, Roger Planchon and Ariane Mnouchkine in France, Ingmar Bergman in Sweden, Andrzej Wajda and the late Tadeusz Kantor in Poland, and in the former Soviet Union, Yuri Lyubimov. (Individual productions by these directors may be discussed in subsequent chapters of this book.) In fact, some of the most striking work in America has been directed by visiting or expatriate East Europeans, especially the Romanians Liviu Ciulei, Lucian Pintilié, Andrei Serban, and Andrei Belgrader. Clearly, European models have had a powerful impact on classical production in this country. The most exciting American reinventions of the classics are not, however, European clones. Let us now turn our attention to the unique history of revisionist classics on this side of the Atlantic.

HISTORICAL CONTEXT: AMERICA

There are no "classic" American plays before Eugene O'Neill's from the 1920s. Most European nations have their own world-class dramatic literatures, but producing classical theatre in America has always meant borrowing foreign plays. This stepchild syndrome may have engendered in the deep recesses of the American theatre an inferiority complex that helps explain why traditionalists cling to old, imported styles and standards and why upstart Americans are compelled to reshape the classics according to native sensibilities. The former group treats these dramas as foreign dignitaries to whom they bow and show respect. The latter Americanize the plays as if to prove the legitimacy of our national heritage or the competence of our theatrical talents. Speculative psychoanalytical explanations aside, Americans have been experimenting with the production of classic plays since Robert Edmond Jones redesigned Shakespeare in the 1920s. The progression from those early updatings to the multifocused, postmodern investigations of today has taken diverse paths, each with its own digressions. Large chunks of this history have been chronicled thoroughly in separate accounts of the theatres, careers, and productions involved, and do not require recapitulation here.[47] What follows is a sprint up to the late 1960s, from which point the ensuing chapters will proceed.

As we have already seen, the earliest classical experiments to be seen on

29

American stages were themselves either European imports or heavily influenced by the antirealistic theatres of that continent. Granville-Barker, Reinhardt, and Jones brought the first examples to America in the decade between 1915 and 1925. In the late 1920s, while much theatrical energy was going to the development of a new American drama, occasional classical offerings were peppered with novelties like *The Taming of the Shrew* in modern dress, directed by A. K. Ayliff at the Garrick Theatre in New York in 1927. Starring Basil Sydney and Mary Ellis, the play was reset in a chic Park Avenue flat and revolved around the domestication of a rebellious socialite. Radios, revolvers, a vacuum cleaner, and an automobile whose tires rotated while a panoramic curtain scrolled in the background were among the updated props. "These productions," sneered Brooks Atkinson of the *New York Times*, "are primarily exhibits of a producer's ingenuity, and it doesn't take so much ingenuity at that. Little sundries furnish momentary pictorial amusement, but are likely to arouse an expectation greater than they can fulfill."[48] W. O. Trapp, the critic for the *New York World,* reported that "one wit guessed it was more Shubert than Shakespeare."[49] Similarly fluffy treatments of Shakespearean comedies continued intermittently through the 1930s. For example, Alfred Lunt and Lynn Fontanne put on a *commedia dell'arte* version of the *Shrew* in 1935.

Apostles of the New Stagecraft, meanwhile, were tending to more serious approaches to new and classic drama. *Continental Stagecraft* had built a case for the designer to assume the role of master shaper of the production. Artists like Sheldon Cheney, Lee Simonson, Donald Oenslager, Norman Bel Geddes, and Mordecai Gorelik were thinking about and drawing old plays with fresh perspectives, even though many of their plans never materialized as productions.[50] "Everywhere the classics are encrusted with traditions, and the public mind bound by preconceptions of them," Kenneth Macgowan had asserted in *The Theatre of Tomorrow* in 1923. "These traditions are hard to demolish, these preconceptions are dangerous things to fight."[51] In America, it was designers who first ventured into that battle. Directors followed their lead. As Lee Simonson would later write,

> the meaning of a classic can rarely be recovered or revived; it must nearly always be re-created. The supposedly universal ideas can never again have exactly the same significance. [Modern scenic designers, therefore] must contrive to imbue the present stage background with the emotional quality of those associations with which this lost audience invested the event enacted.[52]

30

Oenslager devised such modern abstract settings for classic plays as a cubist steel scaffolding for Aristophanes' *The Birds* and a chalk-white box pierced with three towering doors through whose openings would emerge wedges of blood-red light for *Hamlet*. Those designs that made it to the stage usually met the same fate as Jones's Shakespeare settings. "Scenic concept" was rarely incorporated into the directing or other aspects of production, which left the scenery vulnerable to harsh criticism. The legacy of the New Stagecrafters to contemporary directors and the designers with whom they collaborate is, however, undeniable.

In one unusual case, Norman Bel Geddes got the chance to insinuate the ideas in his set design into the total production when he directed his own *Hamlet* at a summer theatre in Skowhegan, Maine, in 1929. His multilevel unit set with a twenty-foot thrust in front of the proscenium accommodated a cinematic scenic montage. A complex lighting plot illuminated individual scenes as they were played in rapid succession on different areas of the stage. Bel Geddes pared the text to the main action, added pantomime sequences, and had Hamlet speak the Ghost's lines. With only twelve hours of initial rehearsal, the show played to packed houses and happily surprised critics. Raymond Massey took the title role when the production went to Broadway late in 1931. Despite the enthusiastic reception that greeted the first version, it lasted only two weeks in New York. "An incoherent, flat and unprofitable narrative," chided Brooks Atkinson. John Mason Brown admired Bel Geddes's flair, but regretted that he had "smothered" the play in scenery.[53] To this day, Broadway critics can be the last to recognize merit in the new or offbeat.[54]

The beginnings of an unapologetically American approach to producing the classics arose with the WPA Federal Theatre Project, in the late 1930s. An enormous pool of artists and production opportunities, low budgets, minimal financial risk, and a mandate to serve the diverse needs and talents of its separate regional and racial units, provided fertile ground for experiments with classic texts (large casts, no royalties). The Negro units in particular presented a direct challenge to tradition. Black actors, professionals who had been denied opportunities to perform major classical roles in the commercial theatre, were eager to prove their mettle. The white heads of those units, apparently unwilling to stage the plays straight with black casts, devised production schemes to accommodate the skills and cultural backgrounds of their companies.

Orson Welles's "voodoo" *Macbeth,* performed at Harlem's Lafayette Theatre in 1936, is the most celebrated example.[55] Welles moved the story to

31

Haiti under the nineteenth-century black tyrant, Emperor Henri Christophe, and lavished upon it all manner of tropical flora and fauna. Coincidence and the young director's prodigious imagination conspired to bring to the production a cast of one hundred thirty-seven players, including forty-three witches and a band of genuine African tribal drummers.[56] The witches took centerstage in this production. It was around them that Welles wove his retelling of the Macbeth story, and it became about a good man struggling against impinging forces of unnatural evil. Opinion is mixed as to whether or not the production's reliance on supernatural rather than internal conflict proves that Welles's revisions reduced Shakespeare's tragedy to the oft-demeaned genre of melodrama. A better argument, consonant with the production's own intentions, is whether or not Welles and company recast the Scottish play in a culturally and theatrically effective new mold. According to Brooks Atkinson:

> The witches have always worried the life out of the polite tragic stage. But ship the witches down into the rank and fever-stricken jungle of Haiti, . . . and there you have a witches' scene that is logical and stunning and a triumph of theatre art.[57]

What the "voodoo" *Macbeth* may have lost in philosophy it more than made up for in verve, color, rhythm, and excitement through its hypnotic evocation of exotic locale. The following year, having moved downtown and out of the WPA, Welles directed *Julius Caesar* in black shirts for his new Mercury Theatre. Detractors still complained that Welles was little more than a showoff, but the production's relatively restrained style and obvious topical relevance convinced many of *Macbeth*'s critics that the impudent director had taken a giant step toward artistic and professional maturity. (In fact, Welles earned more credit for originality than he deserved: A less-publicized Federal Theatre unit in Delaware had staged *Caesar* in black shirts the year before.) Today, however, racist overtones have been detected in the critics' condescension toward the "voodoo" *Macbeth,* and the production is considered a more significant landmark than *Julius Caesar* in the emergence of an idiosyncratically American classical theatre.

The notoriety that surrounded this *Macbeth* spurred other WPA Negro units around the country to attempt similar adaptations. The Chicago branch set *Romey and Julie* in Harlem amid a tense rivalry between African Americans and blacks from the West Indies. In this little-known precursor of *West Side Story,* Friar Lawrence was a rhyming preacher, the balcony scene was played on a fire escape, and an appended epilogue sent the couple, denied entry to heaven because of their suicides, directly to hell to join a rollicking party for fallen angels. The same group presented *Swing Mikado* in 1939. In 1937, the Los Angeles black unit transferred *Macbeth* to the jungles of Africa and decked its cast in bones and beads and bamboo skirts. The Seattle troupe added musical numbers to *The Taming of the Shrew* and relocated its action to New Orleans. Jazz novelty adaptations of classics, featuring popular black performers, proliferated in the commercial theatre in 1939 as the Federal Theatre came to its sudden and sorry halt. Louis Armstrong played Bottom "the fireman" in an 1890s New Orleans musical called *Swingin' the Dream*. The show included music by Benny Goodman and leading performances by "Moms" Mabley and Butterfly McQueen. Bill Robinson and Gwendolyn Reyde headlined in Mike Todd's *Hot Mikado*.

Race reversal has since become a common strategy among directors seeking to Americanize classic plays. In the conservative, war-torn 1940s, conceptual revision went into hibernation as classical production in America reverted to more traditional forms in the hands of the Theatre Guild and Broadway producers. For the most part, a cautious theatre tended to observe the classical status quo. One of the few exceptions to emerge during that decade was *Carmen Jones*, the 1943 black-cast adaptation of Bizet's opera that preserved his music but substituted new lyrics by Oscar Hammerstein II. Its heroine worked in a war plant, manufacturing parachutes in what "use ter be a cigarette fac'ry before de war," according to the script. Her lover, Joe, contended in a boxing ring instead of a bullfighting ring. The *New York Times* reviewer praised the Billy Rose production as a "parallel" not a "parody" of the original and declared that its ebullience made "going to the theatre seem again one of the necessities of life."[58] Race-related musical adaptations have since become an American specialty. *West Side Story* (1957), the black and Puerto Rican *Two Gentlemen of Verona* (1972), and *Sleep No More*, a black comedy based on *Macbeth*, produced by the Los Angeles Inner City Cultural Center (1982), are examples of the scope and diversity of these projects.

It was not until the sixties, however, that directors began contemplating American race relations through the classics without converting them to musicals. Simply by casting black actors in white roles, directors in the wake of the civil rights movement drew parallels between America's racial hypocrisy and the situations of oppression and prejudice depicted in classic plays. Sometimes a block of related roles was assigned to black actors. In other productions, the casting of a single part made the point.[59] After *West Side Story*, the sixties saw dozens of interracial productions of *Romeo and Juliet* in professional and university theatres across the country. In 1968, Zelda Fichandler cast a black actress as the Stepdaughter in Pirandello's *Six Characters in Search of an Author.* Hartford Stage offered an all-black version of Max Frisch's *The Firebugs* that implied disturbing parallels between Frisch's Nazi villains and white America.

The practice of cross-racial casting has evolved in the intervening decades into a more inclusive practice, commonly called nontraditional casting. Nudged along by the Actors' Equity Non-Traditional Casting Project, and the political pressure of multiculturalism, producers and directors have begun to cast creatively members of other racial and ethnic minorities, as well as women and the physically challenged in the hopes of generating opportunities for a pool of actors who represent the changing demographics of this country. In the fall of 1989 at Arena Stage in Washington, D.C., Ruby Dee (who in the 1960s had "passed" for white as Cordelia and Kate the shrew in American Shakespeare Festival productions) played Amanda Wingfield in an all-black cast that won accolades in the national press for their unusually poignant, humorous, and affectionate portrayal of Tennessee Williams's *The Glass Menagerie.* Except for the color of the actors' skin, though, and whatever cultural associations attach to that, there was no reworking or reorienting of the play.

With colorblind casting, productions that feature minority actors may not even invoke issues of race. In fact, by the 1990s, interracial casting is a nonissue in many productions, although the presence of racial difference may have unintended resonances. Nontraditional casting at its most progressive aims to assign roles to the best-qualified performers regardless of race or ethnicity. Colorblind casting reflects the diversity of the American population – the spectrum of peoples one might see walking down the street in any city – and discounts race as an actor's key identifying feature.

Although there was little classical experimentation in the 1940s, the fifties saw a surge of activity. In the first months of the decade, Broadway welcomed Joshua Logan's *Wisteria Trees,* a Deep South adaptation of *The Cherry Orchard,* starring Helen Hayes. "He who tampers with a classic," Logan anticipated, "is apt to infuriate the self-elected authorities of the world."[60] Logan's new script was far enough removed from Chekhov, however, to generate little controversy. Script-intact reimaginings of the classics would develop over the next few years under the influence of more classically minded directors like Tyrone Guthrie, John Houseman, and Joseph Papp. With men like these at the heads of new Shakespeare festival theatres in Stratford (Ontario), Stratford (Connecticut), and New York City, with postwar European drama making its way to the States, and the articulation of the *auteur* theory in cinema providing a model for an all-controlling directorial presence, classical production in America took a decidedly directorial turn.

During Guthrie's long tenure at the Canadian festival and regular visits to Broadway, he had revived Orson Welles's impulse to transpose the classics to more accessible milieus. Like Welles, Guthrie was a consummate showman whose theatricality at times masked a hollowness at the core of his productions. One theatre historian describes "The Guthrie Style" thus: "lavish detail, many extras, muted color-schemes, excellent acting, and a curious vacuum at the directorial center."[61] The Guthrie style, then, had its merits, foremost among them a zest for classical productions and a capacity to make them fresh and immediate to the modern audience. Its obvious downside, like that of Welles's and Reinhardt's styles before him, is that in many cases vast amounts of energy spent on theatrics seemed to leave too little for deep meditation on the play.

In Guthrie's own terminology, not all the classic plays he staged warranted "jollying up." Of his many productions, the 1956 *Tamburlaine,* based on a 1951 production at London's Old Vic, is a typical example. Guthrie lavished opulent scenic effects, a cast of more than sixty doing primitive chants and barbaric dances, and a balletically choreographed battle sequence on a severely abridged text of Marlowe's sprawling plays, frequently considered unstageable. The effect was spectacular, but critics complained it never added up to more than that. "Guthrie applies effects *to* the text . . . but theatrical effects must come *out of* the text, they must seem to be a part of it," wrote Harold Clurman.[62] Richard Hayes, reviewing for *Commonweal,* called the main character as depicted here "a great beast pawing in lust in the diminished world," but regretted that the director had supplied "only a montage of images of barbarism, no imposition anywhere of an attitude, merely the exploitation of sensation."[63] Eric Bentley would later sum up his impressions of Guthrie as "the most expert sheepdog that ever came out of Ireland . . . blasé, apolitical, and trivial."[64]

Guthrie's influence on the American scene would, of course, intensify in the early sixties with the opening of his own theatre in Minneapolis. Guthrie opened his new theatre in 1963 with the vaguely anachronistic *Hamlet,* starring George Grizzard and Jessica Tandy (Gertrude), that was a landmark in American theatre history. With its potpourri of nineteenth- and twentieth-century elements, including Ophelia's tennis racket and Hamlet's blue satin smoking jacket, the four-hour-long production was almost unanimously considered overwrought, although few could resist admiring its grandeur. Richard Gilman called it "a boon to traditionalists, an exceedingly unpleasant production, gimmicky, heterogeneous, inconsistent, and without any style that derived from sources other than a vulgar, obvious theatricality."[65] Walter Kerr, on the other hand, found it flawed but appealing. "To see a Hamlet captured by a posse carrying flashlights suggests that he has been misbehaving in a movie theatre and has been rounded up by the ushers,"[66] Kerr sneered, but ultimately enjoyed what he called the director's "free invention" on that most famous play. The effect, he wrote, was like "looking at the entire play naked, of watching its bones dance on the graveside, or hearing what it is saying without remembering that it is old."[67] Kenneth Tynan dismissed any of the production's serious intentions and announced that the only reason Guthrie could get away with it was because Shakespeare was dead and had no agent to protect him. In the three decades since the Minneapolis center opened, it has played host to a long line of innovative directors, including almost every one featured in the following chapters.

The American Shakespeare Festival Theatre and Academy in Stratford, Connecticut, was established in 1954 to compete with Guthrie's Canadian venture, but it did not find its own voice until John Houseman, Orson Welles's partner at the WPA and Mercury Theatres in the late thirties, took the artistic reins in 1956. "Shakespeare must be saved from culture" if he is to compete successfully with Broadway, warned John Gassner in a preview of the first season.[68] The management of the ill-fated 1955 season did not come to that rescue. When Houseman, by now a Hollywood producer who understood the demands of the box office, was hired to revamp the project, he told the press his "only hope for this hazardous second season lay in the bold, imaginative production of unfamiliar, contrasting plays."[69] Houseman quickly established the tone of the festival with simile transpositions that brought Shakespeare's plays into American settings with high spirits and big stars in the leading roles.

The 1957 season presented Katharine Hepburn in *The Merchant of Venice*, with Morris Carnovsky as Shylock, and in a nineteenth-century Texan *Much Ado About Nothing* costarring Alfred Drake. The Southwest theme had been suggested by Hepburn and proved a hit with audiences and critics alike. Brooks Atkinson said it was "not only shrewd but fresh and joyous and admirably suited to the personality of our leading lady."[70] Gassner was delighted with the "lively mingling of Spanish grandees, Mexican peons, American cowboys, and Western sheriffs,"[71] and with Virgil Thomson's pop-Hispanic score. "Where but in the United States," he mused, "would a theatrical organization stake out a claim to being our more or less official Shakespearean theatre with a Southwestern *Much Ado*? . . . [whose purpose was] not to *instruct*, not to *preserve* Shakespeare, but, without a doubt, solely to make 'theatre' with Shakespeare."[72] Gassner qualified his enthusiasm only by pointing out that it had been applied to one of the "lesser" comedies. He was less confident that similar "modern and American coaxing" would work with Shakespeare's tragedies or high comedies. Still, the production, and the prestige it lent to the Festival Theatre, raised serious questions in Gassner's mind about Shakespeare on the American stage.

> Are we going to "Americanize" Shakespeare in institutionalizing him? How far can modernization go and still be Shakespeare? . . . There is also a danger in succumbing to the seduction of a conceit or 'production idea' in being strenuous when there is little to be strenuous about, in relying on 'Amerikanski tempo' at the expense of language, and in wanting a bright new look in everything just for the novelty of the impression.[73]

Still, a year later, Gassner succumbed to his own delight:

> I'm afraid I must parade myself as a veritable lowbrow in academic circles in praising . . . Mssrs. Houseman and Landau for the playfulness with which they stage Shakespeare's non-tragic plays. . . . We are surely not preposterous in maintaining that Americans have a perfect right to try to make Shakespeare their own by staging the plays in their own way – provided they don't butcher the script, something that was perpetrated for centuries, not by irreverent modern Americans, but by those reverent Britons, the Shakespearean actor-managers from Betterton to Irving.[74]

Stratford became the American capital for simile concepts. Its numerous directors, including over the years Jack Landau, Michael Kahn, Gerald Freedman, and many others, came up with scores of conceits with which to inject novelty into their Shakespearean fare. The 1958–9 season included *The Winter's Tale* in a tarot-card motif and an *All's Well That Ends Well* dressed up like a "Medieval soap opera."[75] Hepburn returned in 1960 to do an Edwardian *Twelfth Night* set on the beach at Brighton. In 1961, Jack Landau directed Carrie Nye in a Civil War *Troilus and Cressida* with toy cannons and mock battle scenes. By 1965, a Spanish-accented *The Taming of the Shrew* prompted Glenn Loney to lament that "apparently Shakespearean productions in the United States continue to invite tours de force regardless of rhyme or reason."[76] Michael Kahn, who took over as artistic director in 1969, has at least paid lip service to the limitations of the Festival's standard approach, although his own early productions, including a "hippie" *Love's Labour's Lost* in 1968, a "mod" *Henry V* in 1969, and *Romeo and Juliet* set in the Italian Risorgimento (1974) followed the transposition model. Looking back, he draws a critical distinction between "concepts," which "mark close and striking affinities with the realities of the text," and "decor," which is no deeper than a cosmetic make-over.[77] Then, in the eighties, Kahn says he realized that his own "messages and ideas were not more interesting than Shakespeare's," and that he might do better

> to stop imposing so much. . . . That desperate need to be different which we had gone through in the sixties was ending. The consumption of ideas had been so rabid that it burnt us out in a way. We didn't want to have to come up with something new again.[78]

Relieved of that pressure, Kahn discovered "that Shakespeare is infinitely more interesting than I am!"[79] Other directors, including Peter Brook, have come to similar conversions at some point in their artistic maturity; having already proved themselves, they are no longer compelled to assert themselves so blatantly. In Kahn's case, the turnabout involved a simultaneous realization that, while occasionally fruitful, the simile technique is more often a director's defense against boredom, repetition, or the daunting task of confronting a classic head on.

If Robert Edmond Jones and Orson Welles can be considered part of the first wave of classical experimenters in this country, the simile makers of the fifties are the second generation, and their method of transplanting classic plays, part and parcel, to novel locales had by the late 1960s become the American tradition. It is partly against that standard model that the third contingent, the group of greatest interest to the current discussion, has been reacting ever since. Joseph Papp, who founded the New York Shakespeare Festival in the late fifties and sponsored scores of controversial rewrightings before his death in 1991 – both fifties-style similes and messier postmodern efforts – can be seen as a bridger of that generation gap. Stanley Kauffmann has characterized the objective of Papp's early career as "matchmaking between Shakespeare and the ghettos."[80] Papp seems to have come to the theatre with a clear civic mandate to make mainstream American culture relevant and accessible to those who had traditionally been locked out of it. In 1961, Papp told *Theatre Arts* magazine that his free Shakespeare audience consisted mainly of people who watched a lot of movies and TV, and that he molded his theatrical offerings to their contemporary, realistic tastes.[81] Another time, he stated that "whenever you do a classic, you recreate life in the terms that now exist, both politically and socially. . . . You have to draw from what exists."[82]

Papp hired many of the same directors who worked at the American Festival Theatre, but encouraged a broader, more urban sweep of styles and production concepts. In 1960 Gerald Freedman directed a *Shrew* in the farce idiom of silent movies, borrowing shtick from the Marx Bros. and the Keystone Kops. Robert Brustein especially enjoyed "the splendid *lazzi,* including pratfalls, beatings, tumblings, and brawls."[83] Papp, Brustein declared, "has created a uniquely American Shakespeare style which is both fresh and faithful to the text . . . volatile, ripsnorting, rough and ready."[84] Michael Kahn's 1966 *Measure for Measure,* set in contemporary Vienna, was marred, in Stanley Kauffmann's estimation, by "Peter Brooklets" the director had appropriated, but its racially mixed cast and serious exploration of the play's "moral-metaphysical dilemmas"[85] brought the text and its updated setting into satisfying register. In 1972, A. J. Antoon set *Much Ado About Nothing* in Teddy Roosevelt's America, complete with brass band and straw hats. Since then, the New York Shakespeare Festival has presented more interesting metaphorical treatments of Shakespeare and a few Greek plays, as well as a number of musical adaptations, including the 1972 *Two Gentlemen of Verona,* but under Papp's leadership it continued to welcome straight simile transpositions as well.

In the summer of 1990, Papp rehired Antoon to direct *The Taming of the Shrew* for the Festival's thirty-six-play marathon. The director transplanted the play to the American West, putting a holster on Kate (Tracey Ullman) and a horse under Petruchio (Morgan Freeman). The director defended his arbitrary transposition in the *New York Times* by explaining that "in the Old West women were a prize because there weren't that many of them on the frontier." He also said his primary directorial motive was "to allow an American audience to find it more accessible. I want the children, the teenagers, to totally understand it."[86] Antoon's simplistic production scheme turned out a slick but shallow performance constricted by the one-time joke of drawling accents and a Kate in blue jeans and spurs. Fortunately, the Festival, under Papp and his successors, has also sponsored directors with more complicated responses to Shakespearean texts. Other marathon entries have included Jo-Anne Akalaitis's postmodernist, pseudo-Victorian *Cymbeline,* Steven Berkoff's monochromatic, ahistorical, and unsympathetic *Coriolanus,* and Michael Grief's tender, time-warped, multicultural *Pericles.*

In the years between Papp's free Shakespeare in Riverside Park and the hip, kaleidoscopic *Hamlet* with which in 1967 he set off a new era in American Shakespeare (see Chapter 4), a series of movements in the American avant-garde changed the course of classical production. Action painting, Beat poetry, Happenings, rock music, and new kinds of dance contributed to the development of an aesthetic that valued spontaneity and juxtaposition over method and unity. Many of these experiments were hybrids that blurred the lines between previously distinct forms, precursors of performance art and strong influences on the impending theatrical revolution of the 1960s. In the broader American culture, the civil rights movement, the Vietnam War, women's liberation, youth culture, drugs, and the sexual revolution burst the seams of tradition and propriety in the arts. America's staunch realism gave way to abstraction and overt presentation as former taboos in both form and content were systematically broken down.

In theatrical circles, the rise and uprisings of the Living Theatre led an emerging counterculture and began a performance style that came to be called the New Theatre. The Becks' work on such modern classics as Brecht's *Antigone* and Pirandello's *Tonight We Improvise,* which the Living played as a rehearsal by some arty little Greenwich Village theatre group, incorporated such hallmarks of the Living Theatre's revolutionary aesthetic as performing in real time, hyperrealism, audience participation, life as art, amateurism, and theatre as protest. The experimental boom that filled shabby Greenwich Village storefronts with performance spaces like Caffè Cino and La MaMa Experimental Theatre Club focused most of its energy on new plays and new styles of performing, but its innovations were soon applied to classic scripts too. Joseph Chaikin's Open Theatre, specializing in improvisational acting and collaborative creation, adapted the Book of Genesis into *The Serpent* and later tackled Beckett's *Endgame.* At the Performing Garage on Wooster Street, Richard Schechner's young group transformed Euripides' *The Bacchae* into *Dionysus in '69,* a participatory, environmental production that invited spectators to have sex with the actors. Mabou Mines, Richard Foreman's Ontological-Hysterical Theatre, and the Wooster Group were part of a second wave of experimental theatres with scaled-down political ambitions and a greater interest in the uses of various electronic media. Most of Mabou Mines' work was based on original scripts or scenarios, or texts by Samuel Beckett, and Foreman wrote most of his own plays, but the performance styles and techniques that evolved from those productions found their way onto the classical stage when these directors, or others reared on their work, later turned their attention to classic plays.

While the experimental scene in New York had slight ripple effect across the country, mostly in the university theatres springing up then, another, separate theatrical revolution was taking place in cities like Dallas, Minneapolis, Washington, D.C., and San Francisco. The proliferation of regional theatres after 1959, when the Ford Foundation handed out its first major round of grants for new theatres, increased exponentially the opportunities to produce classic plays in this country. Financially lackluster, the classics had less and less appeal to Broadway producers and their musical-happy customers. Regional theatres, with more serious repertory intentions, subscription audiences, lower overhead expenses, and less income to pay for big-name royalties, could include at least one classic play in every season. By the 1980s, practically every major city in America had at least one professional theatre and enough support to withstand the risks of hiring daring directors with strong personal visions of the theatre.

In the early years, visionary artistic directors included Zelda Fichandler at the Arena Stage, Tyrone Guthrie in Minneapolis, William Ball at the American Conservatory Theatre in San Francisco, and Robert Brustein at the Yale Repertory Theater. In the 1980s, heads of major regional theatres included Liviu Ciulei and later Garland Wright at the Guthrie, Brustein at the American Repertory Theatre in Cambridge, Mark Lamos at the Hartford Stage Company, Adrian Hall at Trinity Rep and the Dallas Theatre Center, Anne Bogart, who led Trinity's 1989–90 season, and JoAnne Akalaitis, who succeeded Joseph Papp at the Public until the beginning of 1993. As artistic directors, they directed their own classics and, equally important, hired such free-lance directors as Andrei Serban, Peter Sellars, Lucian Pintilié, Lee Breuer, and Akalaitis to invent their own versions of classics at their theatres as well.

Clearly, the question of whether or not directors have a right to press their own theatrical ideas against established texts is by now moot. The history of directing in Europe and America has cleared the way for directorial innovation with the classics. As the American theatre stumbles toward the millenium, self-possessed directors abound and show no sign of abating. At this point, their directorial licenses cannot be revoked. Productions by this latest wave of director-innovators will be the focus of the next four chapters.

3

GREEK AND ROMAN PLAYS
▬ ◈ ▬

CONTEMPORARY REVISIONIST DIRECTORS burrow into Greek and Roman plays as tunnels to primal emotion in the theatre. They mine the seminal Western dramas for intensity, community, and catharsis – dramatic attributes diluted on subsequent stages and in the cooler media of film and television. In the mid-1970s, Andrei Serban created a holy theatre masterpiece from three plays by Euripides and called the work *Fragments of a Greek Trilogy*. Later in the decade, Richard Schechner brought a rough environmental-theatre sensibility to Ted Hughes's remarkable translation of Seneca's *Oedipus*. Lee Breuer's *The Gospel at Colonus,* a product of the mediated eighties, went after grand emotions American-style by recasting the Greek tale in our most vibrant folk-music idiom, presented in full electronic amplification. In these productions, contemplation gives way to visceral response as directors try to reincarnate the piercing, sensuous theatrical experience Artaud had in mind when he reminded us that "it is through the skin that metaphysics must be made to re-enter our minds."[1]

A paradox awaits directors who undertake new productions of classical plays. Whereas we have established a theoretical framework that shows a wide margin of play between the playtext and the director's theatrical response, grandeur, symmetry, rhetoric, poetry, narrow focus, and tight construction are salient features of Greek and Roman drama. Part of their persistent appeal lies in the tension between formal structure and heightened emotional content. Savage passions seem barely contained within each text. Dramatic tension is sustained by a sense of imminent danger, of the protective barrier threatening to burst. Such textual rigors impinge on the postmodern ideal of almost infinite directorial leeway, especially when the director seeks to create a spiritually liberated theatrical experience. Revisionist productions necessarily stray from traditional tragic formality, but they can succeed only when an equivalent structural core is established in its place. Just as an ingenious architect must master sound principles of physics and engineering to keep his soaring, asymmetrical towers from crashing to rubble, so the director must craft a rigorous and disciplined performance format to withstand the forces these plays exert on the stage, both as monumental works of art and as cultural monuments.

Marianne McDonald has noted how well the random, vengeful caprice of the Greek gods and the wanton havoc they wreak on human beings suit the postmodern perspective. In Greek tragedy, she says, there are "no patterns, no sense to the suffering. Everything is just bits and pieces."[2] Postmodern proclivities toward conflict, collision, disruption, and opposition hold sway over aesthetics, too, but a relatively high degree of theatrical coherence is required here. Successful concepts fly in the face of traditional styles, settings, and interpretations, but the new production aesthetic and its execution must have equally high aspirations or risk reductionism or, worse, parody. Directors undermine their own intentions when they try to unleash primal passions by strewing the contents of Pandora's box haphazardly over the stage. Stagings that do not recognize the structural integrity and elegant simplicity of these texts and the powerful myths they depict wind up sloppy, trivial, and ultimately unworthy of the plays on which they are based.

Historical examples that demonstrate this principle can be traced to the striking modernism that Granville-Barker brought to Gilbert Murray's translations of Euripides, or the mass environmental spectacle Max Reinhardt orchestrated for *Oedipus Rex* at the Circus Schumann. Brecht, of course, took a more pointed political stance when he adapted *Antigone* in Switzerland in 1948. As usual, his interpretation was based in contemporary politics and Marxist theory. Brecht's Kreon was a Hitler, an ambitious tyrant murdering his way to power. Antigone's defiance showed how the individual could resist totalitarianism. The stage, designed by Caspar Neher, was almost bare. The actors, wearing plain black robes, entered at the opening and remained on stage, seated on benches in a semicircle at the back of the stage. Four tall poles topped with horses' skulls defined the square playing area. A rack of masks, used to represent the Theban Elders, stood at one side. A huge gong hung opposite.[3] The production, perhaps Brecht's most elegant, created the *Verfremsdungeffekt* through a formal minimalism in which nothing was included that was not essential to the actors' telling of the story. Nothing that was not onstage at the beginning was added later; nothing was removed. The stage was sealed into a self-contained and self-sufficient uni-

43

verse. "The spectator is not supposed to share an experience but to come to grips with it," Brecht wrote.[4] He wanted the theatre to view history and social life with the objectivity of the scientist. Here was Greek simplicity drawn with the clinical precision of an anatomical rendering.

In the 1960s, amid Happenings, the Vietnam War, and experiments in the New Theatre, Greek and Roman dramas were infused with topical allusions to American politics, especially the war, sexual liberation, and the evolving counterculture. When the Living Theatre revived Brecht's *Antigone* in 1967, it became a play about civil disobedience and an indictment of its passive but not assertively pacifist audience. The same cast that stared down the spectators at the beginning of the performance finally retreated from them in terror after they had watched in silence as Kreon (Julian Beck) tyrannized and tormented the righteous heroine (Judith Malina). Malina, who also translated the text from German, stated her objective clearly and simply: "How can I make it clear that civil disobedience is an old and very good idea?" But the Living's antiart aesthetics generated the usual divided critical response. Gordon Rogoff wrote that "The Living Theatre is now the most beautiful acting company in the world. . . . [T]hey are beautiful, I suppose, because they do not look like actors."[5] Margaret Croyden, on the other hand, declared the acting insipid and the whole effort garbled into "amateurish mishmash."[6]

The final years of the sixties proved prolific for the adaptation of Greek plays into the experimental-theatre vernacular. In 1968, Tyrone Guthrie staged *The House of Atreus* in Minneapolis and brought it to New York. The lavish production relied on such heavy-handed theatre-historical artifacts as masks, robes, formal declamation, and an all-male cast to revive the spirit of the ancient amphitheatre. Richard Schechner, reviewing the production in the *Educational Theatre Journal,* called its trappings "tinsel" and renounced its effect as "operatic in the worst Wagnerian way."[7] The same year, Jan Kott "confronted" Euripides' *Orestes* in a New Theatre experiment at the University of California, Berkeley, that transferred references to the Peloponnesian War to the more immediate and volatile situation in Vietnam.

Two productions at Yale in the late sixties (when Brustein headed the Drama School) also made significant contributions to rejuvenating the ancients for the modern stage. In 1967 Jonathan Miller directed *Prometheus Bound,* adapted by Robert Lowell, in an abstract setting based on the idea of a seventeenth-century chamber used in the Spanish Inquisition. "Classics are simply residues," Miller told his cast, "maps left over from earlier cultures; they invite you to make some sort of imaginative movement."[8] The director saw the seventeenth century as a historical hinge between the ancient and modern worlds because our knowledge of classical antiquity is largely based on the inheritance of Renaissance discoveries. The setting was meant to conjure up images of tyrants from Zeus to Cromwell to Hitler and "perhaps even Lyndon Johnson," wrote an observer.[9] "I wanted to escape from that deadening limbo of metaphysics," Miller told an interviewer, referring to the white robes and chanting choruses of traditional Greek productions. "It has less and less resonance for us. . . . We thought it would be far more exciting if we could set it in some institution that represents tyranny."[10] His production scheme reduced the gods to fallible human form, and the characters, dwarfed by the imposing set, were prisoners who acted out the story to pass the time.

In 1969, also at Yale, Andre Gregory directed a "hippie" version of *The Bacchae* that bombarded its audiences with sensory stimuli. The set, a skeletal steel scaffold, was meant to represent both the palace and the skull of Pentheus. Electronic music by Richard Peaslee, burning incense, and contrasting scenes in dark and bright light enhanced the feeling of sharing the hero's stormy internal experience.

The most notorious Greek-play adaptation of the period, however, was *Dionysus in '69,* conceived and directed by Richard Schechner. A practical demonstration of Schechner's "Six Axioms for Environmental Theatre," the production filled a huge, converted garage on Wooster Street with scaffolding, spectators, and sexuality to create a powerful and emotionally raw experience of the ancient myth as contemporary allegory. It struck familiar countercultural chords and attracted a lot of attention for its daring use of nudity and environmental staging. Essentially an original piece based on *The Bacchae,* the production billed itself as "somewhat like Euripides," and was subjected to unfair criticism for neglecting its classical source. A detailed photobook documents the performance and describes the deep personal commitment of the group's members as they worked toward an emotionally true yet presentational mode of characterization that openly acknowledged the actor in the role. Performers alternately identified themselves by their own and their characters' names. In the book, Schechner articulates the group's objectives: "Most important by far is our struggle to expose our feelings, to reveal ourselves, to be open, receptive, vulnerable; to give and take hard and deeply; to use impulse and feelings in our work."[11]

The punning title itself suggests that the piece was really about contemporary sexual politics and breaking away from social and theatrical norms and taboos. The words "theatre," "actor," and "audience" are conspicuously absent from the whole enterprise and Schechner's writings about it. "The Performance Group" played to "spectators" in "the Performing Garage," in

what can only be taken as a rejection of established theatrical habits and definitions. Rumors of nightly sexual encounters between members of the cast
and, on some nights, with members of the audience, were common, although
the director insists there were no opportunities for sexual intercourse during
the performance. He admits that there were one or two incidents early in the
run, but that when the company sensed that audiences were coming to see
the play out of purely prurient interest, costumes were kept on throughout.[12] Still, some willing participants later admitted to feeling they had been
manipulated or violated.

Dionysus in '69 also took some hits for poorly articulated language, a tendency toward self-indulgence, and mistaking physical for psychic contact. Its
eleven-month run suggests, however, that the production touched a nerve in
the youth-oriented and sexually rebellious spirit of its times. Writing for *The
Nation* magazine, Julius Novick praised the director and his company for
"not just playing around with this year's modish theatrical techniques. They
are for the most part remarkably faithful to their incomplete, even distorted,
but still cogent conception of what *The Bacchae* is all about."[13] Others found
the production reckless and intellectually empty. "What was missing in
Schechner's frenetic production was any sense of [Kott's] 'collision' with
Euripides' text," according to a later assessment.[14]

FRAGMENTS OF A GREEK TRILOGY

Derived from similar impulses and sources as *Dionysus in '69* and the other
late-1960s productions, Serban's *Fragments* (1972–4) achieved a beauty and
clarity that far exceeded all earlier – and most subsequent – attempts. In
1970, Ellen Stewart used a Ford Foundation grant to rescue Andrei Serban,
then in his late twenties, from the brutal censors in his native Romania. Serban's mentor, Liviu Ciulei, had managed to get out a few years earlier.[15]
Serban's first project at La MaMa, in 1972, was the first part of the trilogy.
Medea immediately established his Western reputation as a major emerging
talent. The other two *Fragments* evolved over the next two years, during
which Serban traveled to Bali and Japan and returned, like Meyerhold,
Brecht, and Artaud before him, intrigued by the highly distilled and ritualized forms of Asian theatre. By 1974 the full cycle was in place, including the
throbbing, environmental *Trojan Women* and an *Electra* infused with the still,
studied intensity of Japanese *nō*. Although it continued to evolve over a long
international tour and subsequent revivals, the contours had been sharply
enough defined in the earliest versions to have renewed the Greeks for the
second half of the century, as Granville-Barker's had for the first.

These productions established a rigorous theatrical aesthetic that was at once alien to and in harmony with impulses in the text. With La MaMa as midwife and Artaud, Grotowski, and Brook as their guardian angels, Serban and the Great Jones Repertory Company underwent a long, painstaking period of gestation as they tried to "scrape down to the psychic-tribal essences that made these legends material for tragedy in the first place."[16] From Artaud's total theatre and Schechner's environmentalism, they adopted the use of speech as pure sound and the animation of the entire performance hall to create a "language in space."[17] The final texts combined passages in ancient Greek and Latin, and interpolated verses in African tribal languages. No one in the audience and few of the performers understood exactly what they were saying, but literal meaning was beside the point. The goal was to retrieve and release the phonetic force of those ancient tongues. Serban believed the Greek dramatists chose specific words for their impact as vibrations in the huge Athenian amphitheatre. "The sounds of ancient Greek contain the potential for a special energy to be rediscovered after two thousand years, to be unlocked and acted out," said the director.[18] He wanted his actors and audiences to "see images in the sounds," and feel their "untranslatable" meanings.[19] The cast projected raw emotions through shrieks, moans, growls, wails, and vibrato incantation.

By abandoning comprehensible words, the performance was relieved of its duty to deliver a logical narrative and offered instead carefully modulated visual, aural, and emotional waves. The style harkened back, past the fifth-century, to a more primitive, pre-Athenian civilization. The actors, clad in simple robes of rough cloth, became Artaud's "affective athletes" revealing "elemental" emotions through sound, gesture, movement, and facial expression. The acting recalls Grotowski's "poor theatre" aesthetic, in which the holy actor's voice and body are the primary raw materials of theatrical production. Serban had spent 1971 with Peter Brook, whom he credits with having reinforced for him Grotowski's insistence on stripping the performance down to essentials, the one indispensable component being the actor. Brook taught Serban that all the powers of the performance must be in the actor's control. As Serban synthesized the teachings of Artaud, Grotowski, and Brook, the company created a technique so secure that the actor, in "a completely disciplined state of rebellion," could submit to the moment as he would to falling in love or succumbing to a voodoo spell.[20]

Acting purged of extraneous movement, business, or narrative value carved indelible, emblematic images of human emotion into the space. Moments in *The Trojan Women* exuded feelings as pure as the ping of lead crystal: Cassandra (Valois Mickens) writhing in agitated anguish as she literally

47

spit out her horrified visions; the Trojan women hissing and clucking with lashing tongues as they torment a cowering Helen; Andromache (Priscilla Smith) trilling a high-pitched, vibrato plaint as she anointed Astyanax before surrendering him to slaughter. The intensity Smith brought to the simple gesture of cupping water in her hands and letting it trickle onto the child's skin, and the bittersweet tinkle of the drops in the otherwise silent hall, cut a deep, raw wound of maternal anguish. The scene took on the aura of the Pietà and similar archetypal icons of suffering mothers. The drowning of Cassandra was another astonishing feat of a simple, controlled gesture transformed into something profound. The guards dropped her onto a wooden ramp down which she slowly slid, head first, hair fanning out toward the floor. Her body gave in to gravity in such tiny increments that she appeared to float and then sink. At the end of the play, the enslaved women were led up another ramp to a raised platform. There, they knelt on the floor between tall, curved wooden beams held perpendicular to the floor by their captors. As everyone on stage swayed in unison, their "ship" began its rocking voyage away from Troy. Precision, simplicity, and hypnotic concentration joined in a disciplined technique that grounded the performers so securely to physical tasks that they were free to release an almost frightening, primordial emotional energy.

The production's carefully selected and tightly knit elements were further augmented by music. Elizabeth Swados's score, inspired by Asian and African tribal music, punctuated and underscored the action, swelling and supporting the rise, crest, and fall of the emotional line. Pipes, bells, and drums created a haunting aura that alternated between pain, poignancy, and exhilaration. Swados has said that she took most of her cues from the phonetics of the text. She saw her job as helping the actors perform a "ballet for the mouth."[21]

Audience arrangement was altered in each of the three plays to invoke a particular atmosphere and level of spectator involvement. Artaud had written of a total theatrical environment in which all four corners of the room and the audience in between would be enveloped in the playing area. Again drawing inspiration from Artaud and Grotowski, who found the ideal role for the audience in the silent witness, Serban and set designer Jun Maeda carved alleys down the center of the room, with bleacher seating against the side walls for *Medea* and *Electra*. Medea and Jason stood on platforms at opposite ends of the long rectangle in the middle of the room, casting their harsh words across the abyss of empty space between them. The audience turned their heads from side to side to watch them, as they would a tennis

Figure 1. The masked chorus of *Medea,* the first of the *Fragments of a Trilogy,* directed by Andrei Serban, performed by the Great Jones Repertory Company at La MaMa Experimental Theatre Club, New York, 1972. Photo © Kenn Duncan/Ellen Stewart Private Collection at the La MaMa ETC Archives & Library.

match. *Electra* was played in the open area between the bleachers. Each slow, studied step or gesture could be seen in three dimensions, and the audience was aware of its other half sitting across the room. *The Trojan Women,* subtitled "An Epic Opera," swirled around and through its roving audience as its episodes unfolded in sequence at various stations around the dark room. Actor-guards bearing wooden poles and flaming torches accomplished a miracle of crowd control that never broke the spell of the action. Their gentle prods directed the focus and formation of the assembled who were thus drawn into the performance as voyeur-citizens of the troubled city-state.

Serban did not have a profound intellectual agenda beyond reawakening the contemporary audience's receptivity to purely theatrical stimuli. "We were not searching for Euripides' ideas about the society of his time, but for an energy which produced those ideas," he said.[22] The *Trilogy* was about theatrical energy. An experience shared among the performers and the audience was both the means and the end. "Serban doesn't play around with new literary interpretations," a reporter later observed. "He simply presents the material in highly unexpected, unconventional ways. His genius seems to be in . . . bringing to life the spirit, magic, and theatrical essence of a work."[23] While that assessment may not hold true for all of Serban's directing since, it captures his interests and intentions for the *Fragments*.

The understanding of directorial risks and responsibilities that Serban brought to his work on Greek tragedy in the wake of Artaud is evident in his criticism of other directors' attempts. The point, he said, is "to do violence to oneself only in the sense of trying to challenge oneself. All the other stuff – actors on stage performing acts of sadomasochism and homosexual delights in the name of investigating Artaud – all that is rubbish."[24] The sixties' New Theatres and their gurus craved intense, participatory rituals in the theatre to replace those that had become defunct with the presumption that "God is dead"; but true rituals are evolved from the lives of communities, not manufactured by well-meaning artists on the fringe. In 1980 Jan Kott wisely denounced "all attempts at the rebirth of the 'ritual'" as flops.[25] The Living Theatre and the Performance Group left gaps in their productions for audience members to jump into the fray, but the ultimate participatory effect had been a sham. The audience's role was as play-acted as the rest of the performance and rarely as interesting.

Aware that "ritual" and "ceremonial" are dangerous terms to bandy about the rehearsal hall, Serban built the *Fragments* from the most tangible elements of theatre, hoping that thoughtfully honed and selected bits would coalesce into something bigger, richer, and more resonant.

> Theater is a medium which opens through the breathing of the actors, the movement of one arm and the sound that accompanies it, the way an audience in a room listens, receives and transmits. Somehow a circle is formed with the audience; and when this circle starts functioning, a new quality comes into being.[26]

It was not necessary for audience members to carry spears or to voice reactions. Here Serban followed Grotowski's example and was able to evoke a sense of ritual, or religious service, by assigning the spectator the active role of passive witness. Like guests at Faustus's dinner table, or the living dead in the Auschwitz cemetery, members of the roving, gaping Trojan mob assumed a part in the performance that paralleled their status as members of the audience. This metaphorical approach to audience participation provides a heightened sense of involvement for the spectator while maintaining the integrity of the performance.

The "equivalent structural core" identified earlier as a critical factor in appraising an innovative production of a classical tragedy manifested itself in the *Fragments* through the completeness of Serban's vision and the minute detail of its realization. From the time the audience was led down a narrow, candle-lit corridor to the finale of *Electra,* in which the cast trotted around the central playing space gently clanging hand-forged bells, a purity of conception took over. Everything fit. Serban met the Greeks on the plane of raw human passion. Tenderness, frailty, rage, vengeance, pride, fear, and sexuality were conjured with a bodily hieroglyphics that Artaud and Meyerhold would have admired and a palette of elemental means – water, fire, mud, smoke, and human flesh – that Serban's mentor Brook has not surpassed. The strong guiding hand of a rigorous and genuinely theatrical intelligence could be felt from moment to moment.

Without the story to hold the audience's attention, Serban built a plot whose suspense depended on varying the mood, pace, duration, and location of sequential elements. A plaintive scene was followed by one of rage, as calls answered calls or drums beckoned across the darkened room. Guards led Helen by rope through the crowd as torches suddenly flared up behind or to one side. The audience reconfigured automatically to adjust its focus. Perhaps the highest achievement of the production was that the adjustments were so finely tuned as to seem natural and inevitable within the production framework, never forced, intrusive, or foreign. The aesthetic Serban imposed on the original texts became intrinsic to the production as an independent work of art.

So solid was the conceptual foundation that the company was able to take some big risks. The Trojan women clucked and spat as they smeared Helen's naked body with mud. She was then locked in a cage and raped by a bear. Clytemnestra entered *Electra* with a snake wound around her neck. Such moments can easily teeter into gimmickry or cliché; here, they blended seamlessly into the overall imaginative texture of the plays. As Stanley Kauffmann noted in a rave review, "Serban's [work] would be *arty* if it were not art."[27]

When Serban returned to the Greeks with a production of *Agamemnon* at Lincoln Center in 1977, his method was similar to that for the *Fragments*. Rehearsals centered on vocal work with the ancient Greek and modern English text that Serban had pieced together. Elizabeth Swados again scored the piece with music from Persia, Africa, and the Middle East, creating what

51

she called a "sound structure" for the lines.[28] Three principal actors were double-cast in the six main roles along with a chorus of twenty-six. The chorus dominated the production as it does Aeschylus' text. The director imagined the chorus as a "bridge between us and higher possibilities," and sought in rehearsals to help the performers get past their individual psychological responses to the text to find and release a "shared collective emotion." The ultimate effect was of a "long oratorio."[29] The *New York Times* critic noted that an arena seating arrangement, accomplished with movable bleachers that put audience members all around the stage area, created a round orchestra for choral dance that was reminiscent of ancient playing spaces. The production seemed to go the *Fragments* one step further in re-creating not just the mood of ancient tragedy, but the actual theatrical environment as well. The *Times* critic credited Serban and company with having revived "Greek tragedy as live theatre rather than poetics in a dead language."[30]

SENECA'S *OEDIPUS*

Richard Schechner's staging of Seneca's *Oedipus,* also in 1977, shared some of Serban's holy-theatre trappings. It, too, dealt in tangibles – earth, flesh, and blood – and aimed to conjure mythic images on a human scale. Of course, Seneca's harsh retelling offers neither the poignancy nor hopeful resolutions of the Greek trilogy. Schechner was attracted to the cruel beauty of the story and to Ted Hughes's magnificently terse poetic adaptation. He wanted his audience "to feel that it was very close, that this was not a cultural icon that was being renacted, but that some immediate passion affected these particular people who were tangled in the web of their actions."[31] Turning once again to an environmental approach, the Performance Group acted out the gruesome tale in close proximity to their spectators, in a set construction that enclosed all participants in a tight, claustrophobic circle.

Peter Brook had staged the first production of Hughes's script in London in 1968. Martin Esslin noted then that the Latin original is clumsy, coarse, sadistic, and bloody, and that is "precisely . . . why, in the age of pop art, the Happening, the so-called Theatre of Cruelty, Seneca should have come to seem more immediately relevant."[32] Brook's starkly horrifying production starred John Gielgud and Irene Worth, and proved that this "unstageable" play was no such thing. In characteristic style, Brook dealt symbolically with the graphic violence and hideous imagery in Hughes's script, an adaptation of a translation by David Anthony Turner. Brook's own set design consisted of a blackened stage with a huge, gold cube, tilted and revolving on one corner. All the actors wore brown slacks or skirts and black turtlenecks. What little movement there was occurred before and after speeches. The style was more like a concert recital or staged reading. Yet it managed to shock its audience. According to a cast member, the St. John's Ambulance Brigade stood outside the National Theatre and was required almost nightly to revive swooning audience members.[33]

In rehearsal, Brook led his cast through ten weeks of exercises derived from martial arts, yoga, nonverbal storytelling, and extensive exploration of the intersections between the horrors in the text and the actors' real-life "horrific experiences."[34] Their technique, heavily influenced by Asian theatre disciplines, involved breathing exercises, chanting, and symbolic gestures. The acting style reflected the influences of Brecht and the Japanese theatre that he admired. It was cool, measured, and deliberate, and all the more gut-wrenching for its pristine dispassion. Oedipus blinded himself with a twist of the wrist, then put black patches over his eyes. Jocasta, in perhaps the most famous scene of the production, committed suicide by lowering herself onto an elongated pyramid, impaling the tainted womb that bore her husband-son and his sibling-offspring. Chorus members were dispersed throughout the auditorium, aurally enveloping the spectators in a communal circle whose purpose was to explore the ugly, violent side of human nature. Martin Esslin noted a "perfect fusion" of Brecht's distance and Artaud's phantasmagoria.[35] The controversial evening closed with a raucous bacchanal satirizing the whole event. The chorus, toting a giant phallus as a Maypole, danced up and down the aisles, satirizing gory scenes from the play and singing "Yes We Have No Bananas" to the accompaniment of a Dixieland band.

In contrast, Schechner's down-and-dirty production scheme seems almost a revolt against Brook's rarefied approach, but the American director denies that he knew much about Brook's production. He recalls having seen a picture of the phallic-dance epilogue, which did not interest him, and he insists that his work was in no way a response to Brook's.[36] Schechner's connection to the text was more personal. The work on *Oedipus* coincided with the breakup of his marriage to Joan MacIntosh, who played Jocasta and was pregnant through much of the rehearsal period. "It was a play of personal anguish for us," Schechner recalls. "And it was the last work we did together."

As with *Dionysus in '69,* Schechner brought an environmental concept and a raw acting technique to the Performance Group's work on Hughes's text, but this time they adhered to the text absolutely. The director drew parallels between the Roman version of the Oedipus story and the gladiatorial contests that were popular in ancient Rome. To him, Oedipus is like an animal "being led to sacrifice." As in a gladiator's game or a bullfight, says Schechner,

> the end is known. As soon as the animal appears, you know it's going to die. There's nothing for it to do but fulfill its destiny in death. The only question is whether the death will be clumsy and slow or quick and more or less beautiful.

The environment Jim Clayburgh designed in response to Schechner's vision was a seven-tiered, circular pit modeled on the Roman Colosseum. The approximately twenty-foot-diameter circle in the middle was filled three feet deep with twenty-seven tons of dirt. Four vomitoria provided the only means of access to both actors and spectators. In the effort to create a sense of communality, Peter Brook had surrounded his audience with performers; Schechner and Clayburgh surrounded the performers with a small but close-range audience of 150. Benches built into the seven rings of seating area were pitched forward toward the central ring. The effect induced a sense of "vertigo" in one observer.[37]

Entrances into and exits from the enclosed space were mediated by a tall, muscular bodyguard (John Holmes), who spent most of the performance beating a rhythm on a kettle drum in the outer ring of the ground level. Stephen Borst, who played Oedipus, had the option of trying to flee the pit at any point during the performance when he thought he could get past the guard. When Holmes heard Borst's footsteps on one of the ramps, he would rush down the vomitorium, block Oedipus' path, and fling him back into the dirt.

A single, 2,000-watt fresnel hung over the stage. It moved at the rate and angle that the sun shifts over the earth, reinforcing the compression of the action into ninety real-time minutes. While the audience filed into the space at the beginning of the performance, two chorus members buried masks (made from the casts' faces) in the dirt. Schechner believes that *Oedipus* is largely about "leaving traces." He was very pleased by the dirty footprints that accumulated on the various ramps each evening as actors and spectators traversed the environment. At each mention of "digging into the past" or "burrowing in that darkness," performers would dig through the dirt with their bare hands to uncover the masks. Sometimes the unearthed masks were packed with dirt and then overturned and pressed into the ground. When lifted away, they left a bas relief of dirt faces. The masks were also used to

Figure 2. The bodyguard and members of the chorus bury masks in the dirt pit as the audience files into the arena for Richard Schechner's production of Seneca's *Oedipus* at the Performing Garage, New York, 1977. Photo © The Richard Schechner Papers/Princeton University Libraries.

abstract major confrontations between the characters. For example, the chorus member who played the Shepherd thrust her mask toward Oedipus but looked out toward the audience while recounting the tale of the ousted baby. Tiresias wore a dark mask of two cut-off hands that covered his eyes. The blinded Oedipus later wore a mask of the same design in a lighter color. There was also a mask of Oedipus' foot.

Whereas Brook had seen the play as an exploration of the ugly, Schechner feels that it deals with the "horrendous, the horrific, the unspeakable, the awful, the awesome, the fact that life can clobber you on the head." Our continuing attraction to the Oedipus legend, and especially to Seneca's graphic version of it, has to do with its perfect, inexorable inevitability.

I think there's a certain kind of beauty about the destiny's fulfillment. It is beautiful, but horrifically beautiful, in the way that the mushroom cloud of the atom bomb is beautiful. If we didn't admire its beauty and its incandescence, we wouldn't fear it so much.

Schechner saw Oedipus as an innocent, a good son, a good king who has done "everything he was supposed to do" but is caught in the web of his fate.

> He knows the truth on some level, but he needs proof. It is psychoana-lytical in the sense that the circumstances tell you who you are, but you don't feel that's who you are, because you're really repressing it and in denial. So once it's proven beyond a doubt that's who he is, his feeling captures him in one rush and he blinds himself.

Stephen Borst in the title role wore a diaperlike garment and kept one foot turned in at all times. As he listened to the final damning evidence, he lowered his face into the dirt. When he looked up again, he saw his fate.

John Holmes, the bodyguard, doubled in the role of the second messenger, who reports Oedipus' offstage self-blinding. As he spoke, Holmes grabbed a fistful of dirt in each hand to represent the king's eyeballs. At the crucial point in his report, he thrust his head back, tossed the dusty piles into the air, and let the muck fall back onto his face. Oedipus then groped his way back onto the stage, blinded by the mask of cut-off hands and naked but for the mud smeared over his body.

For Schechner, Jocasta's story is quite different. One of the unique features of this adaptation is Jocasta's appearance in the first scene of the play. She urges Oedipus to stop his pursuit of the truth even before any of the evidence surfaces. Schechner is convinced that she knows Oedipus' identity all along, and that her tragedy lies in the fact that she seals her own fate through a series of conscious choices. Oedipus' name, his marked foot, his age, his resemblance to Laius, Schechner believes, all point to Jocasta's indeniable knowledge of who he is. "She knows as soon as he walks in, but taking Oedipus as her husband is the greatest vengence she can have against Laius." The queen's murdered husband had exiled her only child and then refused her any more children. She exacts her pent-up rage at him by marrying their returned son and having four babies in quick succession. Joan MacIntosh's Jocasta, pregnant for the fifth time in ten years, wore heavy, stylized makeup (another kind of mask) and an exposed rubber body cast of her full breasts and swelling belly. (The cast was made on MacIntosh's own pregnant form.)

When Oedipus finally accepts the truth, says Schechner, Jocasta must kill herself because she is truly guilty and cannot face her self-mutilated husband-son. MacIntosh dug Oedipus' sword out of the dirt and plunged it upward into her tainted, swollen womb. Amniotic fluid poured out and soaked the dirt into a thick, bloody puddle.

Unfortunately, the critical record suggests that these rich ideas and images did not coalesce into a penetrating exploration of the text, although Clayburgh's environment was universally admired. Again, as in *Dionysus in '69*, reviewers complained of a lack of directorial editing and the actors' awkward speaking of the text. Only Joan MacIntosh received appreciative notices. The rest of the cast were considered technically and emotionally underprepared to cope with the demands of Hughes's text. Critics balked almost unanimously at slurred, urban articulation by Stephen Borst as Oedipus. They were baffled by Caroline Ducrocq's gender switch and impenetrable French accent in the role of Tiresias, and irritated by Ron Guttman's stuttering Creon. "If verbal distortion is part of an esthetic strategy, it must never appear arbitrary or insignificant," wrote Gerald Rabkin.[38] The *New York Times* reviewer said the language suffered in both "sound and sense."[39]

Schechner is quick to defend the work. While he admits that he is never completely happy with his productions, he was satisfied with the performances of *Oedipus,* including the speaking of the text, which he found "explosive" and "full of interior tension." He attributes some of the critics' distaste for his work to his own long-standing opposition to the whole process of journalistic reviewing. Press critics, Schechner claims, "are stupid":

If they're not stupid, they're stupid to be in such a dumb profession. They are forced to pass judgement rather than to evaluate in a deeper sense. They only see something once, and they write under an impossible time pressure.

Because he has been open about his distaste for press critics, the director expects that reviewers come to his work predisposed not to like it.

Whether or not this animosity is indeed mutual, the anecdote reminds me how difficult is the business of writing honestly about works of art and trying to make judgments about theatrical events one has not actually seen. So glaring are the disparities between Schechner's recollections and the critic's reports that I can only reconcile them by believing and doubting both sides of the story. A fair appreciation of the work should acknowledge the seriousness and creativity that went into its development. For example, the cast went to a slaughterhouse, bought a calf's head, and gouged out its eyes, to imagine what it would be like to be Oedipus. In an early phase of rehearsal, they held an open rehearsal on a gritty sandbar in what is now Battery Park City. I'll bet few, if any, critics knew of these activities. On the other hand, spectators can only respond to the finished product as presented to the audience in the heat of performance. As professional spectators, *Oedipus*'s critics seem to have been confronted with a thoughtful and passionate but poorly spoken enactment of this exquisitely awful play. "Vigor," as one relatively balanced account put it, was "better sustained than vision."[40]

THE GOSPEL AT COLONUS

Vigor is inseparable from Lee Breuer's vision of *The Gospel at Colonus*, first produced at the Brooklyn Academy of Music's inaugural Next Wave Festival in 1983. "It's always been my interest to find a way toward a classic theatre that doesn't imitate a European model," says the director.[41] The American language, the rhythms of life in this country, especially urban life, our immigrant culture, he believes, deserve a crack at the classics on their own terms. In the pounding urgency of the black church, Breuer detected the seeds of a contemporary and authentically American equivalent of tragic catharsis; and in Sophocles' *Oedipus at Colonus*, he saw an opportunity to reflect the internal exile of American blacks.

> I wanted to make a statement that a white man can work not just with a bunch of black intellectuals who have gone to Yale, but with the real performers – that I could respect their art and they could respect mine and that we would not rip each other off, thus disproving the idea that never the twain shall meet. In other words that I could make an integration statement in terms of this country by making it happen on stage.[42]

The director was not overly concerned by discrepancies between the Greek philosophy espoused by Sophocles and the contemporary situation to which he meant to draw references. "I try to mount the work *as* a political statement," says Breuer, "not that *says* the political statement."[43] *The Gospel* revived catharsis in uniquely American terms by weaving Sophocles' *Oedipus at Colonus* into a parable recounted at an evangelical service.

Breuer's earlier direction of *The Tempest* and Wedekind's *Lulu* also grew out of his desire to find uniquely American responses to classic texts.[44] He peopled *The Tempest* with impersonations of contemporary pop stars and celebrities in whose images he saw the echoes of Shakespeare's characters. Disney tunes, a helicopter instead of a ship in the storm scene, a samba band in the masque scene, and other references to the icons of our mass culture transformed Shakespeare, according to Robert Brustein's gentle review of this 1981 New York Shakespeare Festival flop, into "an idiomatic glossary of our time."[45] *Lulu*, adapted by Michael Feingold and produced at the American Repertory Theatre earlier in 1981, transformed Wedekind's Berlin to Hollywood in the 1970s. As in *The Tempest*, Breuer represented the characters as film stars. Lulu was a punk-rock queen; other characters appeared as William Randolph Hearst and Marion Davies, Douglas Fairbanks, Carmen Miranda, and Esther Williams. The music ranged from rock to reggae and samba. The story unfolded in a postsync studio during a dubbing session for a new film. Filmed scenes from the play, often shot in extreme close-up, were projected upstage while the live actors behaved in sync with or in contrast to the looming background images. "Real people," wrote the production dramaturge, "[became] insignificant compared to their fantasies."[46] Neither Breuer nor the critics were happy with either of these productions. The director's inventions never coalesced, but, with the wisdom of hindsight, they can be seen as valuable warm-ups for *The Gospel*.

In both previous attempts at classics, in Breuer's continuing experimental work with Mabou Mines, and in *The Gospel at Colonus*, popular culture and electronic media served as liaisons between difficult or remote plays and contemporary audiences. *Tempest* actors wore microphones until the final scene, when Raul Julia, as Prospero, removed his, relinquishing the final implement of his magic powers. The use of film in *Lulu* lent Brechtian distance to the performance. Breuer's Beckett productions relied heavily on electronic devices to dissect, interpret, and concretize abstract images. When composer Bob Telson invited Breuer to a concert by gospel stars Clarence Fountain and the Five Blind Boys from Alabama, the director recognized a live vein of ecstatic ritual into which he could plug an electronically mediated, aggressively contemporary staging of a classic play. The group's blindness immediately brought Oedipus to mind. Affinities between the passion of Christ and the final days of the doomed Theban king led him to select Sophocles' *Oedipus at Colonus* as the source text.

"As the experimental theatre world was interested in a kind of conceptual coolness," Breuer says, "I became more interested in cathartic theatre. I really feel that if you go one step further with cathartic theatre you might find pity and terror turning into joy and ecstasy."[47] Artaud, Grotowski, Brook, and Schechner had traveled to the remotest corners of the third world in

Figure 3. Morgan
Freeman presides over
The Gospel at Colonus,
featuring the Brooklyn
Institutional Radio
Choir and Clarence
Fountain and the Five
Blind Boys from Ala-
bama, directed by Lee
Breuer, at the Brook-
lyn Academy of Music,
1983. Photo © Johan
Elbers.

search of tribal rituals on which to model Western theatrical events. As if
taking his cue from Dorothy in *The Wizard of Oz,* Breuer needed to look no
further than his own backyard. To find the key to tragic catharsis, he discovered, there was really no place like home.

"What we found in *Colonus* was that we had a wonderful new key to
classical narrative – a didactic and oratorical device – by using the preaching

rhythm inherent in the Baptist and Pentecostal churches."[48] He was convinced that gospel music and its secular offspring, rhythm and blues and rock and roll, had the power to excite genuine catharsis in a contemporary American audience, and that the music could push the tragic tale through pity and terror into joy. With Telson as composer, Breuer transformed Robert Fitzgerald's translation of *Oedipus at Colonus* into a gospel opera disguised as a star-studded revival meeting. The story of Oedipus' death was narrated and acted out as a parable told within the service.

Breuer read Sophocles' text, written just before the poet's death at age 90, as a "sermon on a happy death."[49] In *The Gospel* the sermon is delivered by a guest preacher, played in the lilting cadences of the black pulpit by Morgan Freeman. The Preacher opened the service with the line, "I take for my text this evening The Book of Oedipus," and referred to page numbers in "your text" as the service progressed. Breuer had just spent ten weeks in Japan when he began work on *The Gospel* script, and he designed Freeman's role according to the narrative tradition used in *kabuki* and *nō*. The Preacher recounted most of the story in the third person, functioning in at least four roles – as *choregus*, narrator, cleric, and sometimes speaking Oedipus' lines. The other characters, who appeared at key points in the narrative, were sung by soloists backed by four well-established gospel choirs. Oedipus was portrayed mainly by Clarence Fountain and the Five Blind Boys from Alabama. Ismene was sung by Jevette Steele of the J. D. Steele Singers. Members of the Original Soul Stirrers and the forty-member Brooklyn Institutional Radio Choir also came forward to portray characters. Isabell Monk played Antigone. Self-conscious acting, another influence from Brecht, enabled them to suggest two layers of characterization. Like the Preacher, they presented themselves as church functionaries contributing to the worship service by acting out parts in the sermon.

Similarly, the audience was assigned the role of congregation, a passive-witness function that fits Grotowski's ideal, and goes it one better without the excess of the 1960s. Breuer remembered having read that "some scholars now feel that the tragedies were close to rock concerts, that there were responses from the audience like choral or choir responses in the church."[50] Audience members responded with "amens" and "hallelujahs," and the final song was a sing-along.

As Brecht and Meyerhold had done in adapting other classical texts, Breuer interpolated passages from other texts to support his revision. Speeches taken from *Oedipus Rex* and *Antigone* reinforced loose parallels with such Judeo–Christian themes as the role of fate in human destiny and the need to make peace with self, family, community, and heaven before dying. Telson's gospel melodies, which a reviewer called "one of the best white-man's capturings of the essence of black music since Gershwin's *Porgy and Bess*,"[51] easily bridged the gap between the Greek story and the Christian setting. Chronologically, according to the narrative, *Oedipus at Colonus* is sandwiched between *Oedipus Rex* and *Antigone*. Breuer's script begins by picking up themes from the end of the first play in the trilogy. "Then may you be blessed, and may heaven be kinder to you than it has been to me!" says the freshly blinded King in *Oedipus Rex*. "But all I can do now is bid you pray that you may live wherever you are let live, and that your life be happier than your father's."[52] Breuer simplified the phrasing: *The Gospel* lyrics read, "Live where you can / Be happy as you can / Happier than God has made your father." The chorus speaks the final lines of *Oedipus Rex:* "Call no man fortunate that is not dead. / The dead are free from pain." Antigone's opening lines in *The Gospel* are "Let no man presume on his fortune until he find life, at his death, without pain."[53]

The second act of *The Gospel* opens after the intermission with a song taken as is from the first choral ode to Sophocles' *Antigone:* "Numberless are the world's wonders, but none / More wonderful than man." The passage is about man's omnipotence in the face of all but his own mortality, and it blends nicely into Oedipus' final hours. It ends: "From every wind he has made himself secure / From all but one . . . all but one / In the late wind of death he cannot stand."[54] Inclusion of this passage also helped suggest affinities to Christian teaching. The church urges its faithful to reconcile themselves to the inevitability of death and to resolve earthly conflicts in preparation for entry to heaven. *The Gospel* shows Oedipus doing much the same thing as he seeks "eternal sleep" in a peaceful "resting place." The significance of the theme was further underscored by set designer Alison Yerxa's baroque, painted backdrop. The huge mural showed dark figures jumping skyward from a ragged cliff. They aimed up, but an abyss of rough water lay waiting below for those who did not make the grade.

Parallels between Christian theology and Greek mythology were not stressed, however, and those critics who looked for profundity in this aspect of the production were inevitably disappointed. Interestingly, few of those who wrote about the original BAM production fell into that trap. Most of the 1983 Next Wave Festival critics were enthusiastic. *Newsweek* ran a flattering column called "Oedipus Jones." The title, referring to *Carmen Jones*, is a reminder that *The Gospel* has precedents not only in the early 1970s' religious rock operas *Jesus Christ Superstar, Joseph and the Amazing Technicolor Dreamcoat*, and *Godspell*, but also in Orson Welles's 1936 "voodoo" *Macbeth*, Oscar Hammersteins II's 1943 adaptation of Bizet's *Carmen*, and other attempts to explore classics in the context of black American culture.

Michael Feingold, writing for the *Voice*, said "the validation of Breuer's daring comes from the striking ease with which all the elements of story and performance blend together." Feingold called *The Gospel* "quite conceivably a turning point for the theatre as a whole."[55] A *Voice* follow-up feature by Elinor Fuchs praised *The Gospel at Colonus* for having returned religious ecstasy to the "ironic and analytical" postmodern theatre. Not since Reinhardt's *The Miracle*, she recalled, had New York audiences been given an opportunity to "embrace the religious mysteries" in the theatre. "An entire branch of theatre is risen again," she exclaimed.[56]

In 1988, when *The Gospel* had a limited run on Broadway, more traditional critics jumped at the chance to fault its ideological weaknesses. "However much of Sophocles can be shoehorned into a church service," Frank Rich complained in the *New York Times*, "the matching up of Christian theology with Greek mythology remains a marriage of glib intellectual convenience that distorts and dilutes both."[57] The *New York Newsday* reviewer called *The Gospel* "philosophical gibberish . . . as irrational as one of those late-night brainstorms that should have been told 'nahhh' in the morning."[58] Because *The Gospel*, like the best conceptual theatre, reinvents the theatrical experience as well as the particular play, the degree of theological agreement between Sophocles' text and the black evangelical tradition is not crucial here. More important is the way Breuer and Telson reformulated the Greek story in gospel idiom as a metaphor for contemporary America.

Not surprisingly, Gerald Rabkin put Breuer's work on *The Gospel* in a deconstructionist context with that of other directors "who have destabilized traditional categories of language and meaning by arguing that every literary text is both equivocal and intertextual, that is, it reveals no obvious or single meaning." In a program essay by Rabkin, Breuer is depicted as the "recuperator" of the text, one who fills in the resonant spaces suggested by the text with theatrical gestures that concretize ambiguous or abstract impulses in the original. The theatrical gestures need not adhere to surface or traditional interpretations of what the play is about. Rabkin quotes Barthes's approval of "manhandling the text" to arrive at a deliberate "misreading" that "rejects the false illusion of absolute and unequivocal meaning."[59] In Kott's metaphor, the play changes meaning in production according to the times, styles, and ideas with which it is brought into collision. *The Gospel* bounces the Greek play off the church, and each is enriched by resonances of the other.

In another context, Charles Marowitz has described the complex symbiosis of text and production in much simpler terms that are worth reiterating here. Marowitz detects a reciprocal relationship between classic texts and reconceived productions, a dialogue that reverberates with the clash of past and present. "A connection develops between a contemporary allusion and the material that has given birth to it," he writes, referring to his own "highly subjective, quirky . . . and occasionally perverse" responses to the plays of Shakespeare.[60] As long as the director's ideas are anchored to impulses in the text, he is confident that script and performance will cast reflections back and forth, each augmenting and clarifying the other. Holly Hill, reviewing the Brooklyn production of *The Gospel at Colonus* for the London *Observer,* said it left her eager both to reread Sophocles and to attend a black church.

In fact, Oedipus' story hit home with unusual poignancy and intensity. His outrage at Polyneices, the tenderness between him and Antigone, the pity of the decrepit former patriarch pleading with strangers for simple shelter, the daughters' heartbreak at their father's passing rang true in images that were at once familiar and timeless. The confluence of the 1960s' civil rights movement and the increasing omnipresence of television in American homes had brought the cadences of black preaching into our living rooms on the evening news. The speeches of Martin Luther King, Jr., popularized and legitimized the idiom for mainstream American audiences. Morgan Freeman's distinct but underplayed depiction of the Preacher capitalized on that foundation and underscored the poetry in the Fitzgerald translation.

The genius of Breuer's transformation was to be found in how the production reflected life in black America. Richard Corliss, writing for *Time* magazine, struck the key to *The Gospel* when he compared Sophocles' theme, "man's acceptance of inevitable death," to Breuer's theme, blacks' acceptance of a "hard life in these United States."[61] Alienated, emasculated, poor, persecuted, and powerless, Clarence Fountain's Oedipus reiterated the status of blacks in this country from slavery to legal segregation to the urban ghetto. The plaintive, angry, tenacious strains of Telson's score, theatricalized and a step removed from its usual context, bared the roots of gospel music and what it must mean to a people determined to survive in the face of hate, repression, rejection, frustration, and fear. The lyrics to the finale, "Now, let the weeping cease," were taken directly from the final lines of the Fitzgerald text, but they broadcast a strictly American message. When Carolyn Johnson-White's solo rang out from the ranks of the full Brooklyn Institutional Radio Choir, the song swelled to an affirmation of strength, persistence, and faith. At that moment, it was possible to imagine a band of Negro slaves gathering for Sunday prayer and singing out to release their pent-up rage, soothe their battered psyches, and find the spiritual nourishment to get through the week. Oppressed but spiritually irrepressible are those who sang and sing the gospel. Artaud expected the theatre to purge the community of festering impulses. In its search for a uniquely American cathartic release, *The Gospel* tapped a native, musical steam valve. The performance aroused and relieved its audience as the Oedipus story, the sermon, and the music came to parallel resolutions.

The aesthetic for redirecting classical tragedy may be borrowed wholesale, as was the black church service for the *Gospel,* or developed specifically for the production, as was the unmediated but sharply honed style of the *Fragments.* Part of the pleasure of *The Gospel* was in recognizing familiar conventions. Even spectators who were not black churchgoers could appreciate the way the director restructured the play according to the protocol of the service. In *Fragments of a Trilogy* we enjoyed a vision of the world as we might never have imagined it. In both productions, the goal was less to elucidate original themes than to revive the spirit and energy of Greek theatre in images accessible to the contemporary audience. What distinguished these two exceptional productions is the extent to which they were able to realize potent, alien stage idioms and still keep in continuous contact with impulses, ideas, and situations in the text. In Schechner's productions, on the other hand, hodgepodges of "poor theatre" effects and topical allusions, punctuated by flashes of good ideas, ultimately dissipated their own energies.

Two of *auteur*-director Robert Wilson's classical forays need also be mentioned in this context – the 1981 *Medea* and 1986 *Alcestis*. Although, in the context of the current discussion, his use of classic texts is more personal, radical, and distanced from the original plays, these productions marked a shift in Wilson's willingness to create theatre from scripted dramatic texts. The *Medea* script, adapted with Minos Volonakis, included passages in ancient and modern Greek and in English. In addition to Euripides' plot, which, typically, opens near the climax of Medea's story, Wilson tacked on an extended prologue depicting Medea's bloody exodus from Colchis and her wedding to Jason. In these preliminary scenes and throughout much of the production, the director used his hallmark slow-motion tempo. Unlike most tempestuous Medeas, Wilson's heroine moved through the events of her extraordinary life with the dignified, almost placid demeanor of one in a trance. Wilson also added a final, silent scene in which Jason watched his house burn down. Visually stunning in its processional style, and adequate in its presentation of Euripides' plot, Wilson's embellished *Medea* was ultimately more like his other, self-generated spectacles than a revisionist rendering of Euripides' play.

The history of Wilson's *Alcestis,* which strayed even farther from its source, suggests that the contract with an ancient playwright is simply untenable to the maverick director. This time Wilson worked with a severely abridged version of the Fitts and Fitzgerald translation of Euripides, prepared by Robert Brustein. When Heiner Müller, whose text for *the CIVIL warS* in 1985 had marked the beginning of significant collaborative relationship, suggested that Wilson again add a prologue and epilogue to his production, Wilson asked Müller to prepare new texts. The prologue turned out to be "Description of a Painting / Explosion of a Memory," a single sentence that goes on for nine pages, describing an imaginary, surrealistic landscape. Coincidentally, images from the playlet echoed several of the ones Wilson had begun to establish in the staging of the main play. They included a giant Cycladic statue and a human mummy who stood on the statue's crossed arms and recited the text "in a pure androgynous voice while other, electronic voices coming from various speakers located throughout the house" repeated sections. For the epilogue, Müller declined to write new material, recommending instead that Wilson stage "The Birdcatcher in Hell," a *kyōgen* farce very much in the spirit of the ancient Greek satyr plays.

Wilson had been unhappy with *Medea* and sought in this production to find a more satisfactory relationship to his text. "I didn't like the question—answer situation," he said of that production's adherence to the dialogue. "I felt I had to make it more my own."[62] So, around the text Wilson created a striking, visual landscape crammed with the artifacts of ancient, modern, Eastern and Western cultures. The set, designed by Tom Kamm and inspired by the vistas Wilson had seen during a 1985 visit to Delphi, focused on a mountainside in which were embedded the prow of a Viking ship and three Chinese funerary statues. The other major elements were a sunken river and three cypress trees. The least prominent element of the production was the story of a young wife's willingness to sacrifice her life at her husband's asking. Instead, Wilson created a multicultural, multisensory theatrical environment in which the unfolding of that story took on universal implications, demonstrating the director's contention that myths belong not just to their own culture but "to all people of all times."[63]

Wilson's statement is probably not specific enough to substantiate the kind of production that truly illuminates an old play for a new stage, but it does cut to the prime motivation for redirecting classical drama. Directors who take on the challenge of redefining these plays are looking to resuscitate the gale force of mythic drama. These several additional examples reiterate the idea that there are many ways to achieve that goal; but, as Richard Beacham has pointed out, the least adroit are those directorial approaches that treat the classical script merely as a "found object" that gets put in the theatre mill and processed.[64] The most effective formulas for reinterpreting these formidable plays for the stage derive their strength from the directors' paradoxical mix of awe and audacity in confronting the archetypal dramas of Western civilization.

4

THE PLAYS OF SHAKESPEARE
≡ ⊛ ≡

ECADES BEFORE Jan Kott declared Shakespeare our contemporary, visionary directors and designers had boldly ushered his plays into the twentieth century. Gordon Craig, Granville-Barker, Robert Edmond Jones, and Orson Welles are among those whose Shakespearean productions struck at the nineteenth-century cobwebs that clung to the plays well into the 1900s. Given that Shakespeare is nearly synonymous with "classics" in the English-speaking theatre, it is no surprise that, at some stage of their careers, American directors of ample ambition are likely to test their mettle against one or more of his plays. Beside the poetic, intellectual, and theatrical merits of any individual work, the Shakespeare plays as a phenomenon are the Mount Everest of Western theatre – a canonical challenge that must be faced simply because it is there. To directors, Shakespeare offers complexity and ambiguity to fire the theatrical imagination and established traditions against which to rebel.

Twentieth-century American theatre history is chockablock with "nontraditional" Shakespeare. Chapter 2 chronicled the early phases: Abstract design, modern dress, and historical transposition were the main strategies in both serious productions and novelty attempts to "jolly up" Shakespeare, as Tyrone Guthrie put it. Most of these productions fall into Brustein's simile category. Up until the late 1960s, neither of the two dominant strains of American Shakespeare production had evolved into a cogent native approach. "Straight" versions could be heavy, overintellectualized costume pieces in which American actors mouthed the verse in pseudo-British accents. "Jolly" romps through the comedies and sleek updates of the tragedies, though popular, were often superficial entertainments, anti-intellectual antidotes to the obligatory Shakespeare considered good for you. Both types of production are still popular on Broadway and in festivals around the country.

In *Recycling Shakespeare,* Charles Marowitz devotes a short chapter to "Seven American Misconceptions" about staging the bard's plays. He includes among them the following antithetical Yankee notions: "The only way to approach Shakespeare is to contemporize him," and "The only correct way to stage Shakespeare is to adopt the traditional approach."[1] Marowitz attributes the American compulsion to update the plays to the fact that Americans cannot speak the verse and thus feel compelled to cover their inadequacies through "gussied up" theatrical "superficies." Never one to mince words, Marowitz vents his spleen at the way "the American genius for innovation and experiment hits its nadir in the weird and grotesque permutations American directors foist onto the plays in their misguided attempts to popularise them."[2]

As for the second wrongheaded American supposition, Marowitz swiftly debunks the very idea of a Shakespearean tradition by recalling that the closing of the London theatres in 1642 curtailed the practices of the Elizabethan–Jacobean theatre.

> The Restoration did not restore the Shakespearian tradition which flourished at The Theatre, The Curtain and The Globe, but created a new one conditioned by a different temperament, one which was the first to "take liberties" with the plays of the past. It is important to remember that, from the very first moment Shakespeare was being revived, he was being rethought and reinterpreted.[3]

Because there is no real Shakespearean tradition, Marowitz suggests, the only remaining obligation to the texts is to "make ourselves responsible for preserving what is essential and unalterable in the works of William Shakespeare," so that "we can exercise the freedom to interpolate and digress as we choose."[4]

Notwithstanding Marowitz's blanket condemnations, Shakespeare's plays have in fact undergone some remarkable experiments at the hands of American directors. A new, antiliterary American Shakespeare style received its first widespread public hearing in Joseph Papp's 1967–8 "Naked" *Hamlet,* a "happening" production that aroused anger, scorn, and admiration and begot a motley breed of dazzling and disappointing Shakespearean rewrightings. Papp's *Hamlet* thrust Shakespeare into the irreverent world of antiliterary, antiestablishment experimental theatre and showed that the two could be completely compatible. His production pioneered the use of multiple focus, disrupted characterization, collage, and pop-cult iconography in American Shakespeare production. Our discussion of revisionist American Shakespeare will begin by recalling Papp's groundbreaking example. We shall then turn to three later productions, from the 1980s and 1990s, that represent how far subsequent directors have taken Papp's initial impulses: the Robert Woodruff–Flying Karamazov Brothers *The Comedy of Errors* (1983–7); JoAnne Akalaitis's 1989 *Cymbeline,* an entrant in the New York Shakespeare Festival's six-year Shakespeare marathon; and Lee Breuer's gender-reversed *Lear,* set in rural Georgia in the 1950s (1990).

CONTEXT FOR PAPP'S *HAMLET*

In the social, political, and artistic turmoil of the 1960s, Shakespearean criticism and production took a decidedly countercultural turn. Anger, skepticism, alienation, and absurdity, integral elements of both European postwar drama and the antiestablishment youth culture in America, were either discovered in or inflicted upon Shakespeare's plays. For better and worse, Shakespeare fell into the hands of the American avant-garde. From there, amid echoes of Artaud, Brecht, Ionesco, Beckett, and Grotowski and the blurring distinctions between high and pop culture, a new Shakespeare style eventually emerged: aggressive, highly visual, often irreverent, and, despite its obvious debts to European influences, idiosyncratically American.

These productions answered the constant plaint that Americans cannot speak verse by supplanting poetry as the primary attribute of Shakespeare's plays. Paramount here were the nonliterary theatrical values that such groups as the Living Theatre were then exploring through Artaud. On university campuses and in the pocket theatres of Greenwich Village, physical action, music, scenic conceptualization, and pop iconography were marshaled to the service of such classically inspired Happenings as Schechner's *Dionysus in '69.* Texts were dismantled, reassembled as collages, and otherwise reworked. Their adapters borrowed the fast-paced, rhythmic, and visual sensibilities of film, television, and rock and roll. The results, often mixed, succeeded in establishing an alternative to both highbrow, snob Shakespeare and the pandering anti-intellectual approach.

Ironically, new voices in literary and drama criticism provided support for the antiliterary Shakespeare movement. Jan Kott published his collection of Shakespeare essays in 1964. His absurdist readings of the plays and recurrent insistence that contemporary Shakespeare productions reflect the issues, outlook, and theatrical practices of the modern world unleashed a new era of Shakespeare production. Peter Brook's 1962 *King Lear,* tragicomic and absurdist, openly acknowledged Kott's "Lear and Endgame" as its inspiration. Brook's white-box, circus-motif *A Midsummer Night's Dream* in 1970 was also prompted by Kott's interpretation. That Kott's astonishing rereadings were so well supported by the texts lent further credence to the directorial license he advocated. The 1960s, Kott wrote, provided fertile ground for a revolution in Shakespeare production because they forced the plays into collision with "mass extermination, terror, and civil wars, and at the same time, with . . . Brecht's theatre and the Theatre of the Absurd."[5] Kott's essay "Hamlet of the Mid-Century" was one of the sources (some might say excuses) for Papp's "Naked" *Hamlet*.

Another possible influence, closer to home, may be traced to the American critic Susan Sontag who, in 1965, declared herself "against interpretation." "Interpretation," she wrote, "is the revenge of the intellect upon art. Even more. It is the revenge of intellect upon the world."[6] Sontag accused legions of "leech"-like interpreters of wedging themselves intrusively between works of art and those who wished to experience them. Interpreters who destructively "excavate" art for "meaning" work under the false assumption that there is a distinction between form and content and that the true value of the work lies in decoding some hidden "subtextual" message. The misguided search for pure content, Sontag argued, effectively dilutes the impact of art by reducing its sensory and emotional powers to intellectual ideas. At the same time that Jerzy Grotowski and his international disciples were seeking the live theatre's raison d'être amid a numbing, electronically mediated environment, Sontag complained that "interpretation takes the sensory experience of the work of art for granted, and proceeds from there. This cannot be taken for granted, now."[7]

What, however, are the implications of Sontag's anti-interpretive stance for the theatre, where the text can never stand alone? She does not address the inevitable interpretative role of directors in staging drama. If every directorial choice implies something about how the director understands, or wants the audience to understand, the play, can directors avoid interpretation? At first glance, Sontag seems to denounce any but the most reverential approaches to text. The forecast gets worse for directors of classics, and worse yet for those of the conceptual school:

> Interpretation is a radical strategy for conserving an old text, which is thought too precious to repudiate, by revamping it. The interpreter, without actually erasing or rewriting the text, *is* altering it. But he can't admit to doing this. He claims to be only making it intelligible,

by disclosing its true meaning. However far the interpreters alter the text . . ., they must claim to be reading off a sense that is already there.[8]

The point is well taken if Sontag's remarks are understood to disparage critics or directors who make rigid decisions about the meaning of texts and then mangle the works till they conform (or refuse to conform) to their readings or production schemes. However, there is a less obvious, more encouraging implication for classic-play directors in her anti-interpretive position: Her laissez-faire attitude toward texts liberates directors from having to delineate productions according to the contours of fixed interpretations. Because directors cannot present pure text on stage, she implies, the next-best anti-interpretive strategy is to use old theatrical texts as springboards for completely new theatrical events with their own organic integrity. Various performance experiments in the 1960s – Happenings, collective creations, collages – had already begun to explore a renewed artistic viability for non-literary theatrical spectacle. Sontag extended literary credentials to directors to leave interpretation of dramatic texts to the enemies of art and to create instead complex, even chaotic sensory spectacles that explored those texts in uniquely theatrical ways.

Not surprisingly, these productions stick in the craw of the Shakespeare purist. Those who rate performances of Shakespeare's plays by the relative beauty of the spoken verse probably do not like much American Shakespeare anyway. Antiliterary productions have dealt with the language in different ways, some radical, others awkwardly traditional, but few would stand on the virtues of their oral interpretation. The subordination of language to other, equally "Shakespearean" achievements is a given in these productions. Further discussion must take account of how language was handled or mishandled in these productions, but comparing them to a traditional poetic standard is pointless. Valid critiques of these productions must accept the re-ranking of Shakespearean elements (action, plot, character, stage pictures) and, to borrow a phrase from Sontag, "proceed from there."

PAPP'S *HAMLET*: A HAPPENING

Joseph Papp had been in the Shakespeare business for more than two decades by the winter of 1967–8. The rise of his nobly intended New York Shakespeare Festival empire is well known. Papp was driven by the desire to bring the theatre to underprivileged and culturally excluded segments of the city's changing population and to reflect those subcultures from his stages. Toward those ends, he had produced plays by new playwrights and both straight and simile stagings of Shakespeare, some of which he directed himself. Other notable Festival Shakespeares included Gerald Freedman's 1960 *Taming of the Shrew* as a Marx Bros. farce and Michael Kahn's 1966 Viennese *Measure for Measure*. Papp had also presented dozens of new plays by emerging American and European playwrights. The record of productions at the Delacorte Theatre in Central Park and at various other mobile and temporary venues around the city was prodigious but uneven. Papp's own work as a director was considered only mediocre. The *Hamlet* he directed in the park in 1964 was beset by casting troubles that overshadowed the director's handiwork in the press notices. Alfred Ryder's voice gave out after the first performance, but Julie Harris won raves for her portrayal of Ophelia. Papp's real talents lay in stimulating and supporting others, as many and as frequently as his energy, connections, and ego could generate underwriters for them.

Papp's big accomplishments in the 1967–8 season began with the opening of the Public Theatre complex in the converted Astor Library on Lafayette Street, in eastern Greenwich Village. Never timid and with a keen nose for publicity, Papp chose *Hair* as the inaugural production. The landmark rock-and-roll musical captured the life-style of the "hippie" generation with references to hallucinogenic drugs, sexual liberation, racial harmony, and resistance to the Vietnam War. *Hair*'s enormous popularity at the Public and, later, on Broadway indicated that audiences were ready for overt presentations of nudity, obscenity, and other manifestations of radical culture. Papp's next production tested their readiness to accept these developments in a Shakespeare play.

The recent death of Papp's father galvanized the work on *Hamlet*. The bereaved impresario of the underdog later recalled that he "needed to throw myself into something. So, I just started tearing *Hamlet* apart, threw the pieces into the air, and waited to see where they would land."[9] Papp's program notes and his introduction to the text he later published as a "handbook" for those who might want to emulate his production, reflect his focus on the notorious Oedipal issues in the play.

Is the death of a father one of the most shattering experiences a son could have? Is the loss of the key male link with the past an irreparable one? Is there fear in the hidden realization that the boy has become the father? Hamlet is "too much i' the sun" and the son is too much in him. So much so that he wants to remain the son in defiance of the reality that, at the death of his father, the boy becomes the man – and

74

has the man's responsibility to fulfill his purpose in nature: to father his own offspring. But Hamlet chooses to remain the eternal son, to hold back the process of nature and live outside the pale of humankind. He will not be reconciled, and chooses his own death rather than fall in line with the common theme – the death of fathers. He dies a son. . . . This challengeable psychological premise is the rationale upon which we base Hamlet's erratic mode of existence.[10]

Psychoanalyzing an artist's motivations is precarious at best, but it is evident that Papp's inner conflicts influenced his work on the play and that he spent considerable energy thinking about the text even though his final version plays fast and free with cherished scenes and speeches.

The *Hamlet* pastiche that emerged under these several influences to open on December 27, 1967, roused the New York theatre community to take arms en masse against the sea of troubles that follows in the wake of directorial prerogative with Shakespeare's treasured texts. Dismissed by the majority of daily critics as another of Papp's follies, the production attracted capacity audiences and vocal scholarly supporters too. Guthrie's modern-dress version of 1963, which had opened the Minneapolis theatre that bears his name, was not universally applauded, but it had assured America that *Hamlet* could withstand updating. In 1964, Broadway had lavished praise on Richard Burton as Hamlet in rehearsal clothes, as directed by John Gielgud. Still, those innocuous updatings had not prepared the way for something as radical as Papp's rending of the text.

Charles Marowitz had disassembled *Hamlet* a few years before, in London, in an experiment that derived from conversations between Marowitz and Peter Brook during their Theatre of Cruelty workshops. The directors wondered whether or not it would be possible to communicate the *Hamlet* story "without reliance on narrative": Could a production "convey the multitude of nuances and insights which are to be found in *Hamlet* through a kind of cut-up of the work which thoroughly abandoned its progressive story line?"[11] Marowitz selected segments of the text and rearranged them into a high-speed, eighty-minute collage in which familiar dialogue, characters, and ideas were forced into new light. The director's underlying purpose was to expose serious flaws in the leading character and the implicit values on which Shakespeare based his play.

Contrary to romantic notions of Hamlet as an agonized idealist, Marowitz saw him as "the supreme prototype of the conscience-stricken but paralyzed liberal: one of the most lethal and obnoxious characters in modern times." The play's "misdirected moral concerns, intellectual analysis as action substitute, etc.," Marowitz found antithetical to the contemporary world, and he argued that such antiquated values "derived much of their respectability and approval from traditional works such as Shakespeare's *Hamlet.*"[12] By "fragmenting" components of the familiar work and depicting Hamlet as a clown-faced buffoon, he hoped to intercept the automatic reverence that prevents modern audiences from reevaluating the obsolete assumptions on which the work is based. The director would later acknowledge that his audience's ability to perceive his indictment of the text was derailed by the fast pace and novelty theatrics of the performance.

> I derive some small consolation from the fact that any artifact which is immediately reducible to its theoretical components must be facile and unworthy, but I am simultaneously chastened by the knowledge that many artists imagine they are communicating clear-cut intentions when, in fact, they are conveying something entirely ambiguous.[13]

Years later, in *Prospero's Staff*, Marowitz denounced Papp's *Hamlet* for its apparent lack of similar thematic thrust.

Without pretending that Papp and company produced a definitive contemporary *Hamlet*, a completely original *Hamlet*, or a *Hamlet* of piercing insight, it is worth resurrecting his production here as the progenitor of a loosely connected line of American Shakespeare productions that emphasize contemporary theatrical imagery and technology over traditional linguistic and thematic content.

Like Marowitz's version, Papp's ninety-minute *Hamlet* was, in current critical lingo, a deconstruction. Papp took his first cues from Jan Kott's essay:

> *Hamlet* cannot be performed in its entirety because the performance would last nearly six hours. One has to select, curtail and cut. One can perform only one of several *Hamlet*s potentially existing in this archplay. It will always be a poorer *Hamlet* than Shakespeare's *Hamlet* is; but it may also be a *Hamlet* enriched by being of our time.[14]

The director cut extensively, rearranged scenes, reassigned lines, interpolated contemporary slang and allusions ("Don't give me any of that Shakespeare crap!" Hamlet answered his elders), and otherwise manhandled the text with a vigor that might have delighted Meyerhold. The composer of *Hair*, Galt MacDermott, contributed a blaring rock score. Papp's was "a play of shattered focus – ambiguous, elusive, contradictory, enigmatic, inconsistent and paradoxical," he wrote in his program notes. It took a "view from underneath, through the side, through cracks in the sentences, through great chinks in the wall of tradition."[15] Clearly anxious to demonstrate his own Artaudian intolerance for masterpieces in the shadow of nuclear disaster, Papp reached for new heights of hyperbole. His defense of the production culminated in the following bit of inflated prose: "This production aims radioactive ididium 192 at the nineteenth-century *Hamlet* statue and by gamma-ray shadowgraphing seeks to discover the veins of the living original, buried under accumulated layers of reverential varnish."[16]

Martin Sheen played Hamlet as a cynical, hyperactive, inner-city chameleon. "The one sure way of creating a dead fish Hamlet is to impose upon him a consistent line of behavior," insisted Papp.[17] This Hamlet did not even have a consistent line of identities. In a series of unexplained transformations (a term not used by Papp but that had been recently popularized by Joseph Chaikin's Open Theatre), Hamlet appeared at different points in the production as Ramón, the Puerto Rican janitor; as a peanut vendor, tossing bags of nuts to "customers" in the audience; as one of a pair of vaudevillian comics; and as a ventriloquist's dummy. Sheen appeared at the opening of the show, dressed in floral boxer shorts, a loosened necktie, and handcuffs, sitting up in a coffin at the foot of Claudius and Gertrude's platform bed. His first action was a tug-of-war for his sleeping stepfather's blanket.

The prison that is Denmark was designed by David Mitchell as a scaffold-like unit set, made entirely of steel bars and consisting of a staircase, second-level playing area, and two downstage ramps inside a black-box stage. A limited number of set pieces were hauled in and out for specific scenes: the first-scene bed, chairs for the court, the garbage can in which Hamlet would later deposit Ophelia's dead body, and a wheelbarrow for her grave. The prison metaphor was echoed again in the costuming of Horatio, who wore prison stripes and, like Hamlet, was handcuffed. Unlike a literal simile transposition of the play, which might have set the action inside a real prison with inmates and wardens, there was no attempt to portray characters or events in prison equivalents. The environment was simply one channel through which Hamlet's sense of captivity and submission were suggested.

One of the production's accomplishments can be measured by the extent to which, without resorting to a direct reference, this *Hamlet* captured the sense of entrapment and absurdity that was being expressed at the time by the nation's youth as they protested their enforced role in Vietnam. The closest allusion came in the substitution of Washington for England as the place where Hamlet is sent when Claudius finds him "mad." "*Hamlet* is like a sponge," Kott observed, ". . . it immediately absorbs all the problems of our time."[18]

Papp had picked up Kott's idea that the young Dane had no choice but to fulfill the "scenario" of his life. "*Hamlet* is a drama of imposed situations, and herein lies the key to modern interpretations of the play," wrote Kott.[19] The end, ordained on one level by the text and another by the actions of his parents' generation, fixes Hamlet's fate. He used the line "And how if I say no?" as a vain threat to resist the plot, but he also referred to a copy of the text to keep the action on course. Papp paraphrased Kott (without citation) in his notes and hinted at a Beckett-like appreciation of Hamlet's predicament. (Many of Papp's written remarks are diluted reiterations of Kott's ideas.)

> The end is always in sight. . . . All that was required of the director and the company was to invent engaging and interesting devices to sugarcoat the agony of a man living out his short span of life. . . . And so we devised burlesque skits, song and dance routines, familiar vaudeville. . . .[20]

The performance style was purely "presentational and [had] no use for psychology"; the various scenes were "ceremonies, games, entertainments. With the eradication of the 'why,'" reported the director, "the work process was dictated by 'what' and 'how.'"[21]

Kott's "scenario" theory also justified the production's other offbeat characterizations.

> This scenario is independent of the characters, it has been devised earlier. It defines the situations, as well as the mutual relations of the characters; it dictates their words and gestures. But it does not say who the characters are. It is something external in relation to them. And that is why the scenario of *Hamlet* can be played by different sorts of characters.[22]

Ralph Waite's Claudius was portrayed as a Central American–style dictator, surrounded by armed guards in camouflage fatigues, white helmets, and mirrored, aviator sunglasses. Gertrude (Anita Dangler), a "hennaed floozy"[23] in a low-cut red peignoir, munched a peanut that had lodged in her cleavage when Hamlet pelted her in the closet scene. Ophelia was a teenage sex kitten in a micro-miniskirt and fish-net stockings who vamped her rock-and-roll soliloquy into a handheld microphone. The Ghost, the dead father with whom Papp was so preoccupied, showed up in long, droopy underwear and stayed with Hamlet as his sidekick throughout the show. Father and son played the gravedigger's scene as a comic vaudeville duet, and Hamlet mouthed "How all occasions do inform against me" as a dummy on his ventriloquist-father's knee. As yet another jolt to audience expectations, Papp revived "Rossencraft" and "Guilderstone," the names given to Hamlet's buddies by the transcriber of the First (or Bad) Quarto edition.

Two scenes contained Papp's most interesting innovations. First, no players visited Elsinore in this production. Instead, "The Murder of Gonzago" was acted out by the members of the royal family during a New Year's Eve celebration. Drunk and surrounded by streamers and confetti, Claudius himself was persuaded by Hamlet to enact the role of the murderer. Horatio's home-movie camera caught the usurper-king in the act.[24] Second, Shakespeare's final, cleansing blood bath was given an edge of contemporary tragicomic chaos. Here the characters encountered death via Russian roulette. After loading just five bullets into the six-shot gun and spinning the cartridge, Hamlet shot Laertes. Hit. He then passed the gun to Claudius, who killed Gertrude. Hamlet took the weapon back and turned it on Claudius, who refused to fall even after two shots were fired. Finally, Hamlet showed him the text of the scene, after which a petulant Ralph Waite lay down on the stage. With no one left to shoot him, Hamlet recruited a volunteer from the audience. The chosen spectator-marksman (not a plant) always triggered the empty chamber. Hamlet then threw down the revolver, turned upstage, leapt in triumph, and tripped over the gun. The one remaining bullet went off, killing him in a freak accident. "The rest is silence" came over the loudspeakers, accompanied by a cacophonous roar. Confetti filled the stage, followed by a blackout. When the lights came up for the final image, a wreath rested against the staircase. "R.I.P. William Shakespeare," read its ribbon.

The most common critical response to this *Hamlet* was condescension. In reviews carried by mainstream journals, dubious protests of tolerance for a strong directorial hand were often followed by denunciations of this particular attempt. "I am not attacking this *Hamlet* for tampering with a holy cow," insisted Clive Barnes in a typical comment, "but for its incompetence."[25] The *Women's Wear Daily* critic said it was "fine" with him that the director took liberties with the play. "Do anything you like. But for God's sake, organize it. There has got to be a point – not even an intellectual point, necessarily, but an ARTISTIC point." He summed up the evening as "a mass of noise, disorganization, and lackluster invention, one foolish inspiration piling on top of another until the entire business collapses in a pile of boredom and stupidity."[26] Audience letters (which Papp included in the book version) were even angrier. One patron called *Hamlet* a "vulgar, noisy, pretentious intellectual production." Others characterized it as a "gutter-snipe *Hamlet*," or "McLuhanism in action, denigration of the world and sensation for immediacy's sake." One Shakespeare devotee lamented, "O judgment that art fled to brutish beasts and Papp has lost his reason."[27]

The production's ragged edges and underdeveloped intellectual premise were acknowledged by its supporters, too, but this group also expressed sincere appreciation for the freshness of Papp's experiment. Letter writers described the production as "groovy" and "a gas."[28] Richard Schechner replied to the *Times'* review with a letter that articulated the emerging revisionist argument: "Like Brook's *Marat/Sade* or the work of Jerzy Grotowski, Mr. Papp's *Hamlet* points toward emerging and liberating forces within the theater," he began, adding that the production "went beyond interpretation toward confrontation. The text of *Hamlet* was treated as material out of which not a new but an obliquely different play was made. The result was a contemporary, ironic, farcical – almost appalling – tone and style that freed *Hamlet* from reverence."[29] Schechner pointed out that "disunity" and "competing and contradictory elements" within the production created an appropriate sense of impending chaos. For all its timeliness, the performance was also consistent with its Elizabethan heritage, Schechner concluded, "in its sense of how to live at a time when things are falling apart."[30]

Months earlier, Robert Brustein had published "No More Masterpieces," his Artaud-based essay in support of conceptual approaches to the classics. Papp's *Hamlet* gave him an opportunity to put his theory to critical practice. In a review, he called Papp's direction "an anarchic assault" on the play and applauded its attempt "to rescue the play from the seminar room, to withdraw it from history, to obliterate the memory of all those beautifully costumed productions that now stand like a wall between us and an immediate experience of the action." Brustein traced the performance style to the "Happening" of its subtitle. In *Hamlet*, as in a Happening, "everything is designed for environmental effect rather than for meaning," he explained. A Happening was "a Dadaist nightmare where language becomes an agency not of communication, but rather of ironic contradiction and comic confusion, and where the spectator becomes one of the most important characters in the play."[31]

Papp was indeed interested in the suspect nature of language in the play. "There is nothing more deceptive than language," he later wrote, going on to explicate the contemporary implications of a number of crucial lines.

"Speak the speech, I pray you . . .," Hamlet instructed his parent-players. "Too many speeches have been, and are being, made trippingly on the tongue" Papp suggested, referring to the federal government's Vietnam doublespeak, "and they are not to be trusted."[32] Likewise,

> "what a piece of work is a man" – sprawled in the dirt of Vietnam – on the beaches of Iwo Jima – in the trenches of Verdun – on 125th Street in Harlem – on the streets of Detroit, Newark, Cleveland – in a grave in Alabama that held the remains of Andrew Goodman, civil rights worker – the death of Roosevelt, of Einstein, Marilyn Monroe, and a fourteen-year-old boy in the Bedford-Stuyvesant section of Brooklyn.[33]

As for *Hamlet*'s Happening attempts to involve the audience, Brustein and others were disappointed. Environmentalist Schechner, who was about to unleash his naked Performance Group members on the *Dionysus* audience, regretted that Papp "held back in directly involving the audience," rendering those interactions "painfully planted" when they "could have been the means by which the farce terror of this *Hamlet* was driven into the audience's consciousness."[34] Albert Bermel, writing for the *New Leader*, extended his sympathy to the actors whose faces, when forced to "mingle with the audience . . . took on a desperate, glassy-eyed expression."[35]

No one considered the production a total triumph. Kott had warned that "there are many subjects in *Hamlet*. . . . One can select at will. But one must know what one selects, and why."[36] Papp's work took more from the spirit than the letter of Kott's rereading, unlike Peter Brook's Kott-inspired productions, which were more fully imbued with the critic's thought. Schechner felt that Papp's *Hamlet* was "sometimes sloppy."[37] Brustein decided it was ultimately "boring" due to overly amateurish acting and an "ultimate lack of coherence" in the directing. "Even absurdity must be organized toward some definable point," Brustein asserted, seeming to validate the complaints of *Hamlet*'s detractors.[38] The critic for the *Village Voice* approved of it as "a hallucinatory *Hamlet* with the clashing styles, jagged emotional tone and image overload of specifically the 1960s," but his enthusiasm was limited to the production's novelty. He found it "as frivolous and inexcusable as painting a mustache on the Mona Lisa but similarly liberating."[39] This comparison works much better if the mustache were to be painted on a reproduction of the painting: Neither Papp's, nor any other production of *Hamlet*, leaves indelible traces on the original. Bermel came up with a much better metaphor: "Now, if some intrepid museum curator chopped a Rembrandt canvas into small triangles and glued the bits to a sculpture by Reg Butler in order to establish Rembrandt's shattered focus, the damage would be irreparable. But *Hamlet* remains available and hospitable in its many editions."[40]

A few months after it opened, Papp's *Hamlet* was scheduled to tour the city's high schools, as NYSF productions had been doing for several years. When word of Papp's radical rewrighting reached the school board, trouble ensued, transferring the critical debate from the culture pages to the main news section of the *New York Times*. Schools superintendent Bernard Donovan questioned whether the production was "suitable for the maturity of high school students."[41] At first, Papp defended his work with the firm but polite argument that "since the 'straight' play is ambiguous, there is no conceivable way to produce it on the stage without some special point of view."[42] A special matinee was arranged for school administrators, teachers, and students to determine whether or not the production was appropriate for high school audiences. Papp took a more aggressive position when he led a discussion following the matinee. While nibbling peanuts left strewn on the stage, he responded to a teacher's challenge with "Don't tell me how to direct, and I won't tell you how to teach."[43] The production played the schools without incident, and another version toured city parks in the summer of 1968.

The parks company was headed by Cleavon Little in the title role, who changed the Puerto Rican overtones to African-American ones. When Polonius asked Hamlet what he was reading, Little replied "*Ebony,* baby." Claudius cut short the gravedigger with "Don't give me any of that Shakespeare crap." This time the *Times* sent a bemused Vincent Canby to review. He called *Hamlet* "an interracial political comedy set in what seems to be Emperor Jones territory." While he did not take umbrage on behalf of the text, he declared the whole affair to have had "as much relation to the original Shakespeare as cole slaw has to cabbage." The interracial elements, he reported, made the audience laugh "nervously, like white onlookers at a Black Panther meeting."[44]

Ultimately, Papp's production has had two lasting effects. The first is that it extended the liberty with Shakespeare's texts already claimed by European directors to Americans. The second is that the production raised, in loud and reverberating tones, the question of whether or not Shakespeare belongs in the hands of the American avant-garde, whose major influences – a curious blend of Artaud and popular culture – tend to value image over word, disjuncture over synthesis, and instinct over intellect. The debate, as we shall soon see, rages on.

Figure 4. Hamlet (Cleavon Little) awaits a final shot in the final scene of the "Naked" *Hamlet,* directed by Joseph Papp, at the New York Shakespeare Festival, 1968. Photo © George Joseph.

THE FLYING *COMEDY OF ERRORS*

The Flying Karamazov Brothers are five unrelated men who share extraordinary juggling and circus skills and a hip sense of ironic humor. The group came to prominence, along with Bill Irwin, David Shiner, and other intellectual clowns, in the revival movement known as the New Vaudeville. The Karamazovs had been playing regional theatres, colleges, and nightclubs around the country since the late 1970s. They were especially popular at the Goodman Theatre in Chicago, and, by 1983, Greg Mosher, the artistic director, was curious to see what would happen if they attempted a real play. "Vaudevillians don't usually do plays," he admitted,[45] so the choice of material would be crucial. The company had long been considering a production of *A Midsummer Night's Dream,* and the idea of the Karamazovs playing the rustics was kicked around for a while and then dropped. Noted comedians had taken those parts before, and Mosher wanted the Karamazov Shakespeare to be something new. It occurred to Mosher that the Plautine

Comedy of Errors, "an incredibly dopey play whose only purpose is to make people laugh," would be the perfect vehicle. Furthermore, one of the Karamazovs never spoke on stage, which left the four main speaking roles – two Antipholi and two Dromios – to be divided among the four talking Brothers.

Getting this zany concept past the Goodman's board of directors was Mosher's most difficult obstacle. "For *King Lear* you'd hire a great tragedian, right?" he asked the skeptics. "Why not great comedians for *Comedy of Errors*? Nobody's funnier than the Flying Karamazovs." Mosher prevailed. With the Karamazovs and the text in place, the next critical task was to choose the right director. "Do we hire a maniac or a disciplinarian?" Mosher wondered. He seemed to find both in Robert Woodruff, who had made his reputation with the first productions of Sam Shepard's *Curse of the Starving Class, Buried Child,* and *True West.* Woodruff's imagination was "way out there," according to Mosher, and he had proven able to "function well in chaos."

Once the director came on board, the general contours of the production began to take shape. Unlike the director-dominated rehearsals common to most of the productions with which we are concerned, the work on *Comedy of Errors* was completely collaborative. Woodruff came to the process with a long-standing inclination toward an open rehearsal dynamic. He once told an interviewer, "I don't try to control [actors in rehearsal]. . . . I try to *encourage.* I have to look and then respond to what my collaborators are finding. . . . Unity is overrated. It can lead to a stifling politeness."[46] The remarks are wise advice for any rehearsal situation. The attitude they reflect was essential to the work at the Goodman.[47]

It was quickly determined that Timothy Daniel Furst, the silent Karamazov, would appear intermittently as Shakespeare himself, alternately anguished and delighted by the shenanigans wrought on his play. Karamazovs Howard Jay Patterson and Paul Magid would play the Antipholi of Ephesus and Syracuse, respectively. The Dromios were assigned to Randy Nelson (Ephesus) and Sam Williams (Syracuse). Avner "the Eccentric" Eisenberg, another New Vaudevillian, was cast to play a janitor figure and Pinch, the schoolmaster. Other, multitalented performers included Gina Leishman, who played Luciana, accordion, and bass clarinet; Sophie Schwab Hayden as Adriana; and Alec Willows, who doubled as Angelo and his sidekick, Walter, in a split-down-the-middle costume, and also played drums, maracas, slapstick, jingle bells, and duck call. (When the production was revived in New York, in 1987, after Mosher became artistic director at Lincoln Center Theatre, cast changes brought in Ethyl Eichelberger doubling in drag as the courtesan and the abbess; Karla Burns as a Tina Turner–esque maid; and a klezmer orchestra. This account is based on the New York version.) Woodruff recalls early rehearsals:

> Basically, it was whoever had the best idea at any given moment. A lot of the time it was just sitting around the table with twenty-one people and saying, "Okay, we have to have a sword fight. What are we going to use for weapons?" Somebody yells out, "Swordfish!" After a certain point I would move from referee to aesthetic arbitrator and then to dictator.[48]

Matching performing skills to lines and scenes was mostly a matter of rhythm. The company would generate "a cacophony of skills" from which the director then selected and orchestrated the whirling elements. Traffic management was a major part of his job, but not the whole thing. Woodruff disagrees that the text was used merely as a pretext for showing off the various circus skills. "I felt we did the play," he says. "We tried to find the spirit in which the piece was originally created – a late-night vaudeville. It appeared that we manipulated the text because there were so many sight gags that are not in there, but it was ninety-five percent Shakespeare."[49] The production would also, it seems, have earned the approval of Margaret Webster, who wrote in 1957 that "[i]t is one of the few plays which may be stylized to the limit of a director's invention and with all the extended artifice of music, ballet, and comedy tricks. . . . The play is not bad vaudeville."[50] In fact, for those who require Shakespeare's nod, a validating remark can be found in Act I, scene 1: Antipholus of Syracuse refers to the people of Ephesus as "nimble jugglers that deceive the eye."

About a hundred lines were cut from the text, mostly exposition from the first scene, and some topical references were interpolated. (The 1987 production took swipes at Vanna White, Oliver North, and Gary Hart.) Otherwise, the lines were left intact. Language, however, was at best a secondary means of interaction in the production. The action was set in a white box designed by David Gropman with the requisite abundance of farce doors. Brightly colored awnings and "a frazzling array of gaudy costumes"[51] by Susan Hilferty helped to create what could be called a "czarnival" atmosphere: part Middle-Eastern bazaar, part Russian folk festival. The performance idiom incorporated the borrowed ethnicity of the self-named Karamazovs but made no attempt to reflect the play's Roman origins. Dressed in harem pants, turbans, sashes, and babushkas, the cast recited Shakespeare's lines while juggling balls, hatchets, ten-pins, bowling balls, and seltzer bottles. Baton twirling, stilt walking, unicycling, belly dancing, fire eating, roller skating, blindfolded knife throwing, trapeze flying, plate spinning, and tap dancing substituted for ordinary human behavior. Ephesus became "a land where *everyone* juggled, juggling became discourse . . . not as a pastiche to the action, but as its essence."[52]

The nearly chaotic, free-for-all atmosphere often upstaged the dialogue, but it absolutely captured the topsy-turvy confusion of Shakespeare's precision-crafted comic mechanism. Identity and perception are juggled in *Comedy of Errors*. The plot moves with increasing momentum, always threatening to spin out of control as complications pile on top of one another. The acrobatics physicalized the action, although not always in literal relation to the meaning or emotional content of the immediate lines.

Any pretense to seriousness was dispelled for the audience before the performance began. Statues in the theatre lobby sported glasses with funny noses attached. On the title page of the program, *The Three Sisters* was crossed out and *The Comedy of Errors* handwritten in the space below. The program notes comprised the following essential tidbits:

The Plot: The plot has something to do with twins and juggling.

Dating The Play: The play generally does not go out on dates. . . . Anyway, it's safe to assume that the play dates sometime between Plautus's *The Twin Menaechmi* and the first episode of "The Patty Duke Show."

Famous Quotations From The Text:

Understudies: Understudies never read the play unless a specific announcement is made at the time of the performance.

A page of photos of odd-looking or unlikely twins were captioned with clever quips:

"We are the same person," Helen Hayes says of she and twin brother Isaac [Hayes, the African-American jazz musician]. "When he's doing something great I can feel it in my bones. And if I'm on stage having a winning night, he can feel it too. I just know it."

The opening scene featured Avner the Eccentric as a janitor who swept the floor, then strewed it with litter over and over again. Once the four principals had appeared, it was obvious that the "twins" looked nothing alike. "One would have to be a fool to confuse them – and that should say some-

Figure 5. The Flying Karamazovs and company in *The Comedy of Errors,*
directed by Robert Woodruff, at the Goodman Theatre, 1983. Photo ©
Linda Schwartz/The Goodman Theatre.

thing about the other characters on the stage," noted Mel Gussow of the
Times.[53]

The entire event was suffused with silliness, near-anarchy, and self-
referential humor, but its methods drew from legitimate theatre-historical
sources. It mixed circus, *commedia,* the Marx Bros., and the Keystone Kops
with Meyerhold and Brecht. If the verse speaking was flat and mechanical
by poetic standards (one reviewer noted two vocal dynamics: "loud and
fast"[54]), its mere mouthing seemed extraordinary when delivered while the
speaker either ate fire or tossed sticks into the air so that they fell, miracu-
lously, on the right notes of a xylophone to play a tune, or executed other,
often dangerous, physical feats.

As with Brecht's detached actors, the performers' concentration had to be
split between the world of the play and the physical realities of their various
shticks. They also kept one winking eye on the audience at all times, as if to
say, "We know just how ridiculous this is, but it's fun, huh?" The production
operated on a tongue-in-cheek theatricalism, overt, physical, and carried out
at breakneck pace. The style was reminiscent of the way Meyerhold treated
classics, although *The Comedy of Errors* contained no hint of the Russian director's political edge. Like Brecht and Meyerhold, Woodruff enjoys tension
between theatrical elements. He compares directing to recording music:

87

"everybody has a track, each designer, each actor has his own score. . . . The work becomes more assaultive because it's denser, but it's not *only* the density of language." Using the language of postmodern aesthetics, Woodruff says he enjoys the way the various tonalities create a "dynamic of disagreement [that] creates an unsettling edge," because the elements are never completely resolved.[55]

Acknowledgment of the live audience and collusion with them in the mayhem were essential ingredients. Lines were delivered out front. Bad puns were read by an actor holding a book entitled, "How to Tell a Joke." Mistakes – some planted, some real – were shouted down with cries of "Wrong play! Wrong play!" Timothy Furst as Shakespeare carried a prompt book, took bows after particularly well-spoken speeches, and held up a hand-lettered "PLOT" sign during passages of exposition. When the stage action teetered toward insanity, Eichelberger came down from the stage in his courtesan costume to plead his case directly to the audience. The monologue was interrupted by the arrival of a pizza delivery boy. Ever the perfect hostess, the frantic courtesan panicked because there didn't seem to be enough napkins for everyone in the house. Eichelberger ran away, urging the spectators to go see *The Boys from Syracuse* if they wanted the whole story. The antics continued through the curtain call, a virtuoso group-juggling effort that guaranteed applause.

The 1987 *Comedy of Errors* created strange bedfellows among the New York critics. One reason might be that the production had already earned a reputation in its two previous runs: in Chicago in 1983, and at the Olympic Festival of the Arts in Los Angeles in 1984. Its novelty may have worn off before it even opened at Lincoln Center. Another possible explanation for the widespread critical appreciation is the undeniably high quality of the performance skills displayed. Many of the reviewers least inclined to approve such ventures got caught up in the playful spirit, although hints of condescension can be detected in some of their accolades. They most likely would not have agreed with the director's assessment that it was "ninety-five percent Shakespeare."

John Simon answered the inevitable "Why?" by saying "the talent of the Karamazovs is the 'Why not?'" His enthusiastic review ended with the assertion that "if some poor souls are still benighted enough to think that Shakespeare was really Bacon, this should conclusively prove to them that he was really ham, glorious ham."[56] Mel Gussow, more susceptible to this sort of thing than Simon but still an establishment critic, also judged the production as deserving of its classical heritage. "As Shakespearean actors the Karamazovs are not about to challenge the Royal Shakespeare Company," he assured his readers, "But can Ian McKellen juggle?"[57] Edith Oliver of the *New Yorker* counted an "inventory of *schtick* all loosely (and appropriately) tied to Shakespeare."[58] Clive Barnes credited the clockwork pacing to the director and called the whole romp "a belly laugh tripping on a whoopee cushion to the sound of a kazoo."

In spite of this appreciation, however, and more consistent with Barnes's antiexperimental track record, the *New York Post* critic did not ultimately find merit in the marriage of classical and New Vaudeville performance elements. "I suppose the laudable intention was to provide Shakespeare for people who do not like Shakespeare," he sneered, "but, be warned, I doubt whether it can provide Shakespeare for people who don't like juggling." Barnes's disapproval comes as no surprise. Harder to explain is the resistance of writers from more theatrically receptive publications.

Michael Feingold, writing for the *Village Voice,* picked up on the Russian allusions and imagined that Chekhov would have liked this *Comedy of Errors.* He noted that the production played on both parts of Shakespeare's "merged tradition." By blending poetry and physical humor, the clever dramatist appeals to all segments of his diverse audience simultaneously. This clever *Comedy of Errors,* Feingold observed, deferred the greater glories of language and character to the more readily accessible delights of "pure shtick." The critic then went on, oddly enough, to criticize the production for neglecting those aspects of the play it intentionally chose to play down. "We can see the Karamazovs juggle anytime, under their own names, but," he lamented, "we don't get to see Antipholus of Syracuse mooning over Luciana all that often." Sure, it would be nice to see satisfying renditions of *The Comedy of Errors* more often, but why hold this entertaining production responsible for the lapse?

The *Variety* reviewer found the evening boring and mechanical, although he did acknowledge the performers' skill. He dismissed the whole production as a cop-out: "Of course this sort of thing is easier to achieve than a faithful rendering of the play." Those who admire this Woodruff–Karamazov achievement may wonder if he's ever written a review while swallowing a flaming sword.

What is disturbing about these persnickety reviews is not that their authors did not like the production: That is their prerogative, although in this case, the inability to submit to the production's exuberance is more pitiful than annoying. The trouble with these reviews is that they refuse to judge the work on its own terms. Here was a production that announced its own lack of Shakespearean pretense at every possible opportunity. It employed one of Shakespeare's least idolized scripts, avoided sustained social or political commentary, and spoofed itself regularly. It got the plot right, which is no small accomplishment with this tightly woven farce, and although the characterizations were unorthodox, they fit the play. Greg Mosher, who put together the *Comedy of Errors*, believes a director's job is to "support the intentions of the playwright."[59] Asked whether or not Shakespeare would have been happy with this production, his answer was a proud Yes: "I'm sure Shakespeare would have said 'U-huh, very good.'"[60]

Perhaps these critics were offended because *The Comedy of Errors* refused to take itself more seriously or apologize for its own exuberance. In any case, it is sad that resistance to such harmless experiments can still be found among people who profess to understand and appreciate the theatre in its many and varied forms. It is even sadder to imagine the peevishness it must have taken to resist the appeal of this highly entertaining production.

JOANNE AKALAITIS'S VICTORIAN FANTASY ON *CYMBELINE*

JoAnne Akalaitis confronted similar critical recalcitrance on a broader and angrier scale when she staged *Cymbeline* at the New York Shakespeare Festival in the late spring of 1989. Akalaitis began her career with Mabou Mines, the New York–based experimental theatre cooperative that she cofounded in 1969–70 along with her then-husband, composer Philip Glass, and Lee Breuer, Ruth Maleczech, William Raymond, Frederick Neumann, and David Warrilow. Mabou Mines earned an international reputation for emotionally truthful acting in nonrealistic, multimedia stagings of plays by Samuel Beckett and a series of original, group-generated works they called *Animations*. In the beginning, Breuer did most of the directing. Akalaitis stuck to acting in the early years, although it was always the ensemble's policy to allow any member to try any job. In 1975, she tried her hand at directing, startling the avant-garde community with her theatricalization of *Cascando*, a radio play by Beckett. *Dead End Kids*, which she directed in 1980, was an original antinuclear collage that she later made into a film. From the start, music, often by Glass, played an essential role in setting the mood, tone, and rhythm of the plays she directed. With little formal theatre education (brief study with Joyce Aaron of the Open Theatre and a month spent with Grotowski), Akalaitis was grounded in the bold visual and physical style she helped develop at Mabou Mines. She brought that sensibility to her later work on fully scripted dramatic texts.

Akalaitis remained a member of Mabou Mines until June 1990, but in 1981 began accepting offers to direct at other theatres. Her first solo engagements were in New York, and later at such regional institutions as the Guthrie and the American Repertory Theatre. *Request Concert,* a 1981 production at New York's Ensemble Studio Theatre, and *Through the Leaves,* a Mabou Mines–Interart Theatre coproduction presented at the Public Theatre in 1984, established her reputation as the country's foremost director of Kroetz's grueling, hyperrealistic, working-class plays.

Also in 1984, she directed Beckett's *Endgame* at ART. Instead of the unlocalized setting called for in the text, she set the action in an abandoned subway tunnel. This perceived slight to the play's integrity provoked Beckett's American agents to sue on his behalf to prevent the production from opening. The case was settled out of court when the theatre agreed to include in the playbill a letter of denunciation from Beckett:

> Any production of *Endgame* which ignores my stage directions is completely unacceptable to me. My play requires an empty room and two small windows. The American Repertory Theater Production [*sic*] which dismisses my directions is a complete parody of the play as conceived by me. Anybody who cares for the work couldn't fail to be disgusted by this.[61]

Mr. Beckett insisted that one vision – his – prevail over the staging of his play. Postmodern challenges to textual authority and authorial intention clearly held no place in this notoriously precise playwright's theatrical schema.

ART artistic director Robert Brustein stood by his director. His rebuttal appeared in the program alongside Beckett's complaint:

> To threaten any deviations from a purist rendering of this or any other play – to insist on strict adherence to each parenthesis of the published text – not only robs collaborating artists of their interpretive freedom but threatens to turn the theatre into a waxworks.[62]

Brustein hired Akalaitis back two seasons later to direct Genet's *The Balcony* (1986). She set this piece in an unspecified Latin American dictatorship, again causing an uproar, this time in the critical press.

By the time Joseph Papp invited Akalaitis to direct *Cymbeline,* then, she had a history of controversial, obstinately idiosyncratic restagings of modern classics. This was to be her first attempt at Shakespeare, and although it played to packed houses, it, too, ultimately incited a mudslinging campaign between its critics and defenders. A close look at how the director conceived and carried out her theatrical responses to Shakespeare's play should help us sort out the nasty war of words that followed.

Akalaitis's initial reaction to the play was less than complete enthusiasm: "The first time I read it I said, 'What is this?'" she recalls.[63] "The second time I read it I saw a whole bunch of things and thought it was very interesting, and I thought it was a great idea on [Papp's] part." Closer scrutiny convinced Akalaitis to direct the play, although the final production retained hints of her original perplexity. Audience members were provided with a complicated two-page plot synopsis that highlighted its melodramatic twists and turns. The convoluted summary seemed to affirm the opinions of those eighteenth- and nineteenth-century critics who derogated *Cymbeline* as an inferior if not impossible Shakespearean product. In fact, Samuel Johnson's infamous diatribe against the play was quoted in many of the 1989 reviews. Despite a few "just sentiments," "natural dialogues," and "pleasing scenes," Johnson had declared the play a disaster:

> To remark the folly of the fiction, the absurdity of the conduct, the confusion of the names, the manners of different times, and the impossibility of the events in any system of life, were to waste criticism upon unresisting imbecility, upon faults too evident for detection, and too gross for aggravation.[64]

One early theory proposed that Shakespeare had lent his name and a few scenes to a script written by someone else. Another denied Shakespeare's hand in it at all. Most modern readers, however, have accepted the text as a problematic but organic whole. Akalaitis followed suit and exploited whatever contradictory elements she found there. It was, perhaps, those very inconsistencies that appealed to her postmodern sensibilities.

In the prerehearsal period, the director came across two essays that corroborated her instincts about the play. Granville-Barker's 1946 "Preface to *Cymbeline*" acknowledges the possibility that Shakespeare may not have written the whole play, but its main thrust is an attempt to rationalize the dramatist's intentions. Granville-Barker imagines a retired Shakespeare, no longer interested in heavy themes, playing with dramatic and theatrical forms and creating "art that displays art." He detects a "fertile carelessness" on Shakespeare's part in the text's anachronisms, improbable behavior, and other "frank artifices." The dramatist seems to be "winking at the audience," as if to say, "'You see what an amusing business this playwriting is; take it, please, no more seriously than I do.'" In a conceit that prefigures postmodern reception theory, Granville-Barker envisions Shakespeare extending an invitation to his audience to conspire with him in creating the fiction. Audience members are cast in the active role of "masters of the illusion, not victims of it."[65]

The other source Akalaitis consulted was a graduate school paper on *Cymbeline* by Colette Brooks, who had served as dramaturge on *Through the Leaves*. Brooks argues against coauthorship of the text and for Shakespeare's complete mastery of this unusual script not as a jumble of old scraps, "a failed tragic-comedy or an imperfect Romance," but as a conscious clash of real and idealized elements. She categorizes *Cymbeline* as a successful "grotesque."[66]

Second and third readings led the director to think of the play as a Victorian novel, rich and dense with plot, character, and intrigue. A little preproduction research disclosed that *Cymbeline* was in fact quite popular with the Victorians. "It was Tennyson's favorite play," Akalaitis says she learned, "and Dickens loved it." Her research also led to the discovery that, contrary to popular stereotypes of strict morals and timid ladies, "the Victorians were a very bold, adventurous, physical people. They were real explorers." *Cymbeline's* strong melodramatic plot, its exotic locations, and its plucky heroine reflected the director's emerging concept of life in England in the mid-nineteenth century. She decided to set the play "in the midst of Celtic ruins – a Romantic fantasy in Victorian England," as the program would ultimately announce.

The careful wording of that program note correctly implied that the Victorian setting was not meant to be an authentic or realistic re-creation of the period. Akalaitis's *Cymbeline* seemed to search for the Victorian past through a late-twentieth-century prism. Such theatre-historical referents as footlights, movable scenery, thick red velvet curtains, and crisply delineated heroes and heroines were counteracted by electronic music, cinematic scene cuts, and interracial casting. Layers of new over old theatrical gestures helped to create a frankly fictional presentation of a fantastical past. The production depicted nineteenth-century, Shakespearean melodrama as only a contemporary imagination, fluent in the imagery of late-twentieth-century American culture, could conceive it. Its beauty lay in the way it seemed to exist, paradoxically, in at least three simultaneous theatrical time zones. Ever-present were Elizabethan language and dramaturgy, gushingly romantic Victorian characters and situations, and an aggressively fast-paced and electronically modulated production style.

Akalaitis's remarkable vision of the play blended nostalgia for old-fashioned, emotional, Victorian melodrama with her own, high-tech theatrical vocabulary. The audience entered the Public's Newman Theatre to the sounds of a raging thunderstorm. The stage was hidden behind a thick, red velvet curtain whose deep folds were highlighted by cones of light projected from footlights at the front of the stage. The performance opened "in one"

93

when two male figures emerged from between the curtains, dressed in great-coats and woolen caps and bearing large, wet, black umbrellas. Their dialogue is pure exposition, and Akalaitis blocked it like the first scene of a well-made play. The two men huddled together, as if taking shelter from the storm, exchanging information in obvious stage whispers, periodically looking over their shoulders to be sure no one onstage could hear them disclose the details of the latest court intrigues. When the curtain finally parted, the stage was filled with dry-ice smoke through which could be seen a family, pale-faced and silent, hurry across the stage and off stage left. These unidentified apparitions reappeared periodically during the performance until the Act V scene in which they appeared in Posthumus' dream as the ghosts of his dead family.

When the smoke cleared, George Tsypin's ingenious set was visible for the first time. The design consisted of two revolving columns on casters, on each of whose several faces was depicted elements of the four basic scenes: Cymbeline's court, Iachimo's bathhouse, the woods, and Imogen's bedchamber. Between the columns was a metal ramp that could be flooded to represent a stream, or left dry for interior scenes. In the upstage right corner hung a huge, papier-mâché bird, wings spread as if in flight. Like Posthumus' ghost family, the bird's significance was not revealed until the dream sequence. Then it became the swing on which Jupiter, played here by an angelic boy soprano, swept in to prophesy the happy ending. In the meantime, its vaguely pregnant presence lent mystery to the atmosphere, like an element in one of Robert Wilson's symbolist theatrical tableaux.

Behind Tsypin's ornate set pieces hung a cyclorama the full width of the stage. Onto the cyc were projected background images designed by Stephanie Rudolph. A garden, trees, decaying ruins, and other landscape collages worked in imprecise perspective with Tsypin's columns to create moody, suggestive locales. The effect recalled in contemporary technological terms the scenic practices of the nineteenth century. "I'm very bored when scenery doesn't change in the theatre," says director Akalaitis. "I'm very interested in the workings of scenery." Tsypin and Rudolph's designs moved and shifted, sometimes in blackout, sometimes in full view of the audience.[67] Each scenic transformation was accompanied by Philip Glass's soaring, swashbuckling electronic score, which drove the rhythm and momentum of the whole tightly choreographed production. The rich juxtaposition of real and fantastic, flat and three-dimensional, stationary and mobile elements conjured up a dense and purely theatrical universe for the unfolding of Shakespeare's deliciously convoluted plot. Akalaitis believes that the complexity of the mise-en-scène confused and angered her critics:

. . . it has to do with the fact that it was designed, and it was thought out, that there was scenery instead of something that looks like the National Bank of Venezuela that actors stand in front of and talk in some generic costumes. What they are used to is a kind of noble, flat [image] and they do not understand design. They don't like design. They also don't like direction. They really don't.

Like Shakespeare's underappreciated play, Akalaitis's production was less a meditation on faith and fidelity than an extreme flexing of its creators' theatrical muscles. Other original directing/design features included a flying throne for Cymbeline; skimpy Native American costumes for the lost princes (basically, loincloths and war paint, a healthy twist by this feminist director on Western art's usual presentations of female nudity); and a bike and a scooter as the transportation of choice for Imogen and Pisanio's journey to Milford Haven. In the Act IV battle scene, Akalaitis displayed a virtuoso command of cinematic staging techniques. The scene was played as a slow-motion ballet with freeze-frame tableaux and synchronized strobe lighting effects. The armies, dressed up like toy soldiers, rode this most exciting segment of Glass's score like waves of energy. Completely nonrealistic, the carefully choreographed scene captured the agony, suspense, and adrenaline of combat in visually arresting, moving stage pictures.

Mistaken critics would later denounce the director's cynical approach to a text whose "flaws" they themselves were unable to reconcile. The irony is that Akalaitis never questioned the integrity of the text. Despite her renegade reputation, the director's professed stance toward dramatic texts could be described as reverential. Her tone of voice lowers when she describes "the play" at hand as the source of all her directorial inspirations. She adamantly denies having imposed an alien interpretation on *Cymbeline* and insists that her objective was to project the characters, situations, and ideas she found in the play:

> Shakespeare gives you everything. There's no subtext; it's all there. All you have to do is figure out how to put it out. For some actors, a lot of work entailed vocal coaching, saying these lines, putting these words out in space. Shakespeare is a great gift. It's all there, you just have to make it clear.

Of course, the lavishness of the physical production conflicts with this declaration. However one might appreciate the theatrical means by which Akalaitis expressed that which she found in Shakespeare's text, it is impossible to

Figure 6. The choreographed battle scene plays out in slow motion in *Cymbeline*, directed by JoAnne Akalaitis, at the New York Shakespeare Festival, 1989. Photo © George Joseph.

cast the generator of such potent theatrical gestures as the subservient conduit for Shakespeare's words. Still, Akalaitis's treatment of *Cymbeline* celebrated the script's most distinct (and controversial) features – an improbable, artificial, roller-coaster plot; the blatant opposition of good and evil characters; repetitions and apparent redundancies; in short, its overt theatricality.

Although textual critics have complained of redundancies in the play, deeper analysis suggests that Shakespeare's method is like that of *Rashomon:* The audience is exposed to multiple perspectives on incidents in the play. For example, we see Posthumus write to Pisanio. Then we hear Pisanio read the letter out loud. The two men react to the same "facts" about Imogen's adultery in completely opposite ways. We may compare Posthumus' rash, jealous rage to his more deliberate servant's cooler-headed reason. The long final scene of the play recounts these incidents a third time, offering the audience yet another opportunity to put the pieces of the story together, this time with all parties present. Each telling changes our perception; it is up to us to put it all together. Akalaitis's multilayered theatrical imagery added more elements to be synthesized. Shakespeare used one set of anachronisms; Akalaitis stretched them closer to our own experience by interpolating allusions to the more recent theatrical past.

The production made no attempt to harmonize or rationalize the play's incongruities. The director accepted the script wholesale. Nothing was cut. Practically no alterations were made to the text. She and Tsypin believed they were creating a straightforward rendition:

> We thought it was very elegant, classical Shakespeare. We were not doing a take on the play. We were not doing a version of the play. We did the play. I think I changed the order of something in it, but we thought it was even rather conservative. We never thought we were doing anything radical.

If, as she proclaims, the director stuck to the text, followed the impulses it stimulated in her imagination, and exploited its own most salient features, why did her production incite such a barrage of accusations and counteraccusations among the critics?

One factor that must be considered is the degree of directorial privilege assumed by a director like Akalaitis, whose background is rooted in the avant-garde of the 1970s. A theatre artist groomed in that milieu simply expects to be able to reset the play, juxtapose styles and periods, and cast actors without regard to race or ethnicity, all based on instinctive responses to the text and a small dose of corroborating research. Another possible source of friction might be her fiercely independent personality. An artist who resists labels, she works from a strong social consciousness. Akalaitis has said that she is always very much aware of being a woman director. "I can't stop seeing myself as a feminist," she says. "Especially because society continues to be sexist, racist, anti-Semitic, abusive of children." She sees opportunities in her role as a director to redress social injustice, both in her choice of material and, especially, through colorblind casting.

In *Cymbeline,* four key roles were assigned to nonwhite actors. African-American actors were cast as the Queen's son Cloten (Wendell Pierce),

Imogen's kidnapped brother Arviragus/Cadwal (Don Cheadle), and Posthumus' servant Pisanio (the excellent Peter Francis James). Jesse Borrego, who is Hispanic, played Imogen's other lost brother Guiderius/Polydore. The evil Queen was played by the white actress Joan MacIntosh, Imogen by Joan Cusack, and King Cymbeline by George Bartenieff, who is also white. A few critics objected to the unexplained mixing of races within the royal family. Others took offense at being asked to believe that Imogen, awakening from a drugged sleep, could mistake the headless body of Cloten for that of her husband, Posthumus, who was played by a white actor, Jeffrey Nordling. Akalaitis found their incredulity incredible. She is impatient when asked why she casts without regard to skin color:

> I don't even know how to answer that question in 1990. It is simply a question of justice. I was asked that question by *Time* magazine on *Endgame,* and I can't justify it, wouldn't even answer it. We live in a multi-ethnic world, and it's also a world which is dominated by white men. So on one level, the level of art, colorblind casting works, absolutely.
>
> The other is the personal level of social justice. Minority actors have to be given work. I think colorblind casting works, and once you make a commitment to colorblind casting, you don't have to do all kinds of talking about why this person's black, this person's white, this person's Mexican, and this person's Chinese. Once you've made that commitment, it's very liberating. If you try to find a way to make it logical, I think you get yourself in all kinds of traps, and you limit your choices.

Another piece of controversial casting in *Cymbeline* was the choice of Joan Cusak for Imogen. Cusak had recently made a Hollywood name for herself as Melanie Griffith's costar in *Working Girl.* At the same time, accusations were being leveled at Joseph Papp for feeding the Festival box office by hiring ill-equipped movie stars for Shakespearean leads. Rumors circulated to the effect that Cusak, whom many considered unfit for the role, had been cast at Papp's insistence. Akalaitis says no. She claims to have cast the broad-shouldered, strong-featured actress against Papp's recommendation and against traditional concepts of the character as a delicate, fragile, and helpless female:

> Joan was not chosen because she was a star. I auditioned a lot of people and I chose her. She is a heroic person [and] actress. . . . I think Joan is

a very Victorian looking woman. I think Imogen is a witty, brave, feisty, humorous person, all of whom are Joan.

Cusack did cut a forceful figure in the role. Her Imogen, passionate and resourceful, never seemed at odds with her lines or other characters' descriptions of her. That her characterization seemed completely at home in the context of the play suggests that "traditional" notions of the heroine have less to do with Shakespeare's depiction than the relics of prefeminist Shakespearean production and criticism. It must be noted, however, that Cusak's speaking of the verse left much to be desired. Her vocal work was forced, throaty, and rasping, her diction mush-mouthed. What the portrayal gained in pluck, it lost in poetry.

American actors are notoriously poor speakers of classical dialogue. In general, the cast of *Cymbeline* was no exception. Two performances in particular recall the frequent complaint that acting tends to be neglected by conceptual directors, who are imagined to be more concerned with scenic effects. Jeffrey Nordling's Posthumus lacked the strength and charisma the character needs to justify Imogen's unwavering attachment to him. Wendell Pierce's Cloten was too much a clod, too stupid to pose a threat to either Imogen's chastity or her succession to the throne.

Outstanding performances were contributed, however, by Peter Francis James, Joan MacIntosh, Michael Cumpsty, and Stefan Schnabel. As Pisanio, the wise and loyal servant, Peter Francis James proved to be the company's most skilled speaker of Shakespearean verse. His gentle portrait of a commoner with the courage and compassion grossly absent in his "betters" elevated the character to a central role. MacIntosh played the Queen as fairy-tale evil stepmother who will stop at nothing to see her own son usurp the throne. Savagely sly and sexy in her low-cut velvet gowns, MacIntosh's Queen seemed to sail over the stage. The red talons of her outstretched fingers danced on air in constant, devious motion. Michael Cumpsty's Iachimo epitomized the melodramatic villain, rotten to the core until his final scene of repentance. Cumpsty manipulated his thick eyebrows and black mustache in the glaring footlights to punctuate his every velvet-tongued prevarication.

Stefan Schnabel exploited every comic possibility in the character of Cornelius, the physician who placates the Queen with a poison placebo. Cornelius narrates the unraveling of the knotty plot in the long final scene, which has traditionally been cut drastically. Akalaitis understood the significance in the scene of each character "retelling the story in his own way." She left in every word and orchestrated the scene down to the last raised eyebrow.

I think it's a wonderful scene and I was very intimidated by it, and I just decided to bite the bullet and do it. It was rigorously rehearsed . . . in terms of group choreography. And I was delighted at how entertaining and funny it was. The actors hated rehearsing the scene because I dictated so much from the outside. We all hated rehearsing it, but I enjoyed its effect. A lot of that rehearsal was drill. We're going to do it over and over, and we're going to do it faster and faster. In performance is when they had fun with it.

The comical approach spoofed the preposterous length and implausibility of the scene's sudden confessions, reformations, and restorations. The precision of its performance was typical for the production as a whole. Painstaking execution is often the key to implementing strong directorial concepts successfully. Its lack is often what undoes productions based on equally interesting ideas. Akalaitis's detailed work here brought the fairy tale to its rightfully artificial, happy conclusion.

American Theatre magazine devoted eleven pages in the December 1989 issue to articles by Elinor Fuchs and James Leverett in defense of Akalaitis's *Cymbeline*. They provide a thorough review of the critics' responses and analyze the outmoded theatrical assumptions that prevented the critics from appreciating the production's considerable achievements.[68] Fuchs attempts to explain the critics' hostility by hypothesizing that they were not yet familiar with Akalaitis's postmodern theatrical vocabulary: layered imagery, juxtaposition of clashing elements, anachronism, and reliance on visual modes of expression. Akalaitis is grateful for the attempts to provide a more balanced appreciation of her work, although she was never consulted in the preparation of either piece. She is a fiercely independent artist who resists any attempts to label or categorize her work. When asked what she thought of Fuchs's theory, she told me

I don't even know what postmodernism is. I don't think about postmodernism, I have never read one word of Foucault or Derrida, or any of these people. I would like to; to my shame I have not. I will some day. But I don't carry a postmodern banner, and I don't care about any of that stuff.

She also recoiled from my use of the adjective "conceptual":

Whenever you do something you conceive it, so I think it's a meaningless word, and a kind of buzzword on both sides of academics to

101

find a way to think about bodies of work and for conservative critics to put it down. I think this sort of categorization is not useful at all. I think it's very dangerous. I mean, when you do the play, you do the play.

There is a certain political naïveté in Akalaitis's refusal to acknowledge that her aesthetics do in fact represent a break with theatrical tradition. Her sense of "doing the play" depends on an acceptance of wide theatrical and interpretative margins. Her expectations of the audience, for example, reflect postmodern ideas of the individual audience member as the locus of synthesis for diverse theatrical stimuli. Her frankly theatrical aesthetic owes debts to such widely diverse twentieth-century predecessors as Pirandello and Joseph Chaikin. She is confident that her audience will accept contradictory and artificial theatrical gestures.

I don't think it is asking a little too much. I think that's what theatre does. When we go in the theatre, it's not like going to the movies. When we go in the theatre, we know we're in the human arena. We sit there, and we are much more conscious of people sitting next to us. We are not entrapped by a manipulated image. We see the actors. We see them making mistakes, flub lines. We see their skin, we see their makeup. We see the costumes, the changing of the scenery.

This is another reason why she found "ridiculous" the critics' unwillingness to believe that Imogen could confuse Cloten's headless, black body for Posthumus' white one. For her, the fiction of character transcends the actor's physical characteristics, and she assumes that her audience shares that perspective. Besides, Akalaitis believed the immediate circumstances of the moment of confusion offered a more logical explanation for those who needed one. "She's drugged. She's taken a powerful drug, and because reason and credibility totally went out the window at that point, I just said 'great, it doesn't matter.'" But here as elsewhere, the critics demanded realism from an unrealistic scene in a patently antirealistic production.

"It's hard to work in New York," Akalaitis admitted to me eighteen months before she succeeded Joseph Papp as artistic director of the New York Shakespeare Festival in the fall of 1991.

It's the feeling of a lot of directors and writers that it's not possible to do anything in New York [because of the critics' economic power]. And that includes the *Village Voice,* who . . . I call the "policemen," the "Guardians of Art," like people from an old régime in Europe. But I hope that I'm not an artist who rants and raves and has my life ruined by critics. You can't be stopped by critics.

As head of the institution, Akalaitis directed both parts of *Henry IV* and John Ford's *Tis Pity She's a Whore*. She spent considerable artistic and administrative energy struggling to renew the Festival's post-Papp mission and financial base amid the severe economic recession that devastated public and corporate funding to the arts in the early 1990s. Her brief tenure ended abruptly, however, when she was ousted from her post by the Festival's board of directors in March 1993.

GENDER, RACE, POWER, AND *LEAR*

If *Cymbeline*'s checkered literary reputation hangs over any attempt to stage the play, *King Lear*'s renown is a gauntlet thrown at a director's feet. That is one reason why Arthur Holmberg has called the play "the postmodern performance script of choice."[69] Robert Wilson has worked on *King Lear* twice. The first encounter, in 1985, was a workshop conducted in a Metromedia television studio in Hollywood. The hypnotic pace and style of Japanese *nō* set the tempo. The stage area was decorated as a Japanese garden. The actors moved through slow, measured, stylized poses. Streaks of red paint ran down Gloucester's white-face cheeks after the blinding scene. Lines were intoned without emotion, and songs, puppets, and clips from silent-movie *Lears* were interpolated. His second foray, in the spring of 1990, grew out of the earlier workshop. The full-scale production, which was performed in an empty depot in Frankfurt, cast the eighty-year-old actress Marianne Hoppe as the King in a reversal of the traditionally all-male *nō*. Costumes and choreography were designed by Japanese artists. Critics were struck by the aura of rarefied stillness. The *New York Times* reported that "everything looked cool yet icily hysterical, like a frozen dream," although, ultimately, the emphatic placidity and dispassion "sapped the play's center of desperately needed life."[70] The consummate postmodern theatre artist, Wilson generated pristine theatrical images from the collision of Shakespeare's play and classical Japanese theatre.

In January 1990, Lee Breuer also took on the canonical challenge, returning to Shakespeare despite the tempest that had swirled around his Hollywood-celebrity version of that play in 1981 (see Chapter 3). Although, oddly enough, Breuer and Wilson both directed women in the title role, their two productions could not have been more dissimilar. While Wilson created dance drama of essence, simplicity, and alienation, Breuer tossed Shakespeare's text into the gaudy, earthy, raucous world of the American "white-trash" underclass.

The initial idea for *Lear* came from Breuer's wife, Ruth Maleczech, a co-founder of Mabou Mines and since the 1970s one of the most respected performers on the downtown scene. "I've wanted to do Lear for ten years at least," she told an interviewer for the *Village Voice* during the run of the show. "I'm not drawn to roles usually, but I *was* drawn to Lear's language. And I couldn't figure out any reason why a woman couldn't say those words as a woman."[71] Another director might have looked for reasons why the lines could not be spoken by a woman, but Breuer seized the opportunity to demonstrate to a wider public the unsung genius of his extraordinary actress-wife. After almost twenty years on the stage, Maleczech's name was barely known outside the avant-garde coterie. The sheer audacity of the undertaking would guarantee the coveted attention.

Of course, there is a tradition of actresses taking on the roles of Shakespearean heroes. Sarah Bernhardt, Judith Anderson, Diane Venora, Siobhan McKenna, and most recently Teresa Budziscz-Krzyzanowska, in Andrzej Wajda's backstage-view production, all dressed in breeches to play Hamlet. Comic actress Pat Carroll donned whiskers to play Falstaff at the Folger Shakespeare Theatre in Washington, D.C. Marianne Hoppe played King Lear as a man in Wilson's Japanese production. The Breuers would not have such transvestism in *Lear:* For them, Maleczech in the title role provided a fascinating opportunity to find out what would happen to the dynamics of the play if Lear were in fact a woman. "When a man has power, we take it for granted," mused Maleczech, "but when a woman has power we're forced to look at the nature of power itself."[72] The concept interested Breuer in exploring whether women "can have love and power at the same time."[73] For that matter, they rationalized, why stop at one character? Breuer and Maleczech ultimately decided to drop the first half of Shakespeare's title and switch the sexual identities of all the characters. "He's" and "she's" were interchanged in the script. Lear's "manhood" became "motherhood," and "son" was either "child" or "daughter" depending on the scansion of the particular line.

Instead of daughters, Maleczech/Lear had three sons: Regan (played by Ron Vawter) and Goneril (Bill Raymond) kept their names; Cordelia became Cordelion and was played by Breuer and Maleczech's son, Lute Ramblin'. Cordelion's fate hung on the whims of the ladies Burgundy (Maya

O'Reilly) and France (Breuer and Maleczech's daughter, Clove Galilee), both of whom wore prom dresses to make their marital pitches to Lear's son. Albany (Black-Eyed Susan) and Cornwall (Honora Fergusson) were the wives of Lear's elder sons, her daughters-in-law. The offspring of the female Gloucester (Isabell Monk) also underwent gender and name changes. The bastard Edmund became Elva, a sultry seductress in tight, black-leather jeans, played by Mabou Mines veteran Ellen McElduff. Edgar was turned into Edna and played by Karen Evans-Kandel. Oswald was renamed Wilda and assigned to Kimberly Scott. Only the Fool was cast the same sex as Shakespeare indicates, but Greg Mehrten played him as a drag queen in spike heels and a feather boa. Playing with and against sex stereotypes, Breuer created a topsy-turvy world of upside-down, inside-out gender roles and identities.

By putting women and men in each others' shoes, the production disarmed its audience's usual response to human brutality. The horrors of the violence in the play were intensified when enacted by women. Sisters Edna and Elva tore at each other on the floor. The female Cornwall cold-bloodedly gouged out the eyes of a sweet old lady. Breuer added a scene in which the antagonist-women lynched the quivering Fool, another act of shockingly cruel female aggression. Michael Feingold, reviewing for the *Village Voice,* watched Lear's daughters-in-law "slug it out with sticks and broken beer bottles, knocking each other across the hood of Goneril's roadster," and sensed that "something primordial appears to be taking its lunatic course."[74] Lear's maternal anguish also seemed magnified. It was almost unthinkable that those drunken, redneck boys could mistreat their harmless, cantankerous, old mama in such shameless fashion. When Maleczech lumbered onto the stage bearing the limp body of her dead son, they comprised a virtual Pietà.

We are a culture inured to male violence by overexposure in news reports, film, and television. Breuer's oblique deconstructive strategy – revealing latent realities by depicting the opposite – could resensitize benumbed spectators. We stomach male brutes in our daily media diet, but it was hard to watch the women aggressors in *Lear.* Likewise, *Lear'*s female victims elicited enormous sympathy. Breuer's device retrains our focus obliquely. That we are aghast at the women highlights our low expectations of and compassion for fathers, sons, and men in general.

If Maleczech's needs provided the impetus for the gender bending in the production, *Lear* also suited Breuer's long-term directorial agenda. Just as he had made accommodations in *The Tempest* and *The Gospel at Colonus* to look at/through them from an American perspective, so the recast *Lear* offered him yet another exploratory field. An appropriate American setting had to be found. The Breuer's would later tell the press that they based their decision for the Southern setting on something they had heard on the public television series "The Story of English." The show reported a theory that, due to the regional migration patterns of early English settlers in North America, dialects spoken in parts of the southern United States probably contain the closest extant accents to those of Elizabethan English. The Breuers set *Lear* in rural Smyrna, Georgia, in the late 1950s.

Alisa Solomon, who served as production dramaturge on *Lear,* says the PBS rationale oversimplifies the justification for the production's "geographical and temporal" relocation of the play. She is not sure why Breuer repeatedly offered that anecdotal explanation, but she recalls discussions early in the three-and-a-half-year rehearsal process that suggest the Georgia setting had deeper roots. She remembers telling Breuer about Maynard Mack's postulation in *King Lear in Our Time* that, for the Elizabethan audience, the historical setting of *King Lear* would have had specific resonances.

> The Elizabethan audience would be familiar with the medieval world, where these codes of behavior existed, as the period right before their own "modern" or "contemporary" age. This was the mythic reality of what came before their time.[75]

According to Solomon, Mack's thesis provided the key to a contemporary American "analogue" for Shakespeare's setting: "The South is a place we associate with chivalric codes, clans, those kinds of ways of organizing society, and the fifties is the era in our imaginations that just preceded our own."

In fact, Solomon's recollection of Mack's point is not completely accurate. Mack's reference was not to the historical period in which *King Lear* is set, but to Shakespeare's allegorical depiction of certain characters, in which the critic traces remnants of the medieval morality play:

> Lear himself, as Professor Harbage among others has pointed out – flanked in that opening scene by "vices or flatterers on the one hand, virtues or truth-speakers on the other" – stirs memories of a far more ancient dramatic hero, variously called Mankind, Everyman. . . . Though the complexity of the play as a whole sets it worlds apart from this tradition, one cannot but be struck by the number of details in *King Lear* that seem to derive from it.[76]

Whether by Breuer's intention or not, Mack's postulation did, in fact, inform the final mise-en-scène. The production was bedecked in pop-cult artifacts from an American subculture most of its audience knew best from pre-1960s fictional renderings. Writers of review headlines capitalized on that relationship with such bons mots as "Lear's Little Acre," in the *Village Voice,* and "Mabou Mines Sets Lear on a Hot Tin Roof," in the *Times.* With his characteristic, electronic eclecticism, however, the director avoided imitating wholesale Tennessee Williams's gauzy realism or any Hollywood depiction of Southern life. His pastiche backwoods Georgia moved to the strains of Pauline Oliveros's synthesized score and was visited by a Kent (Lola Pashalinski) disguised as Juanita, a serape-swaddled Mexican peasant, and an Edna/Edgar who subsumed her identity in that of a dreadlocked Jamaican sorceress.

Whether "The Story of English" or Maynard Mack motivated the selection of the Georgian locale, the Breuer–Maleczech Lear was portrayed as the matriarch of a working-class family. In the opening scene, Mama's birthday barbecue provided the occasion for her to divide her run-down acreage among her three beer-guzzling sons. King Lear uses a map to indicate how he will divvy up his lands among his daughters; Maleczech/Lear indicated how the land was to be distributed by cutting her children proportionate wedges of birthday cake. Breuer designed his own whimsical, dilapidated setting. At each of its far ends sat the porches of two ramshackle wooden houses. The interiors of the houses receded beyond the wings of the wide, floor-level thrust stage of the Triplex Theatre in Manhattan. Upstage of the stage-right dwelling was an outhouse, and, upstage center, a green mound topped by a droll papier-mâché miniature-golf-course castle, painted in the bright, iridescent spectrum of period convertibles. Breuer left empty the large, unlocalized, centerstage playing area, which served alternately as backyard, battlefield, heath, and parking lot. Two miniature electric cars (converted golf carts, commissioned at a cost of approximately $7,000 each) were driven onstage and off to reconnoiter with allies, mobilize troops, and transport Lear's mangy entourage: Instead of knights, Lear's despised retinue consisted of a pack of large, if not particularly handsome, dogs.

The Southern setting also gave the director yet another opportunity to deal with issues of race in America. Giving work to nonwhite actors is a priority for Breuer, as it is for his Mabou Mines colleague JoAnne Akalaitis, but he does not practice colorblind casting. When Breuer casts a female or minority actor in a traditionally male or white role, he uses the substitution as an opportunity to comment on the represented group's standing in society. "Most of my large work," Breuer says, "has a political intent, but I don't mount works with leftist dialogue and fist-shaking. I try to mount the work *as* a political statement, not that *says* a political statement."[77] In *Lear,* Gloucester and her daughter Edna were played by black actresses; Elva, the illegitimate daughter, by a fair-skinned blonde. Besides the all-too-obvious symbolism of casting a white actress as the black sheep of the family, the racial overtones brought out subtle subthemes in the production. Through images of white-on-black Breuer generated meanings Shakespeare could never have intended.

Picayune reviewers objected to the plausibility of a close friendship between the white Lear and black Gloucester, but black–white relations in the rural South cannot be judged by the norms of cities in the North, where contact between the races is mostly limited to public accommodations. Closer quarters and a blemished but long-standing coexistence in the South more often breed good neighbors and friends. Racial hate and violence are also facts of southern life, however, and the subordinate treatment of Gloucester by Lear's children in this production was based not on her lower aristocratic rank, as in the original, but on her race. When Lear's white offspring invaded Gloucester's home, demanded her cooperation against Lear, and then plucked out her eyes, the production echoed familiar scenes of white-on-black brutality, such as lynchings and police beatings of black suspects. Elva's whiteness, despite her mother's protests of "good sport at her making," evoked a disturbing history of white men taking sexual advantage of black women as far back as slavery. Like the tenderness that infused the female Lear's suffering, the social implications of cross-racial casting hinted at resonances we might not otherwise have detected in the text.

Gone from this production were the royal trappings of *King Lear,* and with them, some wrote, its tragic dimensions. However, if *King Lear* is indeed applicable to the universal human condition, as its classic stature suggests, its themes cannot pertain only to royalty: Were that the case, the play would have lost rather than gained popularity in the twentieth century. To say that *King Lear* is about royalty is like saying *Hamlet* is about Denmark or *The Cherry Orchard* is about fruit trees. If there are fundamental human truths in these great plays, they are only symbolized by the circumstantial facts of their settings. It is the task of the contemporary director to build conceptual bridges between the allusions, social dynamics, and assumptions in old plays and the common reference points of the modern audience. We do not sit in the theatre with history books in our laps. The production must speak to us in the first person and immediately. By the time we summon the relevance

Figure 7. Ruth Maleczech confronts her surly offspring in the title role of *Lear*, directed by Lee Breuer and performed by Mabou Mines, at the Triplex Theatre in Manhattan, 1990. Photo © Beatriz Schiller.

of some remote historical fine point in the text, the rest of the scene has passed us by. The director must substitute evocative approximations for the details in order to give the audience entrée to the subtext as it applies to their own experience. Lee Breuer was more interested in the ways *King Lear* explores power, trust, and betrayal in families and friendships, and how they are affected by age, race, and gender, than in reproducing Shakespeare's obsolete social and political order.

Breuer's Smyrna, Georgia, became an accessible microcosm of Shakespeare's medieval state, with its own hierarchies, allegiances, and ceremonies based on an old, strict social contract. Its backwoods community was duly shattered by the events in Breuer's production. Parents were devastated by cruelly ambitious children. Unchecked sibling rivalry divided the citizenry into armed and murderous mobs. Denizens of the twentieth century cannot discount the symbolic significance of these upheavals simply because their sufferers lacked royal pedigrees. Breuer demystified the setting, lifted the aura of divine right, and made the play about plain folks.

Despite its blatant appropriations of humorous American pop-cult iconography, Breuer's *Lear* would seem to have had some solid intellectual
foundations. Casting and characterizations were primed to bring feminist
and multicultural perspectives to the play. Offbeat but apt parallels between
old and new instances of social and economic injustice, inhumanity, and betrayal bore the seeds of a powerful reinterpretation of the familiar text. Preproduction publicity and Mabou Mines' reputation had generated excited
anticipation of the production. In performance, though, *Lear* turned out to be
a seriously flawed three-hours traffic. "Steer Clear of This Lear" rhymed the
heading of one stubbornly unimaginative review in the *Daily News*. Alisa
Solomon, the dramaturge, who is also a theatre critic for the *Voice,* understands how tempting it is for critics to go back after the show and "beat the
production over the head with the script." But blanket condemnations miss
the point: Any meaningful assessment of this production would have to separate its admirable goals from its unrealized achievements.

Postmodernism encourages tolerance for disruption, collage, and incoherence within a theatrical performance. The richness of Breuer's *Lear* lay in his
unlikely but fundamental juxtapositions. The performance went astray in the
theatricalization of his new and compelling responses to the play. Like a box
of mismatched jigsaw-puzzle pieces, bits of Breuer's ideas rolled out onto the
stage in tangled knots. Sloppily executed and superficially explored directorial inventions ultimately drowned out serious attempts to address the issues
Breuer said interested him most. A review of the production history should
shed some light on what went wrong.

According to Solomon, the director never articulated a thematic scheme:

> There was no programmatic idea: "Let's make a feminist production."
> There was no intention when we started out to prove anything or to
> show anything. The intention was to ask, well, what if? Now, some of
> us had different ideas about what we expected would happen . . .

It is all well and good for a director to begin rehearsals with "what if." Peter
Brook would applaud Breuer's willingness to approach rehearsals with only
questions in mind, but at some point in the process, the questions need to be
answered. *Lear*'s erratic rehearsal schedule may account in part for its problems. The work evolved over a sporadic, nomadic series of residencies at five
different theatres and colleges, over a period of more than three years. The
process began at the Theatrical Outfit in Atlanta, in September 1987, and
was then abandoned until February 1988, when the company was invited to

the George Street Playhouse in New Brunswick, New Jersey. The visiting-artists deals always included some kind of public workshop or performance of the work in progress. Solomon remembers confused and agitated New Jersey audiences leaving in droves before the end of those sessions. The artistic staff of the George Street Playhouse was fired in toto shortly thereafter, although the management denies any connection between the two events.

Six weeks that summer were spent in the bucolic splendor of Storm King, a private academy in one of Manhattan's more remote northern suburbs. Scenes in progress were shown at the Public Theatre that fall, and work resumed in the spring of 1989 at Smith College. Then, after frantic fund-raising efforts finally attracted ample support from AT&T and other sources, the finished performances ran from January through March of 1990 at the Triplex in Manhattan. It is conceivable that the director had trouble imagining the jumbled cumulative effect of all the scenes in rapid succession. The company had only three weeks prior to performances at the Triplex. Most of that time was devoted to ironing out myriad technical details.

In rehearsal, says Solomon, "Lee has a thousand ideas a minute. If four of them are brilliant, and the other 996 are awful," it can take some time before he sees the difference. She also reports that his approach to solving staging problems is often short-term. His first impulse can be a cheap, quick fix. She says a large part of her responsibility as dramaturge – in addition to helping Breuer change gender and royal references in the text and helping the non-classically trained actors understand and speak their lines – was to keep track of continuity, to make sure the production was "telling the story all the time." During rehearsals for the scene in which Goneril expressed his anger at the presence of Lear and her dogs in his home, Breuer had Bill Raymond "pacing back and forth in a farcical, almost vaudeville way." Solomon pointed out that it was clear that the character was angry, but that his movement did not indicate exactly what he was so angry about. "Yeah, you're right," Breuer agreed. He then turned to the prop master across the room and shouted, in all seriousness, "Can you get me some of that plastic dog shit for tomorrow?" The *faux merde* stayed through several rehearsals, but was deleted, fortunately, before the public performances.

Some of Breuer's wildest ideas came to rich fruition in the final version of *Lear*. Goneril's retreat to his outhouse during an argument with his domineering wife was petulantly perfect. A lesbian embrace between Cornwall and Elva/Edmund concretized a latent homosexual attraction that justified Cornwall's immediate and intense attachment to the young dissembler.

111

Here Solomon notes that Breuer exercised good editorial sense when he realized that the original blocking for the scene, which involved several minutes of wriggling and fondling, was overkill and cut it down to a single, passionate kiss. Inevitably, the characters' black-leather duds merely reinforced
butch stereotypes. Elva also conducted heterosexual trysts with Cornwall's
husband and her brother-in-law in the back seat of one of the miniconvert-
ibles, the bisexuality underscoring the character's indiscriminate use of sex to
accomplish her destructive ends.

Breuer's direction of the Fool embodied some of his best and worst ideas.
Whereas literal-minded critics complained that a gawky, urbane transvestite
would never have been tolerated by Lear's backwoods sons or neighbors, the
presence of a sexually ambiguous provocateur helped to crystallize the fundamental relationship between gender and humanity within the production's
nonrealistic mise-en-scène. Solomon was especially pleased with the Fool's
camp rendition of the 1970s pop anthem "I'm a Woman." Mehrten pranced
out of the latrine, vibrator in hand as a microphone, crooning inane lyrics
about how juggling household chores certifies the singer as a "woooman,
W-OOoo-M-A-N." In that incongruous moment, Solomon believes, the
production posed the essential question of "what it means to be a woman, a
female human." "Is gender essential to our being?" she heard the performance ask, or is it another human "accommodation"? Less resonant was the
part of the storm scene during which the Fool intoned Shakespeare's difficult
lyrics to the tune of "Singin' in the Rain." The production team had given
up trying to figure out what the lines meant, the dramaturge says in defense
of the "easy yuck." Besides, they felt the melody provided the actor with a
structure for speaking the verse.

Perhaps the most consistent fault with Breuer's *Lear* lay neither in the director's outrageous imagination nor the company's aggregate lack of classical
experience. It seems rather that the director was unwilling or unable to bend
and sway with the same elasticity that he demanded of the script. He insisted on several of his favorite effects despite evidence during rehearsals and
previews that they were not working out. Here, as in nearly all of his previous works, Breuer insisted on amplified speech. "Lee doesn't like unampli-
fied sound," says Solomon. "He thinks it's dead. Nobody questions anymore
rock musicians plugging in their instruments to amps and singing at microphones. [So, he wonders] why shouldn't this be an option in the theatre
too?" The facile answer to his query is that in the theatre unmediated human
contact and the spoken word are higher priorities than at rock concerts.

In all fairness, however, Breuer had good theoretical reasons for wiring each actor with a small, headset microphone. He was looking for a way to present Shakespeare's asides and soliloquies to the contemporary audience, and thought the mikes could achieve the theatrical, aural equivalent of a cinematic close-up. Instead, the actors – nearly all inexperienced and not particularly confident speakers of Shakespeare's verse – mumbled their lines (Monk, McElduff, and Maleczech excepted). Much of the time, it was nearly impossible to tell who was speaking. The mouthpieces, floating black splotches in front of every face, made it seem as if flies had been brought in to authenticate the Georgia backwater setting, or that the characters were really telephone operators or air traffic controllers. Solomon agrees that Breuer may have had a valid idea, but that he should have dropped it when the technical obstacles proved insurmountable.

The *Village Voice* ran two opposing reviews of *Lear* side by side on the same page. Erica Munk got right to the heart of what went wrong when she observed that Maleczech's "strong, surprising, monstrously maternal, eloquent" performance was "subverted from the start" by Breuer's technocracy. "How expressive can a face be, with its human power so subordinated to electronics?" she wondered. How affecting can an actor's nuances be when they are "half drowned by overamplified music?"[78] Breuer's misuse of Brechtian alienation devices resulted in annoyance rather than intellectual distance. On the other hand, the second *Voice* critic, Michael Feingold, was convinced that "cutting *Lear* down to a tantrum in a black-eyed-peapatch, oddly, doesn't diminish either the power of its violence or its nightmarish, despairing vision of a hierarchical order torn to pieces by willfulness and greed at the top, willing servitude and hunger below."[79]

The conflicting reactions reflected in the pages of the *Voice* reflect accurately *Lear*'s mixed results. The feminization of the characters successfully softened the emotional landscape of the play and thus made its horrors that much sharper. Watching Maleczech's Lear being tossed among the elements was, at times, like watching one's grandmother being tortured. The racial undertones were a sly reminder that the feudal mentality persists today in less obvious, more insidious forms. On the down side, the increased sensitivity of Lear's loss as a mother hinted by negative implication at something sad about paternity in our society. How ancillary do we consider fathers that a mother's pain should seem more affecting? Women as a group lost, too, when in their quests for power they resorted to traditional male acts of violence and aggression. Lee Breuer had some wonderful ideas and impulses for *Lear,* but he bears the burden of responsibility for its ultimate disappointments. Thematic incoherence may be the hallmark of the fragmented, deconstructed, postmodern aesthetic, but, as we have seen, sophomoric cop-outs, incomprehensible speech, and intrusive technology can undermine the cleverest of directorial conceits.[80]

Contrary to the trepidations of tradition-minded critics, revisionist productions have strengthened Shakespeare's secure place on the American theatrical agenda. His renewed theatrical popularity is spilling over into other dramatic media as well. Kenneth Branagh's Shakespearean films are big box office. Cable television is running half-hour cartoon treatments of Shakespeare's plays for children. Performance artists are deconstructing Shakespeare, too. Fred Curchack's one-man *Stuff As Dreams Are Made On* is about as radical as Shakespeare performances get; yet it proves that a talented and disciplined conceptual artist can cut, paste, jumble, deconstruct, strip bare, and poke fun at a Shakespeare play and still evoke its story, themes, theatrical effects, and poetry.

Subtitled "*The Tempest,* changed into something rich and strange," *Stuff* uses such "poor theatre" means as masks, dolls, puppets, mime, and a pair of disposable cigarette lighters to conjure a performance magic as wonderful as Prospero's own. Curchack is an accomplished actor, director, and teacher who has studied with Grotowski and Alwin Nikolais as well as at traditional schools of *Kathakali, nō,* and Balinese *topeng* dance. His ongoing training allows him in this performance piece to toggle instantly among the five characters he portrays simply by altering his posture or tone of voice. Curchack embodies Prospero, Ariel, and Caliban, and throws his voice, like a ventriloquist, into a muscle-man puppet Ferdinand and a whining-brat doll Miranda. The character transformations are enhanced by imaginative latex masks and shadowplay against a single gauze curtain that hangs at the back of the playing area.

The transformations cut to the play's essential questions about character, self, and identity. The island inhabitants are made to seem like quarrelsome aspects of a single personality, who periodically bursts out of the fictive world to harangue the audience about their ignorance of the play or to reassure them that this is not some overintellectualized, academic deconstruction. As Curchak toggles back and forth among the various characterizations and his own persona, the essential theme emerges: How extraordinary it is that contradictory human beings somehow manage to reconcile the schizophrenic elements of self into a coherent sense of personal identity.

Shakespeare will continue to be a vibrant force in the American theatre. Who knows what theatrical techniques will be brought to bear on his plays in ten, twenty, or a hundred years? Whatever their twenty-first-century destiny may be, it will rest in the hands of innovators who trust that the plays contain still-hidden treasures for the modern world and who are either brave or foolhardy enough to let their imaginations wander off in search of them.

5

THE PLAYS OF MOLIÈRE
■ ● ■

MOLIÈRE'S COMEDY crackles with serious implication. Even the most literal interpreter cannot ignore the fierce anger seething dangerously close to the surface. The survival of La Troupe du Roi and its author-director-star depended on royal favor. Molière had to mask the sharp social criticism in his plays. He managed to expose the decadence and hypocrisy of Louis XIV's court by tempering his honesty with pragmatism. He cloaked his rage in farce and drew such exaggerated characters that an audience unwilling to recognize itself could dismiss them as inoffensive comic ploys. Of course, his barbs rarely went undetected. The targets were often stung, and Molière suffered for insulting them. Critical subterfuge was the impetus for Molière's comic machinations, and its undercurrents remain, like buried treasure, waiting to delight those who delve beyond the surface structure of his texts.

Overt sexuality, greed, deceit, jealousy, false piety, social posturing, immediate gratification, all taken to extremes, are Molière's concerns – mostly taboo topics in polite seventeenth-century discourse. The measure of his genius is that he was able to get them on the boards in the first place. "There is nothing else that theatre is but risk," director Peter Sellars recently observed in defense of his own controversial theatrics. "The minute that Molière is no longer risking the King's displeasure, he becomes like all of the boulevard comedians of his era, and we can't even think of their names."[1] Today, however, Molière's are common themes and not only on the stage. The explicitness of current film, television, fiction, biography, and the news media suggests that we have lost our squeamishness about airing the underbelly of social life. Far from recoiling, post-Freud, post-O'Neill society revels in contemplating its own neuroses. How, then, to do justice to the dramatist's

116

edge, nerve, and ingenuity, when his satire is as apt as ever but his sleight of hand is no longer required? Directors address the problem by exploding Molière's veneer of civility and rewrighting the plays to unfetter the characters' urges, passions, compulsions, and venalities. Lust erupts in scenes of graphic lovemaking, sets materialize the physical and moral decay of blindly avaricious communities, and mild horseplay takes on the deadly overtones of brute farce.

Americans are relative latecomers to experimental stagings of Molière's plays, although Douglas Campbell directed Hume Cronyn in a *commedia* version of *The Miser* at the Guthrie in 1963. Campbell's *commedia dell'arte* format was both historically relevant and theatrically exuberant, but the result was more akin to the way the Lunts popularized *The Taming of the Shrew* in the thirties with their own *commedia* stylization than a fresh or penetrating new response to the material. Revisionist directors in France and the former Soviet Union have a longer track record of reconceptualizing Molière. Molière's country of origin is also the birthplace of deconstruction; and there are obvious parallels between the repressive atmospheres of seventeenth-century Paris and the pre-Perestroika cultural milieu. A brief detour into some distinguished French and Soviet productions will provide context for the American stagings that will be our major focus a little later in the chapter. It is no coincidence that three of the American Molière directors who will be discussed are in fact Eastern-European emigrés.

INFLUENTIAL FRENCH AND SOVIET PRODUCTIONS

French director Roger Planchon claims never to have read the classics in school, so he swears he approached *Tartuffe* as if it were a new play. His 1962 production, at his Théâtre National Populaire, in Villeurbanne, broke away from tradition and can be seen as having cleared the way for subsequent iconoclastic directors of Molière. French New Criticism and the early stirrings of deconstructionist theory seem to have influenced both the way Planchon understood his role as a director and the way the critics reviewed his work. Planchon's groundbreaking version of Brecht's *Schweyk*, in 1961, prompted the magazine *Théâtre Populaire* to observe that

> Planchon is no longer seeking to situate and explain historically a certain dramaturgical practice; he is substituting one form of writing for another. He is replacing a play, that is a narrative and a meaning, by a symbolic system with multiple meanings.[2]

117

In Planchon's *Tartuffe*, scenery and gesture conveyed a topical political sub-text distinct from Molière's own. "I've become Molière's co-author,"[3] he said at the time, only partly tongue-in-cheek, claiming his directorial right and responsibility to stage the classic text according to the issues and images of his own cultural and personal context. "Everything is and remains open. There can be no other orthodoxy."[4]

A Marxist, Planchon wanted to show the turmoil of a society in transition from one form of totalitarianism to another. Orgon became "*un grand bourgeois*"[5] whose substantial house was being renovated "from Renaissance fortress to showy Louis XIV mansion."[6] Rene Allio's setting, in which one wall flew up and disappeared at the conclusion of each of the first four acts, suggested the dismantling of the old order. Paintings laden with almost grue-some Catholic iconography took up most of the wall space, echoing Tar-tuffe's grotesque fervor.[7] By the end of the play the stage was empty, the theatre's back walls exposed. The violent invasion of the Sun King's forces in the final scene evoked images of Stalin's "all-pervading tentacles" that reach into the parlors of its citizens' homes. Tartuffe was gagged and taken away, but the stark environment and the cruelty of those who delivered justice re-placed Molière's neatly tied resolution with lingering doubt about what could be expected in the new regime.

The interpolation of Planchon's own political agenda within the seven-teenth-century text can be attributed to the dual influences of Marx and Brecht; but his other major alteration was more subtle, more Freudian, and perhaps even more significant a precedent for future directorial reworkings of Molière. Latent homosexual attraction was suggested as the motivation for Orgon's attachment to the monk-poseur. Tartuffe became less the aggressor than the passive beneficiary of Orgon's ever-intensifying advances. The re-versal of perpetrator and victim, or the equal distribution of power, blame, and responsibility for absurd behavior, forced the audience to grapple with characters who were not easily, dismissibly ridiculous, but rather more com-plex, real, compelling, disturbing, and thought provoking.

Planchon imbued *Tartuffe* with contemporary politics, philosophy, and psychology by responding to impulses in the text with images that reflect his contemporary associations. By 1986, the director had fully adopted the lan-guage of the literary theorists whose influence pushed him past "copying" Brecht into developing his own style and methods. If, he postulated in a preface to *The Miser*, "each new period 'reads' the works of the past differ-ently and reveals itself through its 'reading,' . . . the director must . . . call at-tention to the process of reading and to the manner in which it is constructed."[8] Planchon "read" *Tartuffe* in a philosophical context that had not been formulated in Molière's day, although parallels can easily be discerned between the circumstances of then and now. His "reading" therefore demonstrated those associations through which a twentieth-century mind may be stimulated by the original text. In that same preface, however, Planchon is careful to caution against the "fashion for 'rediscovering' classic authors in a new light." Planchon's stagings of Molière do not so much subvert the original as exploit the various plastic theatrical media to amplify contemporary themes he discovers embedded in the text. A recent evaluation concluded that "often critics have been too misled by Planchon's bold redefinition of a play's visual field to see that the text itself was perfectly respected."[9]

The next French director to have a major impact on the staging of Molière was Antoine Vitez, who consolidated four of the major plays into a four-evening, twenty-act cycle, in 1978–9. Similar in conception to Orson Welles's *Five Kings* and John Barton and Peter Hall's *Wars of the Roses,* the Molière Cycle was first performed in the courtyard of the Carmelite cloisters at Avignon and later brought indoors against the backdrop of an Italianate trompe l'oeil set. Vitez's telescoping of *The School for Wives, Tartuffe, Don Juan,* and *The Misanthrope* explores the four plays and their four central male characters, all of whom Vitez believes to be projections of Molière himself, as variations on a single theme. The central figure, besieged by the other characters, especially the women, cries throughout for "absolute passion in a rigidly repressive world." His frustrations embody the "sexual and metaphysical impotence of the exceptional man."[10]

Using deconstructionist technique akin to Planchon's, Vitez signaled allusions and associations among the four parts of the piece with an "ensemble of signs," comprised of repeated gestures, costume elements, and six props that were recycled throughout the four sections: a walking stick, a table, two chairs, and two candelabra. These props reappeared at calculated intervals, "each accruing meaning and thus retrospectively assigning meaning to previous performances."[11] Silent pauses, halting or mumbled speech, and exaggerated gestures were also repeated by the successive incarnations of the Molière figure. Vitez's focus was psychological rather than political, but his emphasis on the darker tones in the texts lent the event a Beckettian feeling, a uniquely "modern tragic" sensibility.[12]

Soviet and Eastern European productions of Molière's plays grow out of Meyerhold's caustic, physical farce. Molière's satires served generations of directors as relatively safe vehicles for social and political commentary. One fine example is Yuri Lyubimov's production of *Tartuffe,* performed at the Taganka Theatre in 1969. The production packed its powerful political punch under the camouflage of historical references and a clever conceptual framework. That the performance received the requisite official sanction prompted one observer to marvel that the director "seem[ed] to have shown a blind spot in the censors."[13]

Lyubimov framed the production in the ruse of a staged reading presented to the authorities for approval. On either side of the stage hung a huge portrait, one of Louis XIV, the other of the Archbishop of Paris. Lining the back of the stage stood framed, life-size portraits of the characters. These were actually free-standing screens slit vertically down the middle, through which the actors could pop their heads or step out to play their scenes. Everyone hid behind a fixed, official mask/facade. The crucial scene between Tartuffe and Elmire was played for high stakes. The table under which Orgon hid while Tartuffe seduced his wife was really his own screen propped on a four-legged stanchion. He did not emerge until Tartuffe had dragged Elmire off the central playing area and behind his own screen, where, it was implied, he raped her. When Orgon finally moved, he stood up through the split in the screen, like a beauty who pops out of a cake to find the party over. A Grand Guignol speed-through of the entire first half of the play opened the second act, reinforcing the harsh, mechanistic edge of pointed farce.

Lyubimov focused the central relationship not on sexual bonds, but on the whereabouts of a strongbox filled with secret documents that Orgon had entrusted to Tartuffe. This reference to domestic espionage and official peril was echoed in subtle implications that the Jesuits, Tartuffe's order, were in fact agents of the KGB. "I strain to make the far-off echo yield a cue to the events that may come in my day,"[14] said Lyubimov, quoting Pasternak, in an interview about *Tartuffe*. Orgon's household became, in effect, "a parable of Soviet life."[15] The end of the production underscored the contemporary allusions. Jazz accompanied Orgon's pardon, an aural "wink" to the audience about the lack of true justice in the USSR. At the first curtain call, the actors waved smilingly over and around their screens, but for the second one, they stood solemnly at the edge of the stage, their stares a silent plea to the audience not to miss the point, to connect the fiction to the sorry state of Soviet affairs. Lyubimov's highly conventionalized framing motif, elements of antic farce, and substitution of internal espionage for religious hypocrisy did double duty, supporting both the angst in the script and the anguish of the Soviet predicament. It will be interesting to watch what happens to Molière in the newly autonomous republics that once comprised the USSR.

ANDREI SERBAN DIRECTS *THE MISER*

American rewrightings of Molière tend to be less political in their comparisons between the seventeenth and twentieth centuries. In this way, they are more faithful to Molière's own preoccupation with contemporary mores. However, the stylistic influence of the French and Eastern European models, which embroider the text with a rich theatrical vocabulary of sets, props, and gestures, can easily be traced in the more adventurous American essays. In addition, almost all of the American stagings let Molière's steamier impulses surge into the open.

Andrei Serban directed *The Miser* at the American Repertory Theatre (ART) in the spring of 1989, and I was very fortunate to have been invited to observe a series of rehearsals and speak with the director and members of the cast and company. What follows is a detailed case study of the director's process as he first responded to the classic text and then translated those contemporary responses into original theatrical signs. His revision would ultimately invert the neat neoclassical structure usually attributed to the play, thereby refuting several hundred years of interpretation and thrusting an accusatory finger at his contemporary audience.

"I love that guy, Harpagon," Andrei Serban told a colleague during a preproduction meeting for *The Miser* at ART in the spring of 1989. "He's the only one who isn't full of shit!"[16]

Harpagon the most admirable character in the play? Tradition holds that Molière's central characters – extremists of various annoying, infuriating types – are not particularly sympathetic. Their obsessions may contain a grain of truth, occasionally even wisdom, but fanaticism renders the characters and their opinions ridiculous. Some, like M. Jourdain, simply make fools of themselves. Others are more than laughingstocks. Orgon, Alceste, and Harpagon, for example, impose their obdurate ways and opinions on their families, friends, and servants. They become thorns, tyrants. Their unreasonable demands threaten the safety and sanity of those who must depend on them.

Corollary to this standard view of Molière's obnoxious central characters is that the other characters, those upon whom the fanaticism is perpetrated, are helpless, virtuous, or at least benign victims. Under this paradigm, Orgon's wife Elmire allows Tartuffe to flirt with her, but only to prove the imposter's adulterous intentions to her hoodwinked husband. Célimène flirts too, but only to play along with and get by in society. Likewise, the miser's motherless children are understandably pressed to maneuver around their father's unjust and outrageous constraints on their behavior: Naturally Cléante takes surreptitious loans to finance an adequate wardrobe. Of course Elise makes a secret promise to Valère: Her father would never allow her to marry a young man without a bank account.

Thus, Molière's plays can be seen to be built upon a neat, neoclassically balanced structure: The crazy individuals around whom the plays revolve disrupt the orderly social worlds around them by forcing others to behave according to their own absurd beliefs and expectations. The central figure is the hub, the secondary characters the spokes of a wheel that spins dizzily around until the resolution of the plot. Molière's endings usually entail a restoration of precraziness social norms. Suppression of the insanity and the restoration of order and balance often arrive via an act or agent of the court – the playwright's savvy if rather obvious homage to his monarch and patron, Louis XIV. Society returns to its status quo once the oddball/irritant is reformed, repressed, or repulsed from its midst.

So how did Serban come to like Harpagon best? What does the director's affection for Harpagon imply about his views of the miser's children and the other members of his extended household? And how did these sentiments inform the director's interpretation and staging of the play? Such a radical opinion of the protagonist must have a domino effect on the remaining characters. The subsequent realignment of their roles in the conflict requires a drastic shift in the internal structure of the play in performance.

The colleague to whom Serban confided his uncommon admiration for dramatic literature's most parsimonious paterfamilias was Albert Bermel, whose cleverly colloquial translation (made in 1986) had been selected as the production text. In the spring of 1989, Bermel had also just completed the manuscript for *Molière's Theatrical Bounty: A New View of the Plays,* which contains a relevant essay on *The Miser.* In fact, significant elements of Serban's production can be traced to the ideas in Bermel's essay. Bermel recalls being impressed by the director's receptiveness during early conversations and pleasantly surprised at the extent to which Serban had incorporated his critical remarks into the performance.

"Harpagon is thus the root and trunk of the play, as well as the feeder for most of its branches," Bermel writes: But the tree draws sustenance from those branches. This is not the one-character comedy with interruptions from secondary characters that sometimes finds its way onto the stage.[17] While it is impossible to unravel with certainty the complex network of ideas and inspirations from which a director draws sustenance for a particular production, Serban might as well have begun with this passage. His was a dark vision of the play that cast an unrelenting glare on Harpagon, his kids, his servants and business associates, the society that tolerates him, and the contemporary audience who might dare dismiss him as an innocuous aberration from a bygone era. The director was rightly uninterested in resurrecting Molière's masterpiece as a historical entertainment. "It's easy to turn Harpagon into a ridiculous figure the audience can laugh at and feel morally superior to," the director told the cast at the first reading. "But I don't want the audience to walk out of the theatre feeling complacent. I want to show there is a part of Harpagon in all of us."[18]

The production refracted the seventeenth-century original through a late-twentieth-century prism in order to shed light on its new, American audience. Harpagon was not the only miser in this production, whose often outrageous visual and behavioral references spanned the more than three centuries between the play's first production, in 1668, and the current one. His obsessive greed seemed here to have been infectious. His paranoid fear of being fleeced became an extreme but rational response to an atmosphere thick with schemes and schemers.

From the first glimpses of Harpagon's children in the opening scene, it was clear that these apples hadn't fallen very far from the tree. Despite the silent, anguished presence of their deceased mother – a life-size cardboard cut-out facing upstage, fists raised in futile frustration – Cléante and Elise were every bit their father's offspring. Elise, played by Cherry Jones clad in a skimpy black negligee, was far from a virtuous maiden quivering lest her father learn she had pledged to marry good Valère. She could barely keep her hands off her lover. She bit his self-proclaimed "golden tongue." The "promise" she had relinquished was clearly not one of maidenhood but maidenhead. She stroked her belly frequently and rebuffed anything that threatened to come in contact with it. Her fears were not merely those of a dutiful daughter who had dared verbally to overstep the bounds of unreasonable paternal control. She was single, pregnant, and at the mercy of a swaggering opportunist who tried to reassure her by bragging about his extraordinary powers of deception. Cléante (Steven Zahn) made his entrance in tight black bikini underwear. As Elise divulged part of her secret to him, his valet dressed him in layers of voluptuous, eighteenth-century finery. As the two bemoaned their father's tightfisted cruelty, it become obvious that they wanted him to ease his grip so they could grab and squander its contents.

Eventually, the servants, the neighbors, Harpagon's business associates, all were depicted as hoarding, thieving variations on the avaricious protagonist. Significantly, Serban included in this lot Valère and Mariane, the estranged siblings with whom Cléante and Elise happen to be in love, as well as their long-lost father and "widowed" mother, who are usually the most sympathetic figures in the play.

In the text, Valère justifies his manipulative treatment of Harpagon, who has hired him as his valet, as a necessary evil:

> I've discovered how to win a man's confidence. You keep agreeing with him, nod and nod until your neck aches – thoughtfully, of course. You praise his faults. You applaud his mistakes. It's impossible to overdo the gush. Even a killjoy turns pathetically grateful when you flatter him. Nothing's too outrageous to cram down his gullet when you season it with compliments. I admit that I cut the corners of sincerity. When you need the help of others, you adjust yourself to them. That's how you win them over. So don't blame the one who flatters; blame the one who wants to *be* flattered.[19]

Serban had actor Derek Smith declare his love to Elise as similar, intentional flattery. The daughter was to this Valère merely another route to the old man's stash. Her unwed pregnancy made her situation more precarious and Valère's more assured. No longer the devoted and deserving suitor kept at bay by an irrational father's fiscal demands, Valère became a gigolo with itchy palms.

Even more surprising, and revealing of Serban's sense of the play, was his depiction of Mariane. In the first scene of Act IV, Mariane begs Cléante to be her advocate at home against her impending marriage to Harpagon. "Please, don't ask me to break the [engagement] contract. I must obey my mother," she says. Serban understood her remarks to mean that everything she had done so far must have been with her mother's consent, that her mother sent her off to entice the old man and get his money. Thus Mariane was played, by Pamela Gien, as a wily, miniskirt-lifting flirt to whom Cléante meant little more than a more attractive package in which to receive the miser's fortune. This portrayal of Mariane also implicated her mother. The impoverished widow to whom the girl is so obedient now appears to have much in common with Harpagon. Both are anxious to sacrifice their daughters to marriages to much older men in order to gain access to their fortunes.

Surrounded by this array of plots and plotters, Harpagon had good cause to keep a close eye on his precious cashbox. Serban's sympathy for the stingy fellow did not lead him to excuse or minimize the character's obsession, however: It was, in fact, elevated to full paranoid psychosis.

One of the most interesting aspects of the play for me as a director is Harpagon's paranoia. The atmosphere of the play reminds me of Kafka and Beckett, authors who, like Molière, are comic but make you laugh in the face of tragedy. . . . One should laugh at Harpagon but also identify with the state of terror he lives in. Like many Americans, he can't relax no matter how much money he has. I hope to dramatize that we are all implicated in Harpagon's neurosis. . . . Rather than laughing at Harpagon from a safe distance, I hope the audience will recognize the delusion that inner peace comes from financial security.[20]

With Alvin Epstein in the title role, Harpagon was played as an impossible, irascible, and irrational domestic despot, but also a tortured soul hounded by nightmares and delusions about the treasure buried in his backyard. Epstein, a keen, resourceful classical actor who is also noted for acting and directing the plays of Beckett, is of short and slender build. Dressed in a long black tunic, his miser displayed a steely will but looked almost frail, as if he had denied himself as well as his children the creature comforts his money could well afford. The dog barks that send Harpagon scurrying offstage in Molière's text here became haunting howls to which the old man responded immediately and frantically, as if his life and not his loot were at stake. The director's objective was to force the audience to experience the psychic consequences of Harpagon's financial fixation.

Through these characterizations, we begin to see the director's modus operandi. Serban's conceptualization of characters alters the familiar roles these characters have played in the social system that is *The Miser* onstage. Traditional analysis and traditional stagings find the miser a lone manifestation of evil in an otherwise rational and moderate world. In Serban's version, the play lost its symmetry but honed its edge. Harpagon was not so much a freak as simply the most extreme example of unrepentant miserliness on a leech-filled stage. There were no innocents in Serban's *Miser*, no one to provide respite from the craziness, no character with whom the audience could comfortably identify and so differentiate themselves from the pack of wolves. The director meant to implicate his audience as the miser's fellow travelers. This interpretation effectively turns Molière's neat neoclassical structure inside out and denies the audience the balm of a return to happy equilibrium at the end of the play. There can be no restoration of order where stealing, corruption, and usury are the status quo. The satire Molière tucked into his script was unleashed as a full-blown indictment of a world – ours – that trades material goods as moral currency.

Those who might object to Serban's innovations as directorial imposition must recognize that the director took most of his cues from an adamantly faithful – even literal – reading of the script. When the company felt compelled to alter the script, they consulted either a literal translation by Bermel or the French original as their root source. For example, in the original, Maître Jacques informs Harpagon that his neighbors call him "les noms d'avare, de ladre, de vilain, et de fesse-mathieu."[21] Serban was not satisfied with Bermel's "Sometimes they call you the vampire and sometimes the leech."[22] As the team tried to come up with a list they liked better, Serban insisted they retain the syllabic rhythm of the French. "Because it is in French four, it has to be four. It's a rhythm." They ultimately agreed on "miser, vulture, crook, leech."

Now that we have seen how the director's reinterpretations of character recast the internal dramatic structure of Molière's play, we may go on to examine how Serban and the *Miser* company translated his responses to the script into a rich vocabulary of theatrical signs and gestures that conveyed his vision and coalesced into an eclectic, witty, and vigorous, if sometimes overstated, farce style, adorned with bold anachronisms and a raucous sexuality. A glimpse into the rehearsal studio will afford some insight into the director's working methods.

Derek McLane designed the set for *The Miser*. A black–and–white, semicircular arrangement of six tall, square columns, depicted a *palais* decaying from neglect. Torn patches of wallpaper revealed old layers underneath; what remained of the topmost layer bore scattered, enlarged images from dollar bills, a reminder that American "consummania" was Serban's real target. Weeds grew through cracks in the floor and walls. Near one of the columns had accumulated a boulder-sized mound of dirt. The only furniture was a worn wooden table with one side chair and an equally tattered stool. This Harpagon was so attached to his ducats that he had not spent them to protect his own investment.

Doors of various shapes and sizes were cut into every column surface, evoking farce tradition, and Serban exploited this old theatrical device to chilling effect. Members of the household eavesdropped on Harpagon all the time. They appeared slowly or suddenly, sneaking an eye or ear into view or bursting onto the stage when Harpagon, thinking he was alone, spoke of his stash. Tiny, free-form doors were neatly hidden in the flats too. At several points, they were opened by black-gloved hands that poked through to grope hungrily at the air as the stage lights dimmed and flashed disconcertingly. These walls had eyes and arms as well as ears. Harpagon's agonizing fantasies were thus projected on stage as plastic theatrical realities. The audi-

Figure 8. Black-gloved hands grope the air above the heads of Cléante (Steven Zahn) and Harpagon (Alvin Epstein) in *The Miser,* directed by Andrei Serban, at the American Repertory Theatre, Cambridge, Massachusetts, 1989. Photo © Richard M. Feldman.

ence was not exactly asked to pity Harpagon nor to forgive him, but they were forced to take him – and his moral disease – seriously.

Making palpable the subtext motivated all of Serban's directorial decisions for *The Miser*. Serban at work is intelligent, intense, and, occasionally, impatient. He presided over rehearsals like a master chef attended by two flanks of assistants, who can be grouped roughly as the stimulators and facilitators of his staging. The stimulators included a personal assistant, Hafiz Karmali, off whom the director bounced most of his ideas; a corps of dramaturges and ART interns; a movement coach; and the lead actors. The facilitators included the stage manager and her assistants; still more interns; and those student actors assigned to nonspeaking roles.

Once the initial readings and discussions were over, each rehearsal began with a brief introduction to the director's goals for the scene at hand. Then he put the actors on their feet. At this point there was little talk of character nuance or motivation with anyone but Alvin Epstein. It was clear that the director already had strong physical and visual images in mind. The work entailed turning his projections into vocal inflections, blocking, and stage business. Suggestions from the company were welcomed and often adopted. The focus of the work was kinetic and pictorial. Much like Brecht, who insisted the audience be able to understand the story without hearing a word of the dialogue, and Meyerhold, who strove for a hieroglyphics of the actor's body, Serban sculpted living stage pictures that told the story of the subtext. The director had already settled on the fundamental issues, tensions, and objectives of each beat. Just how those impulses would become manifest in theatrical dimensions was worked out through brisk, improvisational trial and error.

Foremost was the director's need to explore the rhythm, visual composition, timing, and tempo of each potential piece of business. If the full cast was not present, various facilitators stood in for absent actors, often having to master difficult or intricate movements that would later be transferred to the designated actor. Surrogate costume elements and props were also swiftly supplied. In one session, Maître Jacques had not been given a rehearsal apron, so one of the interns literally gave him the white T-shirt off his back to tie around his waist.

Movement coach Thom Molinaro was one of the most influential of the stimulators. A veteran choreographer and dance historian, Molinaro transformed Serban's ideas into the actors' gestures. The director wanted highly stylized and animated acting, but not according to any single period or tradition. Costumes, by Judith Ann Dolan, included everything from powdered wigs and a pirate's eye patch to leather pants and platform heels. Serban wanted the movement to be similarly anachronistic to emphasize the timeless relevance of the text. "The movement, what would you call it classical? Modern? It is neither. Sometimes it's modern, and sometimes they make a flourish."[23]

"Where are you, Thom? He can't just stand there and say the line!" became Serban's rehearsal refrain. Counting each movement pattern in measured time, Molinaro sprinkled the production with physical quotes from classical dance, romantic acting, silent movies, burlesque, vaudeville, Italian cinema, and musical comedy. His ideas were always clever and often hilarious. In the first act, Harpagon inspects La Fleche's hands to be sure he hasn't stolen anything and then demands to see his "other ones." Actor Thomas Derrah and Molinaro worked out a bit in which Derrah removed his jacket, put it on backward, and showed his hands behind his back. When the Miser went on to check La Fleche's pockets, Derrah pulled his pants down around his ankles and Epstein stuck his head between his partner's legs. Later, in Act II, Harpagon instructs La Fleche to be careful when washing and handling stemware for the engagement party. Molinaro decreed immediately that handling Harpagon's glassware would make anyone a nervous wreck. He devised a clumsy, fumbling, near-pratfall to serve as the servant's acknowledgment of his orders.

Frosine the "matchmaker" says she is in the business of "finding love" for people. "I love all the world," she says in Bermel's translation.[24] In the context of this amoral universe, where Serban believed "there is no love," what she procures can only be sex. Frosine will arrange Harpagon's marriage for a price, but her true calling is to the oldest of professions. As embodied by the very funny and resourceful Mary Lou Rosato, Frosine fortified her machinations from a flask and stroked the Miser's cane with less than subtle innuendo.

"Comedy relies as a rule on the deployment of the characters' will power, whereas fate in the form of coincidence, or synchronicity, the imposition of the author's willpower signals that a funny play is a farce," writes Bermel in his analysis of *The Miser*. "A director who means to do justice to the play should keep in mind that the forces of fate loom over the action."[25] Molière resolves the young lovers' trials in Act V with a deus ex machina in the person of Anselme, the wealthy Neapolitan nobleman who turns out to be the father of Valère and Mariane. Serban presented his sudden, fortuitous appearance in appropriately farcical, exaggerated style. He envisioned Anselme's arrival as the proverbial ship coming in for everyone. As the old gentlemen appeared suddenly from behind a door concealed high in one of the columns, a huge, gilded, cutout of a boat descended from the flies. Valère automatically assumed an Italian accent, and money rained from above as the assembled, sans Harpagon, joined in a happy jig.

Clearly, Serban's method in *The Miser* was not subtle. Except for a focus on the actor's body as the primary theatrical signifier, the director of the *Fragments of a Trilogy* can barely be detected here. Where the *Fragments* explored minute gradations of feeling and drew its audience into its rarefied aura, *The Miser* was drawn in bold, shock-value strokes. "Oedipal rivalry is ferocious in this play," Serban had told the cast.[26] When Cléante and his father finally have it out, in Act IV, an enraged Harpagon insists that Mariane is his "territory." Epstein was directed here to grab his unyielding son's testicles to prove who was boss. Cléante retaliated in kind until they were both red-faced and winded. The fusion of wordplay and overt physicalization of psychic and emotional states climaxed here in an outrageously apt theatrical moment.

There were less effective moments in the production, however, when gesture simply replicated a verbal image in the script. For example, Harpagon walked his fingers across the table on the word "spider." Likewise, Mariane's tenuous virtue had been well established by the final scene: It was unnecessary for the director to add an aside in which Valère, having just discovered his Neapolitan heritage, calls her a *"prostituzzione."* Fortunately, Serban was convinced to cut the addition during previews. In such instances, word and gesture became redundant, and the result cartoonish. Several critics zeroed in on these minor lapses to accuse Serban of either mistrusting the text or indulging in a narcissistic desire to eclipse it.

Bermel again, in a more general comment on the production of Molière's plays:

> If modernizing directors now and then use Molière to make a statement about late twentieth-century conformists and nonconformers, they invite rebuke only when it turns into an overstatement that makes the playwright appear naive.[27]

Serban's "modernizing" never strove to show up Molière's timidity or innocence. Instead, the production seemed to tap a live vein of outrage that the playwright himself might have liberated had the court's and public's approval not been crucial to his personal and professional survival. In other words, this production felt like one Molière might have put on if he were here today.

Perhaps the most successful of Serban's innovations for *The Miser* were two pantomimed sequences that ended the first and second halves of the show. Movement coach Molinaro was instrumental in developing these interpolations to help realize the important theme of Harpagon's near-psychosis. The director wanted to lead into the intermission with one of the miser's nightmares brought to life. A brief discussion with Epstein determined that Harpagon is most afraid of thieves stealing his money, guests eating his food, and his son prevailing with Mariane. Molinaro was asked to "do a workshop" on those ideas. Ten minutes of improvisation with the cast produced such mimed images as dancing with a cashbox, savoring grapes, and various suggestive embraces between Mariane and Cléante.

Serban edited and blocked the movements into a three-minute sequence. By opening night, the scene had been distilled to less than a minute. The corps of extranumeraries appeared in long black gloves, capes, and hoods. The Harpagonettes, as the company came to call them, were grotesque figures, insatiable and unrelenting. They were like free-ranging ids, slithering and gyrating to fulfill their greedy urges without conscience or restraint. Dark, anonymous, hallucinatory, they became symbols of the intoxicating, intimidating power of greed.

Bermel and others have correctly pointed out that *The Miser* is unusual because Molière never really ties up all loose ends in his happy ending. Harpagon goes unpunished. The scales of justice remain unbalanced. Serban recognized this structural oddity, but took it to mean that Harpagon, not having learned his lesson, suffers a severe punishment in the perpetuation of his internal turmoil. So severe and chronic is Harpagon's moral and emotional disease, according to Serban's reading, that "the end of the play should be linked with a mythological image that devours, suffocates, takes away life."

The "mythological image" turned out to be a pantomimed epilogue. The script calls for the miser to stand apart and fondle his beloved cashbox while the others celebrate and the curtain falls. Serban sent the revelers offstage to bring the happy news to Mariane and Valère's newly unwidowed mother. This left Harpagon onstage, truly alone. As per the original stage directions, he contentedly nuzzled and cooed to the box. Then the sound of dogs barking and howling sounded again. The stage went dark as Harpagon's ecstasy turned quickly, via Pavlovian response, to terror, despite the fact that he held his booty in his own hands.

Epstein's body crumpled as he sank to the floor, hugging the box. He crawled upstage where he began clawing the ground with his fingernails to dig a new trench for his box. His movements slowed gradually as he poured dirt from between his wiggling fingers onto the buried treasure. In the final

131

image Harpagon knelt alone in a cone of harsh white light as, one by one, the doors opened to reveal behind each the masked face of one of the other characters, peering silently, spying on the bent old man and his pitiful ritual. "The more you are insured and assured, the more insecure you are," said Serban. "You have that much more to lose."[28] Haunting, ceremonial, and solemn, Serban's coda put the finishing touch on his pessimistic interpretation of the play.

"Serban drives Molière's point home," wrote the *Boston Globe* critic Kevin Kelly in a typically mixed review.[29] "Whatever our distance from Harpagon's obsessive greed, we're really just as interested in money as he is, if, perhaps, less maniacally." There was no mistaking the contemporary relevance Serban took pains to underscore: "When [Harpagon] sits in the audience next to you [searching through bags for his 50,000 ducats], he's first cousin to the Helmsleys, the Marcoses, the Trumps." Nor were the director's more somber warnings overlooked. The final image, Kelly reported, "has the power of the final scene in *The Treasure of the Sierra Madre*, gold dust blowing away in the wind."

Of course, the warning to beware the worship of money was not something Serban discovered or grafted on to the original: Molière had much the same intention in 1668. Serban merely pulled out the seventeenth-century stops. The stage imagery through which the director expressed his response to Molière's play can be seen to have projected a simultaneous system of theatrical signs (sounds, gestures, intonations, etc.) that bounced off the text to amplify and intensify its darker tones. Serban's direction did less to update or transplant the play from one historical period to another, in what ART Artistic Director Robert Brustein would call a "simile" production, than to shake it loose from the social and artistic strictures of the period in which it was written so that it might speak more emphatically to its postmodern audience.

Kelly and other reviewers objected, however, to what they felt to be an overload of contemporary license. "In italicizing the play's essential crassitude with explicit sexuality, Serban has staged a *Miser* that more often seems sex-obsessed than money-grubbing," wrote Kelly, parenthetically and incorrectly postulating that the production "may be the most erotic Molière ever."[30] He objected to the blatant theatricalization of Harpagon's nightmares and described the lascivious depiction of Mariane as evidence of the director being "smirkingly vulgar." He did, however, praise Serban's sense of adventure, Bermel's "breezily apt translation," and the performances, especially that of Alvin Epstein, who was almost unanimously well-reviewed. Negative criticism of the production was leveled mostly at the extent of directorial outrageousness. Serban's basic intent was too obviously connected to Molière's to have elicited objections.

While Serban violated Molière's seventeenth-century etiquette and inverted Molière's structural balance by painting all the characters in various shades of Harpagon's hue, the aims of his production were clearly in sync with the original. Serban's rewrighting extended the Miser's obsessive greed, paranoia, insensitivity, and insincerity to the whole community in a way that resonates easily with life in these United States, both thematically and in its audacious performance aesthetic. The audience, unable to dismiss Harpagon as a freak, was forced to accept him as an extreme manifestation of a still-potent and painful communal neurosis. The appearance of the Harpagonettes reinforced the idea, as did the complicity of the audience members who clung to their purses when the Miser swooped into the aisles. Just as the *Globe* reviewer was reminded of contemporary paragons of avarice, the audience was reminded of the ways we revere/revile their ingenious knavery. It was through such recognition that Molière's and Serban's farcical barbs connected, both with each other and with the ART audience.

OTHER AMERICAN MOLIÈRE LIBERATORS

As might be expected, Serban is not alone among his colleagues in underscoring the darker aspects of Molière's plays. Despite their renegade reputation, concept directors tend to take their texts very seriously, even when their productions turn out irreverent or satirical. Other directorial attempts at Molière present a surprising concurrence of themes and strategies in what would at first appear to be quite different conceptualizations. Productions by Liviu Ciulei, Garland Wright, Richard Foreman, and Lucian Pintilié have shared the transposition or manipulation of place and period; the full venting of extreme sexual and religious passions; the tendency to see the world – and not just the main character – as mad; the paranoid sense of being watched or spied upon by malevolent forces; and an overall emphasis on the scarier aspects of Molière's farce. Although there is great stylistic variety in the ways these directors theatricalized the various motifs, their repetition suggests that they tap into live veins running through both Molière's plays and the contemporary world.

The Misanthrope

Garland Wright has directed two solid productions of plays by Molière, neither of which seemed, on the surface, to have taken exceptional textual or conceptual risks but were in fact powerful reimaginings. Wright's *The Misanthrope* opened his tenure as Artistic Director of the Guthrie Theatre, in 1987. He updated the setting from the 1660s to the summer of 1792, five months before the execution of Louis XVI, under the premise that the play is "about the myopic people who caused the French Revolution." Although Molière is not normally credited with the prescience to have written *The Misanthrope* as a Revolutionary warning, Wright had at his disposal the wisdom of hindsight. He used that knowledge both to illuminate meanings the playwright could not have known would accrue to his text and to alert the contemporary audience that history repeats itself.

The director's conceptualization operated on the basic deconstructive strategy of asking what is missing from the text, what is not being mentioned, who is left out. His answer was the multitudes starving in the streets while Molière's upper-crust characters gossip and pose and anguish over their petty, pampered peccadillos. The production brought that left-out segment of the dangerously divided society into the world of the play through offstage hints that an angry mob was assembling and growing increasingly agitated in the street below Célimène's window as the play's action unfolded. As the scenes progressed, the sounds of revolution intensified. What began as vocal protests and the singing of the Marseillaise escalated to the sounds of gunfire and, finally, cannon blasts that shattered the heroine's windows and set the Parisian cityscape ablaze.

In what again would appear to be a minor alteration that ultimately had great impact on the play, Wright also moved the setting from Célimène's parlor to her bedroom. Here, the coy, girlish widow became a sexually active woman whose inability to extricate herself from the superficial rituals of social discourse seemed more pitiful than irritating. The parade of guests ambled onto Joel Fontaine's glossy, colonnaded set in voluptuous costumes by Jack Edwards, spouting Richard Wilbur's highly polished verse translation, an overrefined, cynically sterile aristocracy oblivious to the encroaching commotion in the streets.

Caroline Lagerfelt received unanimously enthusiastic reviews for her portrayal of Célimène, which exposed the dangerously conventional and vulnerable woman beneath the powdered wigs and petticoats and painted face. Alone with Alceste, stripped down to her dressing gown and her own short, matted hair, she expressed a genuine longing for him as they slid to the floor in the early stages of passionate lovemaking. (The sexiness of this scene surpassed the hot-lipped groping in Serban's *The Miser* because Célimène and Alceste were played with real emotions at stake.) The embrace was interrupted by the announcement of the arrival of the other suitors, however, and

Figure 9. Célimène (Caroline Lagerfelt) receives Clitandre (Richard Hicks) and Acaste (Richard S. Iglewski) in *The Misanthrope,* directed by Garland Wright, at the Guthrie Theatre, Minneapolis, 1987. Photo © Joe Giannetti/The Guthrie Theatre.

135

she jumped out from under him, an automaton so steeped in the foolish ways of the world that she could not resist the pull of convention, even when faced with a more meaningful alternative.

The apocalyptic ending of the production found Célimène alone, having "virtually commit[ted] suicide by refusing to leave Paris with the still-loyal Alceste."[31] As her windowpanes shattered, she tried in vain to shut out the chaos by drawing the curtains. Dressed in a deep-red gown, she then gathered roses strewn across the floor and curtsied. This awkward and futile gesture, carried out with blank expression, underscored her terror and desperation. By then, it was too late to repent or undo the abuse the precious Célimènes had wreaked on so many misérables. "Most of my productions have a parallel theatrical imagery going on," Wright has commented about his staging of Célimène's exit. In her final humiliation, he says, "she realizes that her ultimate destiny is to be the butt of a joke in a Molière play." Her eerie, inept curtain call signaled her vague realization too late that she was in some way responsible for her own fate.

Thus Célimène became the target of Wright's criticism, while Alceste, contrary to traditional interpretations, was "not a nonconformist outcast, but an unrecognized hero of the revolution."[32] Molière's ending casts Alceste as the loser who must forgo the comfort of companionship because he refuses to reconcile himself to the little white lies that smooth over the bumps in human relationships. The character's comic choler probably cloaks the dramatist's own similar distaste, but director Wright expresses an even stronger aversion. His production subtext suggests that seemingly benign interpersonal hypocrisies can mask more insidious forms of social denial and can, thus, have dire consequences. Alceste may be an obstinate pain in the neck, but his truth is far less of a threat to the general peace than the self-imposed blindness by which the others allowed a violent revolution to sneak up and destroy them.

Wright's hundred-year dislocation of *The Misanthrope* added layers of resonance to the text. By attributing to Molière almost mystical powers of foresight, the director resituated the play in historical context as an unwitting premonition. At the same time, and without direct contemporary references, Wright also turned the play into a perfect cautionary allegory for Reagan's America. The production sounded an analogous warning to the 1980s' American Célimènes, those self-absorbed, Yuppie strivers who gorged themselves on designer meals while the gap between the poor and the superwealthy grew increasingly, dangerously wider. Drug abuse, street crime, all those pesky "social problems" brought on by economic inequity, Wright implied, could very well erupt in a full-fledged revolution as bloody as the September Massacre with which he ended his production.

If Molière's accidental prognostication followed in the ensuing century, Wright's forecast came true just five years later when the streets of Los Angeles erupted in 1992. The Rodney King verdict, in which four white L.A. police officers were acquitted of wrongdoing in a bloody, videotaped beating of a black motorist, may have ignited the riots, but their fury was fueled by long-term, blatant social, political, and economic disparities in the city, and across the country. It seems no small coincidence that the other major *Misanthrope* update of the last decade, Neil Bartlett's translation-adaptation, reset the play among the rich and famous of Hollywood. Wright got it right. His was not a meaning the author intended, but rather an extrapolation of the text that, like Serban's *Miser,* cast new light on both the play and the new world in which it found itself produced.

Three Don Juans

A few years before *The Misanthrope,* Wright directed *Don Juan* for the Denver Center Theatre Company in 1984. The script has been both popular and controversial among concept directors for many of the same reasons *Cymbeline* attracted and bedeviled JoAnne Akalaitis (see Chapter 4). A hastily written and somewhat sprawling text, *Don Juan* lacks the tight construction of many of Molière's plays. These critical "problems" with the play would seem to offer an open field for directors. Thumbnail sketches of three very different productions within a six-year period, by Wright, Liviu Ciulei, and Richard Foreman, suggest that some plays, like stubborn clay, resist the sculpting hands of a wide range of directors.

Garland Wright addressed the politics of class and gender in *Don Juan* through the presence of a gallery of overpainted aristocrats who were stationed on a retractable upper level parallel to the front of the stage. Revealed intermittently, the gallery watched Don Juan's escapades with frozen, bored expressions. They appeared at once menacing and remote, disapproving and yet unwilling to intervene as Don Juan assaulted each subsequent social and sexual contract. The Don's insatiable appetite for women was here portrayed as a pure and unquenchable thirst for defiance. The country lasses, usually portrayed as fresh-faced, unblemished fruits begging a first bite, were dirty, bawdy farmhands plucking the feathers out of real chickens.[33] Don Juan's indiscriminate pursuit of these two proved him not so much an incorrigible lover of women and pleasure, but a fanatic flouter of social rules. At the end of the play, during the final confrontation, the women the Don had abused assembled onstage, a silent chorus of witness-victims. They stood behind him in the face of Don Carlos's accusations and the statue-Commander's ultimate revenge. In the production's final moments, a resigned Don Juan plopped himself down in the Commander's stony lap. The statue then descended into a fiery pit of hell. Wright undermined the melodramatic, evil-are-punished ending, however, by having a statue of the Don reemerge from the trap. The chorus of women bowed before the statue, a shockingly benign specter of a culture that has come not only to tolerate but to venerate the libertine.

Liviu Ciulei's *Don Juan* (Arena Stage, 1979), essentially a simile production, displeased reviewers, but, ironically, inspired an absolutely spectacular set design by Ming Cho Lee. Of course, opponents of the conceptual approach might argue that overemphasis on design is the quicksand into which sink so many productions of this ilk. Ciulei moved the play forward two centuries to Paris in La Belle Epoque. The architect-trained director and his designer erected a glistening, lavishly appointed, two-tiered glass gazebo with its second story a few inches above the usual stage floor and its lower level a full flight below. The upper level doubled as Don Juan's salon and a beach where his first seductees were a couple of female fishmongers who looked as if they had wandered in off the set of *Pygmalion*. The lower level was used as the entry hall for the Don's flat and as the Commander's tomb. A double-bottomed fishbowl through which the audience could see simultaneous action had enormous potential as a setting for this play about duplicity and the contrast between social and religious norms and personal desires. One reviewer called it "a set so ingenious and riveting that one has to keep reminding oneself to stop gazing at it and pay attention to what the actors are saying."[34]

Unfortunately, many of those who bothered to listen were disappointed. The period to which the play was moved is renowned for sensuality and loose morals. Ciulei's program notes strain, with well-pedigreed quotations from Pascal to Aleksandr Solzhenitzyn, to justify an implicit comparison among the seventeenth, late-nineteenth, and twentieth centuries, but setting dramatic literature's most flagrant abuser of conventional morality in such a hospitable environment apparently backfired. The new milieu effectively wiped out any dramatic tension between Don Juan's actions and the society against which Molière intended him to rebel. It is possible that Ciulei was aiming for a more Svengalian Don Juan, a hypnotic rather than swashbuckling seducer, but critics complained that the play seemed to have had the life drained out of it.[35] Ciulei's gimmicks "ought to be punishable by a Molière Defense Society," scolded Judith Martin in the *Washington Post*.[36] Even

Julius Novick of the *Village Voice,* who asserted that "Mr. Ciulei's inventions are never vulgar, or dismissive of the play," and that "Mr. Ciulei has found a way for American actors to bring this refractory classic to life," conceded that the production was marred by "a vast sea of by-play" that pushed the evening past three hours long. "Someone," Novick suggested, "should buy this director a watch."[37]

Richard Foreman first directed *Don Juan* at the Guthrie Theatre in the fall of 1981 and was invited by Joseph Papp to revive it for the New York Shakespeare Festival the following summer. Foreman applied to the play the techniques he had developed for his own Ontological-Hysteric theatre pieces in the 1970s: curtains that suddenly reveal or conceal tableaux, blinding quartz lights, mirrors, strings that represent "lines of force" bisecting the stage, bursts of disorienting sound and music. In a gesture similar to Wright's gallery of onlookers, Foreman also added a chorus of ghastly white-faced aristocrats who stalked the main character and commented on his every line and action. When Sganarelle tells his master "you talk like a book," the chorus wheeled out a lectern. At the mention of heaven, there was the pounding of an organ. When the Don insists that the only thing he believes is that "two and two make four," a blackboard with sums appeared beside him. Foreman used these Brechtian devices and other seeming redundancies to draw attention to "a series of articulated echoes and reflections" in the text, "as the characters mimic both each others' and their own language and gestures."[38]

Foreman's dense and difficult treatment of the play found few sympathetic receivers. Gerald Rabkin found himself in a small appreciative minority and so defended the production in an analysis in the *Performing Arts Journal.* According to Rabkin, the director began the rehearsal process, his first assay at staging a classic text, with the belief that "language is still treacherous – indeed even more so when it is encrusted with the sedimentation of history." From his viewpoint, the historical text is a series of remote verbal cues that can no longer bear their original implications. Like genetic material, the words have mutated over time. Foreman thus had no need or desire to discover or interpret meaning in Molière's slippery text. His interest lay, rather, in staging the sequence of mental images the play's language aroused in his mind, as if the text were a series of Rorschachs and the production a display of the director's associations. The approach, Rabkin decides, is a brand of theatrical deconstruction.

[The] production aims not at a univocal reading of the play or the myth, but at a synthesis of opposed values . . . Affirming Derrida's deconstructionism, [Foreman] aims to show the text to be woven from different strands which can never result in a synthesis, but continually displace one another.[39]

Like the reader who in the act of reading inevitably writes his own text by fulfilling the author's indications with his own referents, Foreman directed a theatrical text in which his own aural and visual signs were used to echo, corroborate, or defy the spoken word. Rabkin again:

> With Barthes, Derrida, Foucault, et al., [Foreman] rejects the realist or authoritarian heresy that the critic (or director) can make definitive contact with some ultimate, residual meaning when, in reality, he is simply transcribing a code – or a series of interlocking codes which can be deciphered but never fully recovered.[40]

Although Foreman's methods had received accolades when applied to his own highly personal and experimental texts, and *Don Juan,* with its noted inconsistencies, must have seemed a suitable vehicle for his style of experimentation, most critics were not pleased to have been invited on the director's subconscious journey through the text. Many were offended at what they took to be an egotistical director's attempt to eclipse the play. "This sort of thing turns the audience into a group of dull-witted students in need of visual reinforcement," balked Allan Wallach of *Newsday.*[41] Frank Rich of the *New York Times* had a field day enumerating the piece's various offenses: John Seitz's physically stylized portrait of the title character, a pastiche of baroque operatic conventions that Foreman intended as a subtle historical allusion to the acting of Molière's day, Rich decried as "a scowling, unattractive gnome who walked like a crab." The chorus were "an avenging mob of crucifix-bearing, chalk-faced grotesques who might have popped out of Peter Brook's *Marat/Sade.*" The ultimate problem "with Mr. Foreman's idiosyncratic visual embodiment of the play's themes," Rich concluded, "was that it sent him into a cul-de-sac when he had to deal with the letter of the text. . . . He settled instead for proving that he could give a four-century-old classic the Foreman stamp, no matter what."[42]

An angry Julius Novick pronounced the director "not inept," but "perverse":

> [Foreman] celebrates himself in a vainglorious demonstration of the destructive power that a live director can wield over a dead playwright.

Figure 10. The Don (John Seitz) recoils from the statue of the Commander in *Don Juan,* directed by Richard Foreman, at the Guthrie Theatre, Minneapolis, 1981. Photo © Bruce Goldstein/The Guthrie Theatre.

I suspect, however, that when Mr. Foreman is just as dead as Molière, Molière will prove to be a great deal more alive than Mr. Foreman.[43]

Even Rabkin, the director's champion, had to concede that "in accepting the textual immutability of the play, [Foreman's] revisionary strategies must all be embodied in his mise-en-scène and hence risk the dangers of imposition and redundancy, dangers plaguing all such experimental versions of 'fixed' classics."[44]

Whether his were errors of ego or execution, Foreman's unhappy reception reminds us just how dangerous is the business of applying genuinely experimental theatrical models to the staging of established texts. It is interesting that, diverse as they are, none of the three *Don Juans* appears to have been an entirely satisfying rendering or reconstruction of the play. Perhaps Foreman was right in his sense of the play as slippery, elusive, ultimately ungraspable. Its misogynous main character seems especially problematic. Or, perhaps the play just has not yet met up with the right director – a woman, maybe? – who can make it speak more emphatically to us.

Pintilié's Triumphant Tartuffe

In contrast to the errant *Don Juans*, Lucian Pintilié's 1984–5 *Tartuffe* is a shining example of how an aggressive directorial plan can liberate and revitalize a classic play without obstructing or overwhelming it. The production was first staged at the Guthrie in the summer of 1984 and then revamped for the square-in-the-square Arena Stage in Washington, D.C., in April 1985. "This is not, one must emphasize, *the Tartuffe,* but *a Tartuffe,*" wrote Mel Gussow in the *New York Times,* "one 20th-century directorial vision of a 17th-century masterpiece."[45] Like Serban's *Fragments* or Peter Brook's *Midsummer Night's Dream,* Pintilié's reimagined *Tartuffe* has met the paradoxical critical fate of being so well received that it is often, oxymoronically, considered a definitive reinterpretation.

Pintilié's method for *Tartuffe,* not unlike Serban's with *The Miser,* corporealized textual metaphors as theatrical motifs, using a progression of anachronistic references to drive home the play's ominous contemporary relevance. Proceeding from a literal reading of Mme. Pernelle's lines in the first scene, Pintilié and his long-time design collaborators, Radu (sets) and Miruna (costumes) Boruzescu, depicted Orgon's home as "a madhouse with the keeper gone." At the Arena, the walls and floor of the whole auditorium were covered with white institutional tile. The title character's metaphorical allusions to self-flagellation and the wearing of a hair shirt were translated to physical realities. Tartuffe made his first entrance from a dark and smoky trap below the stage, his hair matted, large red welts on his back visible beneath a coarse tunic. The sounds of thunder and organ music accompanied him to the stage, where he squinted at the sudden harsh light like a bedlamite emerging from a long confinement.

A simple theatrical gesture in the opening scene introduced the director's other thematic threads. The scene was played as a picnic at which a basket of apples was overturned. The red fruits that rolled across the floor, conjuring images of the Garden of Eden, later "turn[ed] up in the darndest places . . . as Tartuffe's calling cards – symbols of carnal temptation and manipulative passion."[46] Beginning here in Genesis, the production's visual references then moved through the ages, past Molière, into the present, and on to Armageddon. As the scenes progressed, costumes were shorn of baroque ornamentation, wigs were removed, and props became more and more familiar. At the denouement, Orgon clutched a ham-on-rye and an oversize VISA card to

Figure 11. Laurent (Peter Francis James) speaks from atop the deus ex Deusenberg in *Tartuffe,* directed by Lucian Pintilié, at the Guthrie Theatre, Minneapolis, 1984. Photo © Joe Giannetti/The Guthrie Theatre.

sustain him in his flight from ruin. Working clocks on all four walls of the Arena auditorium kept real time until the production hit the twentieth century, when the hands twirled round and round – pairs of spindly dervishes hurtling themselves toward a chaotic millenium.

The pace of the action sped up, too. As the antic momentum accelerated, the characters rushed about the stage. Brisk slapstick routines spilled over into the audience. Frenzy – religious, nervous, and sexual – permeated the space. The members of Orgon's household, cracking under the dual pressures of Orgon's false and repressive bourgeois morality and the imposter's increasingly impossible demands, went crazy. They became, or revealed themselves to be, true inhabitants of the "madhouse." Reviewers inferred analogies with the mercenary piety and corruption of America's religious right. Pintilié seemed to wonder how long the delirium of the followers of the Moral Majority would last, before they realized that their ministers wore no clothes?

Pintilié ended both of his versions of *Tartuffe* with outrageous *dei ex machinae.* In Minneapolis, a 1936 Deusenberg crashed through the back wall

143

bearing the King's minions. At the Arena, a roaring helicopter descended from the flies to make a crash landing through the stage floor. Its turbulence literally shook the tiles off the walls. The landing left a crucifix-shaped hole in the floor. Pintilié's technological coups would soon turn out to be the progenitors of a spate of technologically dazzling grand finales. Large, loud vehicles became the late-1980s' *dei ex machinae* of choice for such diverse theatrical productions as Bergman's *Hamlet* and *Miss Saigon*.

Machine-gun-toting thugs poured out of the Arena chopper, led by Laurent, a silent figure added by the director, who had acted as Tartuffe's servant until the end, when he was exposed to have been an agent of the state all along. Pintilié's ending "converts the monarch from a protector to a tyrant who will let his citizens suffer to increase their awe and dependence," wrote William Henry in *Time* magazine. "Perhaps it takes an East European, schooled in the ways of the surveillance state, to grasp the political implications of that conventional element of farce."[47] Perhaps it was the director's Eastern European origins that allowed him, like Serban, the distance to see connections between Molière's play and the particular and insidious insanity of mid-1980's American fundamentalism. Even the helicopter, a gratuitous special effect in *Miss Saigon,* was here a manifestation of the decade's extremism and excess.

If dramatic classics are distinguished by their capacity to seem continually relevant across time and distance, the preceding directors have given Molière's plays a leg up in the American theatre. Time and again, critics of their productions lament the scarcity of opportunities to see Molière onstage. By shaking off the reputation of mannered posing and tepid, if witty, chatter, revisionist directors have led audiences to grapple with the genuinely outraged and outrageous Molière. His plays have been proven minefields set to explode our most deeply held illusions about the organizations and institutions that govern social life. It is thus no great surprise that directors who enjoy exposing givens as fallacies have been attracted to Molière. As the literary world dismantles received interpretations of the great books, so the theatre, in order to keep its masterpieces on the stage, is in the process of dissecting, rediscovering, and rewrighting its own past. The trick, as Julius Novick reminds us, is "to dance with Molière, not to trample him underfoot."[48]

6

PETER SELLARS'S MOZART–
DA PONTE TRILOGY

IN THE PAST, opera, more than any other theatrical form, adhered to a deeply entrenched performance tradition. A limited active repertory, extraordinary technical demands, and an elitist reputation conspired to keep the ranks of performers and audiences relatively low, especially in the United States. Historically rarefied and exclusionary, opera remained in the hands of a chosen few. Within that coterie, singing techniques and production styles, lovingly handed down through generations, were preserved substantially intact until the first decades of the twentieth century. Remnants of those traditions can still be seen and heard in period productions in opera houses throughout the world. Audience members, not unlike those who bring copies of the plays to performances of Shakespeare, know the works and take pleasure in comparing subtle nuances of vocal technique or variations in small bits of business.

Opera's insularity has been augmented by the relative infrequence with which new operas enter the performing repertory. Company managers, daunted by the economics of mounting even a modest production, tend to schedule box-office reliables again and again. Such occasional new works as *Nixon in China* (1987) and *The Death of Klinghoffer* (1991), both of which were directed by Peter Sellars, tend to premiere in alternative opera houses, like the Brooklyn Academy of Music. In the theatre, where new plays (of admittedly uneven merit) are spawned like guppies, an intermittent trickle of new scripts feeds into the mainstream. For both artistic and financial reasons, serious theatre companies balance their classical offerings with new work. The New York Shakespeare Festival, for example, is as committed to producing new plays as to the canon of its namesake. The dedicated closed circle of opera mavens may be credited with the preservation of a noble tradition, but it can also be faulted for fossilizing the operatic repertoire and discouraging the rediscovery of those works in light of contemporary sensibilities.

It is neither necessary nor possible here to cover the history of opera in the twentieth century. The immediate purpose is to consider directorial reinvention of classical operas as part of the wider theatrical trend.[1] It is interesting to remember, however, that it was in response to encrusted artificiality in the opera that Wagner, and Appia in his service, envisioned a synthetic performance genre including music and drama that could do justice to both without slighting either one. Their ideas inspired superficial changes in design, but their spirit of radical reform has had a long-delayed and hotly contested effect on the performance of the classic repertory. What could be further from the synthetic ideal than a common practice that provides for a small, international pool of superstar singers to flit from city to city all over the world to sing the leading roles in productions that are rehearsed entirely without them until days or hours before the performance? This system imposes severe restrictions on creative and interpretative leeway; received meanings and methods necessarily prevail. Opera history includes few visionaries like Otto Klemperer, whose Kroll Opera in the late 1920s merged the talents of performers from the Berlin theatre and designers from the Bauhaus with the great classic operas. Much of what has been considered revolutionary in this otherwise homogenous global opera world has consisted in abstract design or "simile" transpositions of sets and costumes.[2] Even this degree of directorial innovation irks traditionalists. A. M. Nagler decries contemporary European productions that require the reading of copious program notes in order to make sense of the "far-fetched" stage presentation. In *Misdirection,* a slim volume devoted entirely to discrediting operatic experimentation, Nagler bemoans the effronteries of "tone-deaf stage directors who seem to suffer from an ailment which can be correctly diagnosed as lack of confidence in the original score."[3] While the efforts of such renegade stage directors may seem like a foul wind to those who cherish opera's insularity, they are a welcome breeze to those who have tired of or felt left out of the tradition.

In a series of reviews, Edward Said provides a useful critique of operatic tradition, in which he links issues in music performance to those that have already been discussed in theatre. Revival according to historical precedent, he explains, is really a search for

some lost or forgotten original. The vogue for early music played on original instruments, the revival of *bel canto* repertoire and style, the re-

turn to Mahler: All these have embodied not just the idea of recupera-
tion, but a usually unstated ideology of authenticity. But it is not generally noted that even so apparently harmless and "correct" a notion as
faithfulness to an original is itself already an interpretation, in which a
slew of unverifiable entities . . . are set up and bowed to as if they were
facts of nature.[4]

Among those "unverifiable entities" must be included both performance
conventions and the underlying social structures and assumptions upon which
the originals were tacitly (or sometimes consciously) based. Thomas Disch
cleverly observed that "stage directors stand *in loco auctoris* to the creator."[5]
As surrogate authors, or rewrighters, of operatic texts in performance, directors have the dual benefits of historical distance from the original and first-
hand experience of the cultural context of the current production. Historical
distance allows today's directors to see yesterday's facts of nature as artifacts
of a specific culture. The morals and etiquette that governed social intercourse two hundred years ago are now perceived as relics of the past, and it is
up to directors whether their productions observe the inherent codes or replace them with more contemporary ones.

What makes this business so tricky is the fact that contemporary life is
based on equally transient assumptions. In the future, our own concepts of
who we are, how we should live, and our place in the universe will seem as
quaint as crinolines and curtsies seem to us. Directors who avail themselves
of this perspective apply insights about the past to a frank analysis of the
present by substituting contemporary equivalents in order to subject them to
the same scrutiny. Productions that refer back and forth from the original
period of a play's or opera's creation to the present performance context can
give palpable evidence of how the original reverberates in our own culture.
Interpretation, Said continues, "has become inventive, a form of deliberate
misreading, supplying all sorts of frankly conjectural possibilities as a way of
rendering the work's historical distance, the author's silence, the critic's [here,
director's] manifest power over the work."[6]

We might begin exploring revisionist approaches to directing opera by
defining just exactly what "opera" is. The *New York Times*'s Donal Henahan
offers this parochial definition: Opera is "drama as expressed in lyrical manipulation of the vocal cords."[7] He summarily condemns acting, scenery, or
lighting that does more than provide a simple backdrop to the voice. While
his rancor over theatrical effects that overtake, obscure, or otherwise detract
from musical qualities is probably justified in ample cases of incompetent directorial excess, he reveals himself to be a snob when he attaches the label

"sophisticated sleaze" to any and all adventurous attempts by "directors from the legitimate theater"[8] to create new stage life for canonical texts. Henahan demonstrates the most virulent kind of antitheatrical prejudice and denies opera its full dimensions. The inadequacy of his perspective becomes glaringly obvious when, for example, he berates musicologists for mentioning staging and philosophical themes in productions of Wagner. "It is a legitimate role of the opera director to rethink conventions and give us the clichés of the future," Henahan concludes speciously: "What is not his legitimate function is to stand opera on its head."[9] No self-respecting artist wants to create clichés of any kind. It is a director's duty to abandon the empty platitudes of stage cliché and forge a fresh and engaged response to the work. Why not turn an art form on its head? You never know what gems will fall out of its pockets.

Into this hotbed of professional Oedipal rage, in which the guardians of tradition cling to the past despite the forceful and inevitable encroachments of the avant-garde, burst Peter Sellars, fresh from Harvard, in 1980. His first assignment out of college was to direct Mozart–da Ponte's *Don Giovanni* for the Boston Opera. Irrepressible, young (he was born in 1957) and energetic, Sellars is tenacious in his belief that the classics can be fully realized on contemporary stages only through productions that unfold in the present tense. He has since mounted such controversial dramatic and operatic productions as Sophocles' *Ajax* set at the Pentagon with Howie Seago, who is deaf and mute, in the title role; Shakespeare's *Pericles* outfitted with an array of anachronistic references spanning the centuries from the Roman Empire to American urban blight; Handel's *Giulio Cesare* around the swimming pool of a Middle Eastern luxury hotel; and a "long, serious, sad musical"[10] that evolved when the director added seventeen Gershwin show tunes to Gorky's *Summerfolk* to create *Hang on to Me*. He received a five-year MacArthur Foundation "genius" grant in 1983 and was quickly dubbed the latest enfant terrible in the proprietary battle over classic texts in performance.

"Whatever you do on stage must = the public at the time that you stage it," Sellars once told an interviewer.[11] He denies imposing an alien "concept" on his productions, but insists that in the theatre "the basic level of honesty is that everybody is alive at the moment and in the same room. . . . That's what's different from movies or television." Live actors and audiences share common experiences and assumptions about the world, some of which might be very different from those of actors and audiences who experienced the classics when they were new works. In the theatre, actors and audiences also share space and air, and Sellars likes to keep everyone aware of each other's presence. He likes to keep the house lights up and play with fourth-wall illusion by combining diverse theatrical modes within a performance. Stylized gesture and movement are performed by actors clad in outfits off the racks of Macy's and the Gap. Performers break out of scenes to address the audience. Blatantly fake scenic elements are added to hyperrealistic sets. Vakhtangov would have appreciated Sellars's theatricality. "Fantastic realism" suits the young director's blend of Stanislavskian sincerity and Meyerholdian graphic physical action. The dual sensibilities involve the audience in Sellars's theatrical process, reminding them that they are seeing the old work through new eyes and encouraging them to shift focus between the simultaneous worlds of the author and the director. Deconstructionists might say Sellars thus demystifies the theatrical event and brings his audience into more active participation.

Dressing the characters in up-to-date fashions, Sellars believes, cuts through the stylistic barriers that separate a late-twentieth-century spectator from the meatier substance of a classic text. He concedes that gifted actors costumed in period might be able to show how their characters' predicaments relate to the audience's own. "But what a pity," he says, "to waste all that talent just to make that statement when that statement could be made so much faster and relieve the performer to concentrate on other things." Like other directors who come under attack for circumventing the time-honored patina of the classics, Sellars is impatient to get at the core perplexities that make classics intriguing again and again. Unfortunately, his means can be deceptively glib. A man of no modest ambition – Sellars told a reporter for the *New York Times,* "My goal is to create in my lifetime a twentieth-century performance tradition of opera"[12] – the director is in fact quite serious about his work. He is thoughtful, well informed, knows his theatre history, and understands exactly how the smallest gesture will read from the stage. (On whether or not some of his more jarring juxtapositions were meant to produce an alienation effect: "It is Brecht, it's Shakespeare, it's medieval." And it is.) He has a rationale for every carefully planned and orchestrated moment and discusses his productions with seductive conviction. He can outtalk any objection. (On the often-noted problems with Act I of *Don Giovanni*: "Everyone will be happier when they see it on video; the camera is able to give you real focus.") His supporters enjoy his startling anachronisms and recognize his involvement in the murkier regions of familiar texts; his detractors take his shorthand as shortcuts around serious material and denounce his work as parody. The truth lies somewhere in between.

The pros, cons, and paradoxes of Sellars's approach emerge in a close examination of his Mozart–da Ponte trilogy, the full cycle of operas created by the composer and librettist between 1781 and 1790, including *Le Nozze di Figaro, Don Giovanni,* and *Così fan Tutte.* The director, his collaborator-conductor Craig Smith, and a corps of singers worked together on these productions for more than ten years, from the Boston *Don Giovanni* to the videotaping in 1989. Initial rehearsals for each piece were divided into two periods. Although Sellars claims he knows "nothing" at the outset about how his productions will evolve, he and the design team went into each three- to four-week rehearsal period with some sense of direction. Those early weeks were spent exploring the material, testing and revising original ideas, and allowing the singers a first crack at the score. "Some ideas are simply not valid and you don't know until you try them," he says. After the first period, the production team finalized their plans, integrating the discoveries made during early rehearsals. Sets and costumes also were constructed during that hiatus. The second phase of rehearsals, a three-week period leading into opening night, was conducted on the set, allowing an unusually long period of adjustment to the physical environment. The performances were never considered finalized, however. Sellars is well known for tinkering with large and small details night by night during the run of a show. Multiple revivals of the Mozart operas generated hundreds of major and minor revisions. It is too early to predict whether the results of the company's persistent reworkings will ultimately add up to a new "performance tradition," but they do amount to a novel, updated approach to the works that is at once vibrant, daring, subtle, obvious, haunting, intense, frivolous, and a host of other conflicting adjectives.

Sellars has said he believes there have been only three great periods of theatre history: the Greeks, the Elizabethans, and the American musical.[13] The sensibilities of the latter and an openly declared love of "show business"[14] shaped much of Sellars's response to these three operas. Like musicals, the productions featured semirealistic acting, choreographed production numbers, and recognizably American characters. Within those trappings, however, were sincere attempts to come to grips with three of the most challenging and enigmatic staples of the operatic repertoire. Summerfare, the Pepsico-sponsored festival at the State University of New York at Purchase, played host to the three evolving productions, culminating in a presentation of the complete trilogy in the festival's tenth and final season in July and August 1989. The following analysis is based on the summer 1989 versions, although the productions continue to be modified and sung in Europe and the United States, and were recorded on videotape in Vienna in October 1989.

The Mozart–da Ponte collaboration is widely considered to have been a pinnacle of classic operatic creation, crossing generic boundaries between

opera seria and opera buffa to produce a tragicomic form that is feisty and witty one moment, darkly ambiguous the next. Mozart's scores often move
into more somber, even ominous, tones than da Ponte's charming libretti.
"One of the great attributes of Mozart's music," writes Will Crutchfield, "is
the way dark, mysterious or foreboding strains will swell up within jocose
movements – sometimes appearing in response to a specific verbal stimulus,
but often appearing without explaining themselves, leaving the memory of a
shadow behind to tint what else we hear."[15] Like Molière and most social
satirists, Mozart and da Ponte had to couch their serious intentions in levity.
Sellars identifies with their methods: "The only way to get people in a basically trivial society to pay attention is to assure them that what you are doing is *fun*," he wrote in the introduction to his extensive program notes for
the 1989 Summerfare marathon.[16] He complains that too many modern
revivals neglect the underside of these operas and gloss over their more subtle and serious implications. "The implied disclaimer of larger ambitions is
maddening . . . because they *did* mean it, they're *not* kidding," he writes.
Between *buffa* and *seria*, he insists, "we are in a new world where the labels
must be checked, re-checked, and finally mistrusted, and we enter a zone of
pure possibility." His directorial style was a glitzy marriage of high- and
pop-cult, opera and show biz, which implied that ours, too, is a "trivial society" that must have its bitter pills dipped in sugar. Sellars himself emerged as
the prototypical product of his superficial environment, except that he tried
to lure us into those uncharted regions of the psyche, "the twilight landscape
. . . [in which] Mozart and Chekhov meet."[17]

The junctures between comic and serious elements in these operas and the
rich interpretative potential of the friction between them were what most
interested this director. "I have seen very few productions that take these
pieces at their word," he writes,

> even to the extent . . . of performing a complete edition, or . . . just
> getting the plot right. . . . We know these pieces through the eyes of
> the generation that chose to revive them in the early part of our centu-
> ry, and dreadful clichés of this period persist in the most cultured pro-
> ductions. I suppose this is why I was so anxious to begin with settings
> that removed all traces of faux rococo, and just start over.[18]

To Sellars, starting over meant using unabridged texts and scores. (Nothing
was cut, but "Vado, ma dove" – a vocal passage Mozart had written for the
original Dorabella to sing in another composer's opera – was interpolated in-

to *Così* to add complexity to the character, and the Adagio from Mozart's E-Flat Serenade, K375, was added as an interlude between Acts I and II of *Figaro*.) The works were sung in the original Italian with no titles. The lack of translation, like so many of the director's choices, functioned as both a subterfuge and an interesting wrinkle in the overall fabric of the productions. The inability of most audience members to comprehend the dialogue conveniently masked discrepancies between what the characters said and what the audience saw them doing. On the other hand, the foreign sounds added another source of friction that worked to Sellars's advantage. He explains:

> I don't know who to ask to come up with American versions that are as dark and as quick, as vibrant, and as deceptively simple, as da Ponte's originals. And, I must admit I enjoy the sensation of being surrounded by the detritus of New York in the 1980s and being constantly reminded and astonished that the text, like the music, represents the 1780s. I also enjoy the fact that for once most of the audience in this verbally-dominated culture is forced to take in information through other pores, be sensitive to other indicators, and ends up projecting its own text into the evening. It is the multiple levels that give pleasure in opera.[19]

The director's heady justifications create an almost Pirandellian paradox for the critical listener. Questions about his motivations are met with seemingly irrefutable answers. Sellars's confident pronouncements on how friction and dissonance function in his productions make sense, yet the inquirer is left feeling duped by sleight of tongue. It is impossible to overlook the merits of Sellars's idiosyncratic juxtapositions, especially when his explanations are so compelling. Smooth, predigested versions of the operas were not his goal. As the director insists, "art should be chewy."[20] But as self-contradictory as were the productions, the responses they evoked were often equally ambivalent. Sometimes the odd mix of elements was surprisingly evocative, but it was impossible to stifle the occasional groan at sophomoric jokes and adolescent sexual innuendoes. The critic must resort to the "yes, but . . ." figure time and again.

Sellars's use of anachronism is itself paradoxical. While he dresses his productions in the accoutrements of contemporary life, his objectives go way beyond drawing parallels between past and present. The initial shock of the familiar setting, he hopes, will prove transparent. He seems to think it has the same effect as driving out of a tunnel: After a few seconds the glare fades back to useful illumination. Once the audience is drawn into the present-tense convention, Sellars expects the outward particulars of our world to be neutralized. The audience's attention can then shift to the deeper currents running beneath the surface. Startling topicalities are placed strategically throughout the production to repeat the process. The director uses style in order to transcend it.

> To me the argument over modernizing is totally a red herring. We don't know what people thought when these operas were first performed, and we have a better chance of being honest if we stop pretending we do. My point is to eliminate the sense of distance so that people can get right to the subject matter.[21]

When directing an old opera, Sellars believes, the subject matter has to include the text, the music, and the context of the time in which it was written, as well as the present situation and the performance history in between. "All that has to be taken into account and find its place somewhere in the production." Updatings that merely change the locale and put on modern clothes but don't shuffle back and forth between the sources and the present "embarrass" him. "It feels cheap and tacky and has no resonance. Like stuffing a square peg in a round hole. I try to let my productions have a lot more air than that and a lot more layers."

There is no doubt that Sellars's versions endowed the Mozart–da Ponte operas with a compelling immediacy that has appealed to segments of the traditional opera audience as well as experimental theatre patrons who followed the director from the theatre to the opera. Moreover, although the familiar debate continues about whether the director was true to the creators' intentions or just showing off, few critics deny that these productions struck deep chords within the three pieces and resonated with their overtones. What remains open for discussion is less the impudence of mixing extreme emotional states with silly topical jokes, than how the productions ultimately managed to rouse the operas' metaphysical rumblings from beneath the productions' patent superficialities.

The company began its work on this material with a revival of the Boston Opera *Don Giovanni* at the Monadnock Music Festival in New Hampshire in 1980. Edward Gorey's sets and costumes were carried over from the Boston production but were replaced by new designs by George Tsypin in 1987, when the company completely restaged the production at Summerfare. Tsypin's wide, shallow set depicted a ghetto street scene, whose elements were inspired by sites within a five-block radius of the designer's home in Queens. In this *Don Giovanni,* the main character was not a Spaniard who prevailed in his debaucheries by virtue of his noble birth, but a coarse, small-time drug dealer who terrorized the denizens of his Lower East Side neighborhood with a coercive combination of generosity and violence. Tsypin's set included the awning and window of a cramped basement bodega, an open sewer excavation complete with Con Ed stanchions and flashing yellow lights, and the fluorescent-lit entry hall of a dilapidated tenement. The front-door glass was broken and looked like a spiderweb, a neat metaphor for the Don's hold over the rest of the characters. The action took place in the course of one night. James Ingalls, who did the lights for all three operas, shrouded the stage in varying degrees of darkness rudely interrupted by the flash of a neon cross from a church across the street. Set, lighting, and costumes (by Dunya Ramicova, who designed costumes for all three Mozart–da Ponte productions) captured seedy street life in a way that was both realistic and intensely theatrical.

Costumes and behavior in the Summerfare *Don Giovanni* were strictly late-1980s. Leporello in a black-leather motorcycle jacket break-danced to the overture; Donna Elvira wore leopard-patterned tights with spike heels and a miniskirt; and Donna Anna required an intravenous fix before her exhausting second-act aria. The Don feasted on McDonald's hamburgers and snorted cocaine with his sidekick. Music for the party scene was provided by a suitcase-size portable radio. The characters, now denizens of the inner city, were racially mixed: Massetto (Elmore James) was black; Zerlina (Ai Lan Zhu) Chinese; and Don Giovanni and Leporello were played by a pair of African-American identical twins, Eugene and Herbert Perry respectively. Even the production's rage at Don Giovanni's brutalization of women seemed more feminist than moralistic. These women did not succumb easily to the Don's advances: They fought back hard and with dignity; their inevitable falls took on greater tragic proportions. Even the musicians in the well-lit orchestra pit abandoned the usual formal wear for black T-shirts and jeans.

"The oppressive class structure that Mozart depicted is alive and well 200 years later in The United States of America [*sic*]," Sellars writes in defense of his choices, "even if the money is from drugs. Addiction is, after all, the theme of this opera."[22] Addiction to power is what Sellars means, especially sexual power. He believes that sexual politics is the real issue in *Don Giovanni* and the other two works in the trilogy. "Mozart concerned himself very shockingly with sexual politics and made the larger point that the various political corruptions of his period were linked to sexual politics," he says.[23] In the interactions of the various initial and reconfigured couples in

Figure 12. The Don (Eugene Perry) snacks on McDonald's as he tries to convince Leporello (Herbert Perry) not to leave him, in *Don Giovanni*, directed by Peter Sellars, at Pepsico Summerfare, Purchase, New York, 1989. Photo © Beatriz Schiller.

all three works, Sellars finds Mozart and da Ponte exploring the dynamics of cultural dominance and subordination. Trust–mistrust, honesty–deception, and devotion–duplicity are all played out within and among the symmetrical pairs of lovers, but the implications reach beyond the domestic situations. "It is the quality of personal interaction, how people really treat each other, that determines the health of a nation and becomes the story of an epoch," writes the director. "It is on this level of fine detail that Mozart and da Ponte have erected these enduring edifices."[24] Not that Mozart and da Ponte were the first to use this metaphor, Sellars adds, "but Mozart does it with such astonishing sensual information, the music . . . reaches one in such strange recesses of sensuality."[25]

155

Even though Don Giovanni was of the same socioeconomic class as the rest of the characters in Sellars's version (with the casting of the Perry twins underscoring the irony), his drug-lord status gave him the power to oppress. As in the original, Don Giovanni's abusive seductions were more than mere sexual conquests. They were the means through which he acquired increasing control over his turf. Both the women and their boyfriends/fiancés/husbands were subjugated to the Don's sexual whims. He was an emasculator as well as a rapist, and each sexual triumph earned him more leverage on the whole community. Drug addiction was another hook he used to maintain their dependence on and subordination to him.

Besides the obvious ways in which the ghetto setting of *Don Giovanni* deemphasized the libretto, Sellars's staging, here as in the rest of the trilogy, was based primarily on his responses to Mozart's score. He explains:

> In an opera by Mozart, the music really takes precedence just because of the way the sheer process of writing an opera works. The words come first and then the music. And so literally, the music is the last word. And so you have Mozart using the text in many different ways, sometimes ironically, sometimes taking it perfectly literally, and sometimes contradicting it utterly to produce a strange, conflicted feeling.

The director followed Mozart's lead wherever the music delves into things less rational, less polite, less easily put into words. He seemed to follow Wagner's prescription for opera, that it show the "deeds of music made visible."[26]

In all three Sellars productions, choreographed movement physicalized patterns in the music. In *Don Giovanni,* the choreography extended past the party-dance sequences, played here with snapping fingers and pelvic gyrations. Arias were sung while rolling on the floor. Singers of duets and quartets moved through formalized floor patterns that traced shifting musical and interpersonal relationships. Movements were often complicated and strenuous, giving powerful physical expression to the interior life of the music and the characters. Lorraine Hunt, as Donna Elvira, crouched and writhed on the floor as she sang out her agonies. As Donna Anna, Dominique Labelle had to sing while her body convulsed in the aftermath of an intravenous injection. *Così* and *Figaro* contained more scenes in which relationships between the singers were echoed in movement patterns. Much of the action of *Così* reinforced coupling, uncoupling, and recoupling among the three pairs of lovers. Neat symmetrical arrangements of men and women in the early scenes gave way to increasingly mixed-up patterns later on.

156

Sellars also played on doubles as a movement motif in *Figaro*. Susanna and the Countess rolled on the floor in mirror image as they sang the duet that prepares them to switch identities to snare the Count. The only segment in the trilogy arranged by a professional choreographer was the Act III fandango in *Figaro*, by Mark Morris. At times, the obvious formality of the movement and the long pauses that Sellars inserted, supposedly to force the audience to think about what they were seeing on stage, "reek[ed] of acting-class exercises."[27] They were, in many instances, oversimplified expressions of complex human emotions, but in the context of the intricate music and the untranslated text, they offered a useful diagram, or map, of the subtext. John Rockwell of the *New York Times* described the choreography as "ritualized synchronization."[28] Andrew Porter wrote that the movement "gave convincing physical shape to the phrases of Mozart's score."[29] Edward Said concluded that the key to Sellars's success was his ability to bring out "what is most eccentric and opaque about Mozart: the obsessive patternings."[30]

It is not easy for singers to execute complicated physical movements and hit the notes in Mozart's demanding vocal score at the same time. Meeting that challenge was part of the experience for both the director and his cast. The technical difficulty of the performance, he believes,

> gives it a kind of extra-moral edge of authority. Because you see a human being challenging himself, not just complacently sitting there lecturing you on how you should improve your life, but somebody who's actually subjecting their life to tremendous discipline, and who's willing to encounter genuine rigor in the aim of purifying themselves and what they're doing. These moments of tremendous purity are arrived at through the most intense [exertion], literally facing danger. You don't know if a singer is going to be able to hit that note; it's very hard, and I just try and make it harder. I make it so daunting for the singers, but it really is an astounding accomplishment when they're able to do it, and the audience senses that and that's one more level at which you're gripped by the performance.

Sellars's nontraditional expectations were well served by the youth, vigor, and dedication of his singers, many of whom had been a part of these productions for ten years. Mainly in their thirties, the lean and limber cast broke barriers with young audiences simply by looking and behaving like the active young characters they were written to be. Typically, though, Sellars occasionally left in too much of a good thing. There were moments, especially in the most serious sections, where the acting felt forced, more play-acted

157

than felt, more maudlin than cataclysmic. Overall, however, the singers were able to handle Sellars's unpredictable mix of stylization and subtlety. The cast sustained complex, psychologically realistic characterizations that redefined expectations of operatic acting.

Over the years, mixed critical reception of *Don Giovanni* reflected the production's daring, its conceptual flaws, and its musical merits. *Opera News* reviewer C. J. Luten called the production's multilayered ambiguity "well beyond what one normally encounters," but thought some of the director's effects "exaggerated and irrelevant."[31] "The most radical recension of an opera that I've ever seen," wrote Thomas Disch in the *Nation*. In the shift to an urban setting *Don Giovanni* exposed the legendary main character as a brute who rules not by virtue of his exalted birthright, but "because he is reddest in tooth and claw, the top of the food chain."[32] Said was bothered by the production's "unflattering portrayals of women" and "a claustrophobic dissonance throughout" that can probably be attributed to the oppressive darkness and a sense that the director had to force his concept a little too hard.[33] Andrew Porter recognized in Sellars's work "something different from the cosmetic refreshment of old operas effected by shifting them from one period setting to another." He appreciated the way the production avoided "big, dull, greasy platitudes," replacing clichés with "the fruit of specific circumstances." Often the most outspoken champion of Sellars's transpositions, Porter felt that "amid so many [opera] conventions, it is easy to accept another: that an eighteenth-century text is being sung, in Italian to eighteenth-century music, in a modern New York setting."[34]

The exploration of domination and intimidation within an urban subclass renewed the familiar *Don Giovanni* for a modern American audience. The production seemed to discover new facets of the music as well. However, there were times when the parallels and contradictions felt forced and self-conscious. The visuals were, perhaps, too consistent, too realistic to let the music in. Sets, costumes, and body movement conjured the sounds and rhythms of the argot of New York's narcotics street trade; the lyrical cadences of Italian strained to wedge their way into that universe. Instead of disco or rock or samba, the party guests swung their hips to what even a willing American audience could only identify as "classical music." Mozart's hits sounded not just odd but ridiculous emanating from a ghetto blaster. Cries of "Viva la liberta!" were accompanied by the cast stripping down to their underwear. Sexual liberation may relate to the work's theme of sexual subordination, but such an overt and unbelievable gesture trivialized an important issue and diminished the characters. Because the subculture in which

Sellars chose to relocate the action has its own indelible linguistic and musical profiles, and because the presentation of that subculture was so compelling, the conflict of rhythms onstage and in the orchestra pit tended to grate, especially in the first act. Later, when the opera itself slows and darkens, the staging and the music settled into more provocative register and Sellars's aesthetic of contradiction vindicated itself.

The ensemble's *Così fan Tutte* was first staged in 1984, under the auspices of the Castle Hill Music Festival in Ipswich, Massachusetts. Two years later Christopher Hunt, who took over the artistic directorship of Summerfare in 1986, invited the troupe to the festival to resume its work on *Così*. SUNY Purchase's 560-seat Theater B proved a receptive space for the intimate, chamber atmosphere the company insisted was integral to their rebellion against operatic bombast. The combination of Hunt's enthusiasm, the college facilities, and the festival's proximity to New York audiences proved fertile ground for Sellars's work. As already noted, *Don Giovanni* joined the Summerfare repertory in 1987, and Sellars finally attempted *Figaro* there in 1988.

The Italian libretto for *Così* sets the first scene in a "*bodega di caffe.*" Sellars's set, designed by Adrianne Lobel, put the action in "Despina's Diner," a typical suburban eatery, complete with fluorescent-lit refrigerator case displaying cheesecakes, pies, and pastries behind sliding glass doors. Despina (Sue Ellen Kuzma) waited tables in the Formica-topped, chrome-tiled restaurant. Her boyfriend Alfonso (Sanford Sylvan), a disgruntled Vietnam veteran, stood guard at the cash register. The metal-shell diner looked as if it had been revealed with a can opener. Its back wall, lunch counter, and a bank of brightly vinyl-wrapped booths ran parallel to edge of the stage, confronting the audience full-face with its playful topicality. Doors on either end of the back wall bore black silhouette cutouts of a man and a woman with ornate eighteenth-century hairstyles. These restroom-door markers added hints of humor and planted sly reminders of the opera's roots. The paradox of Sellars's work is that such rich details, simultaneously accurate and symbolic, can create distracting inconsistencies. For example, a character who exited through the upstage-right bathroom door did not reappear until several scenes, supposedly several hours, later. This and similar small glitches disturbed the continuity but, in yet another layer of contradiction, also reinforced the theatrical context of the performance. The dissonance kept the updated setting from slipping into simple transposition. The world onstage may have looked like the world in which we live, but it was out of kilter, strange, unsettling, and mystifying, too.

Figure 13. Despina's Diner is the setting for the young lovers' (Susan Larson, Janice Felty, James Maddalena, Frank Kelley) separation, as Don Alfonso (Sanford Sylvan) advances his scheme, in *Così fan Tutte,* directed by Peter Sellars, at Pepsico Summerfare, Purchase, New York, 1986. Photo © Beatriz Schiller.

"That a system of contemporary references is an essential ingredient to the functioning of these pieces seems relatively obvious,"[35] Sellars contends. Mozart and da Ponte included numerous topical references on which to hang their larger themes; Sellars extended their impulse by interpolating contemporary references he knew his audience would understand. It was on the basis of those substitutions that Sellars was accused in some circles of tak-

160

ing cheap shots at the opera. Of the three productions at hand, *Cosí* contained some of the boldest and baldest visual puns. The notary arrived with a
cellular phone and laptop computer. The "Albanian" disguises look more
like costumes for the "wild-and-crazy guys" from "Saturday Night Live."
Guglielmo's Act II aria, "Donne mie," which asks rhetorically why women
mistreat men, was handled like an episode of "Donahue." Sellars had the

character grab a cordless microphone and run into the audience, where he shoved the appliance in people's faces as if to invite their opinions on this ancient and unanswerable query. Obviously, Mozart did not compose for Phil Donahue, but bringing the talk-show host into the scene underscored the notion that no facile answer could be better than woefully glib. Typically, the audience laughed in recognition but quickly grew quiet: Once the giggly shock of recognition settled down, deeper implications sank in.

Sellars's work is marked by brilliance jutting up against banality. Facile jokes precede painfully frank confrontations with human anguish, but, as in the Guglielmo–Phil Donahue bit, there is usually a more serious intention. The spectator has to look for connections. Sellars believes the friction between silly and sublime generates energy in the theatre:

> You don't know something's profound unless you've just come from something that isn't profound. We're capable of being in a really profound state and doing something really silly. . . .
>
> You know Mozart does that very deliberately, as does Shakespeare or Chekhov or Hitchcock. It's a very specific strategy. It's time for Cleopatra's death scene, we need some asps, lets have a clown come out and tell snake jokes. In fact, that's how you can tell you're at the moment of deepest intensity, the crisis moment of the piece, because the silliest, goofiest things happen just before it.

The appearance of Despina disguised as Shirley MacLaine at the end of Act I of *Cosí* demonstrates how Sellars layered meaning into a seemingly banal incident. According to the text, the disguised Guglielmo and Ferrando pretend to be so devastated by the girls' rejection that they drink poison. In Sellars's production, the lads emptied squeeze-bottles of ketchup and mustard down their gullets. Mozart and da Ponte then bring Despina on stage, disguised as "Dr. Fatalis," a parody of F. A. Mesmer, the famous doctor who based his practice of hypnosis on theories of animal magnetism. Mesmer was a friend of the Mozart family; the reference alluded to the possible connections between the couples' sexual attraction and Mesmer's hypotheses. Sellars explains the satirical evocation of a controversial, contemporary celebrity as Mozart and da Ponte's lighthearted way of dealing with a larger issue with which that individual was popularly associated. Mozart, as Sellars understands, establishes

> the idea that people have other lives than their material lives, and that we don't even begin to understand the limits of the human psyche, by using the figure of Mesmer as a huge joke. So the audience laughs, and

162

then they stop laughing because we're in a zone that truly is interplanetary, is cross-generational, that does go between lives people have lived, and where we do wonder what we did before we arrived on the earth, and how we learned what we learned here. How much do we really know ourselves and do we really understand any human response?

Of course, Mesmer was no longer a popular celebrity when Sellars directed *Così*, and the director's here-and-now philosophy demanded a more immediately recognizable personality. Not that the interjection of current celebrities into the casts of classic plays is Sellars's invention: Among many examples, Lee Breuer did it in his Hollywood *Tempest,* and Joseph Papp did it in his 1968 *Hamlet.* Sellars's initial choice to substitute for Mesmer and to heal the languishing lovers was media sex therapist Dr. Ruth Westheimer, who was aped in the 1986 version. By 1989, however, Dr. Ruth was passé. Shirley MacLaine had become the reigning queen of home-video spiritual healing, and Sellars thought her cosmic aura fit Mesmer's image even better. So, out came Despina in short auburn wig and flowing magenta caftan, an unmistakable MacLaine clone that was both funny and surprisingly resonant. It called up images of cosmic wonder but poked fun at them at the same time. As Sellars paraphrases Mozart's own ambivalence: "Was Mesmer a quack, or are all living things connected across time in a mysterious interaction of fluids and electricity?"[36] The production substituted MacLaine for Mesmer and left the question open for audience members to mull over on their own.

Sellars likes to toss issues into the ring and leave them lying around unresolved. One interpretation of this habit is that he expects a lot from his (usually upper-class, highly educated) audience. At other times, however, his directorial overkill suggests that his faith in them is less than complete: Sellars had Alfonso hold up a hand-lettered sign inscribed "S-H-I-R-L-E-Y M-A-C-L-A-I-N-E" and point to her with his finger. The audience could have gotten the obvious joke without such explicit explanation. Small judgment calls are pivotal in executing risky production concepts. They can alienate sympathetic spectators who are willing to ride the adventure so long as they are treated with respect.

Sellars was aware that the sign was a potential problem, but decided to use it for several reasons, including valid theatrical precedents.

We debated the sign so much. It is Brecht, it's Shakespeare, it's medieval. It's very didactic and very obvious, but it also does two things.

163

One, it completely objectifies what's going on and makes it presentational. It's not just Despina dressing up as Shirley MacLaine to please the girls within a diner frame; it steps out of the diner frame in a deliberate device that we're using to address the audience. It breaks the fourth wall and reiterates that what we're seeing is a construction and that we are at any moment capable of scraping away the veneer.

There were also practical, "show business" reasons why the sign stayed in. Problems with the wig and costume had apparently prevented early audiences from identifying MacLaine right away. The company felt insecure, and the sign made them more comfortable. The director also liked the way the sign worked rhythmically.

> The other thing [the sign] does is concentrate the laugh. People are laughing at different times as she's coming around; then the sign is produced, and there's one big, strong laugh, and then we move into the [rest of the] scene. As show biz tactics, it's how to start the scene on a very strong laugh when the whole audience acknowledges to themselves – together – that they already know this. It allows the audience to hear itself. It unifies the whole audience to say this is a joke, and then we move on. But there were huge debates about that sign.

Just how delicate is the distinction between directorial excess and the successful, satirical use of repetition can be seen in a third MacLaine reference in *Così*. "Dr. Fatalis" appears just before the Act I finale, which has what Sellars calls a "shocking B-flat minor section that musically lets you know that the piece is about to move into extremely strange, private, and undiscussable regions." The act ends on that mysterious note, and Sellars's intermission followed. Video monitors in the lobby played one of MacLaine's meditation tapes. Instead of reiterating the same joke, this time the MacLaine reference added a layer of irony and healthy, self-deprecating humor to the heaviness of what had just been sung. It seemed to mock the arrogance of our asking the same unfathomable questions, confident that somehow our generation will successfully unravel the eternal mysteries.

Minor plot alterations magnified the moral ambiguity of Sellars's modernized *Così*. For example, a nod to twentieth-century feminism could be detected in the portrayal of the sisters Dorabella and Fiordiligi. Doublemint Twins in floral slacks and brightly colored T-shirts, these girls were not the innocent dupes of da Ponte's libretto. They were aware of their fiancés' deception from the beginning, and their willing participation in the scheme made their eventual disillusion that much more painful. They shared equal responsibility for the harm done to their idyllic, naive relationships. Thus, all could not be resolved neatly at the end with male regret and female forgiveness: No one could deny or forget the frightening sexual stirrings they felt when they had swapped partners. Sellars left those disturbing memories hanging in the air at the end. The couples' reunions were tentative, haunted, and fragile. The brides and grooms played musical chairs, confusion on their faces, as they sat down to sign their marriage contracts. No easy happily-ever-afters here. John Rockwell, in the *New York Times,* described the ending as "brilliantly ambiguous . . . all six characters crisscrossing hysterically, winding up with everyone apart, flapping like broken dolls."[37]

The critics identified Sellars's *Così* with a trend toward more serious interpretation of this opera, but several complained that too much of the light-hearted spirit of the original had been eclipsed. Rockwell lauded Sellars's "attempt to rescue it from its still-prevalent reputation as a silly farce," but cautioned that the director seemed to be "thinking so hard that he clutters up his emotional effects with cleverness."[38] In a similar vein, the *Times'* Will Crutchfield, who liked the production, complained that "art in our century has been ready to see beauty as false and ugliness as truth, and in this Mr. Sellars is an authentic spokesman for his time, but he is shouting our message at Mozart so loudly that we cannot hear part of Mozart's to us." He also felt that long passages of "toneless, numb-sounding recitative" did not necessarily illuminate obscure knots in the opera, but were "only a more sophisticated dodge of the genuine than the more usual empty histrionics."[39] On the positive side, Peter G. Davis of *New York* magazine found that "every response, no matter how extravagant, arises directly from Mozart's sublimely ambiguous but deeply human musical interpretation of da Ponte's witty libretto."[40] Moira Hodgson called the production "a deep response to Mozart's ambiguous text."[41] And fan Andrew Porter appreciated the way Sellars had "directed the score rather than the libretto. He brought onto the stage – 'underlined' is perhaps not too strong – all the marvels that he found there; left nothing unexplained; tweaked and twisted the plain sense of the words when it didn't match his perceptions of the music." Porter's final sentence lends credibility to some of his more adulatory remarks and is a delightfully candid response to revisionist directing in general: "I can understand resistance to this *Così* as easily as my surrender to it."[42]

As bold as were Sellars's restagings of *Così* and *Don Giovanni,* the director had never intended to conquer the full Mozart–da Ponte trilogy. He felt intimidated by the musical mysteries of *Figaro,* and it wasn't until 1988 that conductor Craig Smith and Summerfare's Christopher Hunt convinced him to undertake this piece. Perhaps because the director came to the project seasoned by his work on the previous two pieces, *Figaro* was the most seamless and satisfying of the trilogy. Richard Trousdell's excellent case study of Sellars's work on *Figaro* is a thorough recounting of the rehearsal process.[43] I will focus, therefore, on the performance itself and its critical reception.

Again working with set designer Adrianne Lobel, Sellars set *Figaro* in a chic apartment on the fifty-somethingth floor of New York City's Trump Tower. Count Almaviva (James Maddelena) and his elegantly coiffed, blonde Countess (Jayne West), an Ivanna Trump look-alike, lived in luxurious splendor with the aid of their maid and butler, Susanna (Jeanne Ommerlé) and Figaro (Sanford Sylvan). The action, as in da Ponte's libretto, took place on Susanna and Figaro's wedding day, but their quarters here consisted of a cramped laundry room with a temperamental sofa bed. Lobel's sets for Acts II and III depicted the apartment's sleek master bedroom suite and a sweeping, duplex living room decorated in ultramodern monochrome beige, centering on a large, swirling abstract canvas à la Frank Stella. Act IV was played on the living-room terrace, a narrow strip downstage of a glass curtain. The clean lines and sweeping spaces in the Count's apartment confirmed his status as a peer of the American capitalist ruling class, enjoying material splendor at the underpaid physical and emotional expense of his servants.

With *Figaro*, the director resumed his political arguments about sexual and economic exploitation. Whereas *Don Giovanni* struggled to discern the pattern of subclass oppression within the lower ranks of American society, *Figaro*'s beautiful-people setting established clear parallels between the opera's landed aristocracy and America's corporate plutocrats. In the program notes, Sellars evokes the image of another, less sympathetic, female tycoon. Court testimony by Leona Helmsley's employees remind him of the

> mutual fear and dependency of servants and masters that is so crisply delineated in *The Marriage of Figaro*. And the notion that a certain class of people is above the law (Leona's "only the little people pay taxes" remark is apropos) or see to it that the law exists in order to protect their own prerogatives, privileges, and power options, with the extravagances, waste and indignities of the rich laid directly on the backs of the poor – these ideas seem in no danger of becoming isolated historical phenomena.[44]

Sellars hears an alarm in the opera's elucidation of entrenched systematic oppression. In contemporary America, as in Mozart's Europe, he notes, "the

Figure 14. Figaro (Sanford Sylvan) admires Susanna, his bride-to-be (Jeanne Ommerlé), in their servants'-quarters-cum-laundry-room in the Trump Towers, in *Le Nozze di Figaro,* directed by Peter Sellars, at Pepsico Summerfare, Purchase, New York, 1988. Photo © Johan Elbers.

historical moment is passing from our hands into the hands of others who have been waiting for a long time."[45] When Mozart and da Ponte wrote *Figaro,* it was already too late for the frivolous aristocrats who lost their heads in the French Revolution. Just months after the final Summerfare season, Eastern Europe took lessons in how and how not to relinquish power to those who have been denied. Sellars seemed to be warning us that America's class struggle may be more subtle, but it is just as dangerous. "All men are created equal," he insists, still applies only to some men and fewer women; and those who are not included may be more clever, more resilient, and more willing to risk what they have for what they want. Figaro and Susanna are clearly their betters' betters in terms of honesty, compassion, endurance, and love.

The opera itself is revolutionary in its frank depictions of complex sexual psychology. Like Don Giovanni's, the Count's dalliances with women from the lower class combine sexual attraction to them with degradation of them. Almaviva affirms his virility through his socioeconomic as well as sexual

167

prowess. Contrary to his professions, love is not the great equalizer between him and Susanna (or Barbarina, or whomever else he has intimidated into performing sexual favors), but another manifestation of a wealthy man's tyranny over other people. Unlike Giovanni, who never repents, Almaviva is tortured by his obsessive need to have other men's women. He is equally tormented by jealousy toward his wife, for whom he appears to have little other feeling. Sellars's production emphasized the Count's and Countess's loneliness, isolation, and despair. They wandered aimlessly through the large spaces in their apartment, whose cool, minimalist decor offered no comforts, no cozy corners to curl up in, nothing soft or fuzzy or warm. They seemed lost in their own home. Conversely, Susanna and Figaro's tiny room, barely furnished, teemed with activity and people and life. Almaviva was more pitiful than menacing as he pursued Susanna. Sellars reworked funny moments in the libretto to make the Count even more foolish. In the original, the Count discovers Cherubino underneath a tablecloth in Susanna's room. Here he found him under the skirt of Susanna's wedding gown. Enraged, he pounced over the open sofa bed to attack the boy, but the mattress collapsed, trapping him in its steel-framed embrace. Maddelena played the Count as a fumbling, self-absorbed, immature lout, an accurate modern antihero for this subversive operatic text.

Sanford Sylvan's Figaro also translated easily to a contemporary figure. He was a passionate and determined fiancé, interested only in securing happiness with Susanna and genuinely heartbroken any time his faith in her was threatened. Sylvan's vocal performance received unanimously excellent reviews, and his handling of Sellars's direction was equally impressive. Infuriated by evidence of the Count's advances toward his bride-to-be, Figaro pitched an egg across the room. Its smashed contents dripped down a pristine, cream-colored wall. An outlandish gesture became a potent symbol: The egg was the opening volley in the battle between the Count and his servant. Figaro thus declared revolutionary war against the appearance of smug propriety in his master's domain. Sylvan's Figaro had all the spunk and resourcefulness of traditional interpretations of the role. He played along with Susanna's schemes, catching on to the latest lies just in time to save the day, and always thrilled to rediscover her constancy after impetuously having doubted her.

The contrasts between Almaviva and Figaro were echoed in the portraits of the Countess and Susanna. The pampered Countess, like her maudlin husband, absorbed herself in her misery, feared her brutish husband, yet pined for his affections. Act II found her in her mirrored bedroom, complete with vertical blinds and thick down quilt, barely able to get out of bed until Figaro and Susanna helped her devise a plan to catch the miscreant in flagrante delicto. Jayne West sang the Countess's long, dark arias about the agonies of a still-loving but rejected wife slowly and with deep emotion. Sellars staged her Act III aria on the living-room balcony. Dressed in formal pink gown, her hair swept up, jewels around her neck, the Countess posed regally, clutching a railing for support.

Meanwhile, a majestic Central Park sunset sank beyond the living-room windows, bathing the stage in dark hues of pink and yellow and blue. It looked too beautiful to be true, and in fact it was. Sellars did not want simply a pretty, realistic sunset: It had to be a theatrical sunset. Lighting designer James F. Ingalls created the spectacular effect by simulating the sunset from two directions at the same time. Most audience members probably never noticed that the image was unnatural but surrendered to its stunning beauty and the way it enveloped the opera's most serious musical passage.

Susanna confronts her own share of woes, but, unlike the Countess, she is able to act resourcefully in her own behalf. Sellars's staging of Susanna and Figaro's schemes played like episodes of "I Love Lucy." The Susanna–Cherubino switch took place in a small closet. The new bride seemed to enjoy allowing her husband to squirm for a while under the mistaken impression that she was betraying him on their wedding night. A lighthearted, everything-will-work-out-in-the-end, sitcom optimism in these sections leavened the production's overall focus on the darker shades of this haunting opera. Practical, capable, level-headed, take-charge, the character of Susanna made the most convincing transition to the updated setting.

Cherubino (sung by Susan Larson) provides another good example of how well this *Figaro* transposed original elements into the updated setting. In the libretto, this alto-in-britches is a page in the Count's mansion. His exploding adolescent passion is a significant foil for the main characters' overwrought romantic plots. In Sellars's production, Cherubino became the quintessential American adolescent male, dressed in jeans and a hockey jersey, swilling orange juice from a cardboard carton, and swooning at his own love letters. Lolling on the sofa bed in the first act, daydreaming about his beloved Countess, Larson's Cherubino lay on his back, pelvis pumping in fantasized anticipation. In the second act of da Ponte's libretto, Cherubino jumps out the Countess's bedroom window, supposedly the second floor of the Count's house. Here, the youth took a more perilous and, symbolically, more emotionally reckless plunge from an upper story of Trump Tower. He landed on the terrace of the apartment below. Da Ponte has the gardener show up to complain about damages to the landscaping; Sellars brought on the building superintendent, who was all worked up about the destruction of a potted poinsettia. After Almaviva banished Cherubino, and ordered him off to military service, the boy turned up disguised as one of Susanna's bridesmaids and flirted with his own rival.

The wedding itself contained the greatest number of topical jokes. Figaro initiated the wedding procession by turning on a portable CD player. The ceremony was recorded by a man toting a videocamera on his shoulder. Household staff bearing wedding gifts included the doorman, a utilities worker, maids, cops, and a chef. The ceremony was held in the grand living room, with the Count and Countess seated on the only two chairs, like throned nobility. The reception took place in pantomime behind the huge picture window that dropped down to define the edge of the stage as the Act IV terrace, where the final trap was laid for the Count.

Here, as with the Shirley MacLaine sign in *Così*, Sellars's impetuosity led to a couple of gaffes in an otherwise thoughtful and illuminating reinterpretation. After switching gowns, the blonde Countess and dark-haired Susanna pulled on ugly, knitted ski hats to aid their disguises. When the Count finally got his hands on Susanna (actually his wife in a bridal gown), he groped her like a schoolboy. Sellars probably meant to make him overeager, but no practiced seducer would be so crude. The high quality of the singing made the silly business look even worse. Trousdell offers a generous interpretation of such events in Sellars's productions: "One strategy Sellars uses to avoid the trap of a prepackaged production is to surround his work with a show of amateur informality, to feature what cannot be fixed and to accept unevenness as a preferable alternative to instant mechanical perfection."[46]

Unlike the ambiguous endings of *Don Giovanni* and *Così*, *Figaro* finished on the high and happy note of Mozart and da Ponte's original. The Countess forgave the repentant Count. Marcellina, who in Sellars's version sought Figaro's hand only to make Bartolo jealous, married Bartolo, and Figaro and Susanna learned their lessons about faith and trust. The finale was danced in a conga line. The cast shimmied and waved to the audience in ritual celebration.

Opera News critic C. J. Luten found the Peter Sellars who directed *Figaro* to be "immensely talented, yet undisciplined, he seems unable to confine himself to the best of his ideas."[47] The *New York Times*' Will Crutchfield described the overinterpretation as the director "jumping in front of the music, frantically gesticulating to tell us that because he has heard it already we need not listen."[48] The critics have a point, yet one is reluctant to suggest that Sellars train himself to be a good editor. His excess may get him into trouble, but his proliferation of clever ideas is also what makes his transpositions transcend themselves. Trousdell identifies this very quality as the thing that makes Sellars's work tick. His core method, Trousdell writes,

> signals its choices through undisguised discrepancies between the text and its anachronous performance, as well as between serious moments and send-ups, realism and subjective poetry, elegant execution and simple plaindealing. . . . To some, Sellars's all-gestures-on-the-table approach is distractingly self-conscious – a kind of showing off. But his style has the virtue of preserving the integrity of an opera or play by clearly distinguishing it from its patently invented production. More-over, Sellars's abrupt shifts in context reflect an important characteristic of his theatre in which the realities of contemporary life and the inven-tion of poetic imagination coexist, not in romantic fusion or classical balance, but in zany and provocative juxtaposition.[49]

Self-constraint might domesticate this director's imagination but not re-fine his final products. There are many hidden layers for alert audience members to mine, but the director is not troubled by the fact that some segments of his audience will miss the deeper meanings. "Art is like anything else in life," he says. "The more you know about it the more you get. If you don't know anything, you can probably get something. If you know more, you'll get more. All the possibilities should be present."

Sellars's productions of the Mozart–da Ponte trilogy realized many new possibilities. They refreshed the images of all three operas by bringing them to life in contemporary frameworks. They furthered the development of op-eratic acting, and they introduced the works to new opera audiences. These achievements were predicated on the director's irreverence, egotism, and profligate imagination, as well as his genuine appreciation for the beauty and complexity of the three operas. Occasionally, those same qualities also led the productions astray. It is easy to fault obvious instances of self-indulgence when the director seemed to usurp authorial privilege; it is trickier to detect the interpretative timidity beneath the director's lofty talk of the interplane-tary and unknowable. The enfant terrible may in fact have erred on the side of too much awe and left some things more vague than was necessary.

In the final analysis, however, Sellars's work with these pieces was origi-nal, vital, and moving. His forceful reinterpretations were meant to shake up the operatic status quo, and so they upset those who see themselves as keep-ers of the traditional watch. "There is a school of thought," writes chief sen-try Donal Henahan, "that pretends to reject the whole concept of durable art, contending that art is ephemeral and progressive by nature and never should reach a point where it can be preserved, like a butterfly under glass."[50] Peter Sellars is a graduate of that school. His productions reflect a sure-footed understanding of the fleeting and temporal nature of the performing arts. The image of a beautiful creature pinned down, dead, inside a hermetically sealed case as a metaphor for live performance would probably, and rightly, make him cringe. Like living things, Sellars's productions of the Mozart–da Ponte trilogy had warts and blemishes, but, both musically and dramatically, they also had depth, humor, complexity, and vibrant enthusiasm.

THE CLASSICS, POSTMODERNISM,
AND THE QUESTION OF COHERENCE
■ ● ■

"A classic is a house we're still living in," Peter Sellars asserted early in the run of his 1993, Gulf War adaptation of Aeschylus' *The Persians*. The most prolific talker of all the directors whose work has been examined in this study, Sellars offers up a neat metaphor for the revisionist stance that undergirds all of their work. "As with any old house," he continues, "you're going to fix it up and add a new wing. It's not an exhibit. It's meant to be lived in, and not admired."[1] Like zealous new tenants, eager to make an old house a home, these directors have repeopled, redecorated, and refitted classic plays with the accoutrements of contemporary American life. They have invited in heretofore excluded guests, ferreted out hidden nooks and crannies, exposed structural inconsistencies, and installed new mirrors to reflect the values, perspectives, and experiences of the latest inhabitants. A final tour of the renovated properties should reveal much about the social, cultural, and intellectual contexts reflected in those mirrors, the essential critical problems posed by the process, and the legacy and prospects of classical theatre in this country.

A worthwhile point of departure would seem to be the situation of classical reinventions in the postmodern landscape. Directorial rewrightings comprise essential contradictions – between the spoken text and the artifacts of the physical production, between high and popular culture iconography, and among internal anachronisms and stylistic juxtapositions. The play of contrasts and oppositions in these works embodies the noisy, disjointed, and fragmentary nature of our daily lives. Peter Sellars, again, describes the experience vividly:

> You are walking down the street and eight transistor radios are playing and fifteen little dramas are playing themselves out. You may have

173

caught a little snippet of one of them and then three others went by and you didn't even notice. That is what it is actually like in this world – not this Aristotelian one-thing-happens-at-a-time situation. We live in a world that is about simultaneity and contradiction.[2]

If a stroll down Main Street bombards the senses and the sense of continuity, the wider world available through communication technologies multiplies and intensifies the possibility for disjointed stimulation.

Raymond Williams, writing about television, the broadest common denominator in late-twentieth-century America, observes and labels a parallel, and I believe relevant, phenomenon. Williams notes that prior to the age of television, readers, listeners, and viewers selected and attended to "discrete events."[3] A person could read a book, or watch a play, or listen to a symphony without continual interruption. The sequence of an hour's television broadcast, however, can consist of program segments, commercials, trailers, coming attractions, news bulletins, and/or other stray video fragments. The borders between and among the various broadcast units are rarely demarcated, so as to reduce the likelihood that viewers will tune out when the all-important advertisements appear on the screen. So, what the viewer takes in is not the drama, sitcom, documentary, or ball game and its discrete interruptions, but the overall "flow" of the broadcast.[4] Williams's study, published in 1975, does not even mention how much more crowded and collagelike is the picture now that dozens (and soon hundreds) of additional cable channels are at one's fingertips via remote control.

The creators and consumers of contemporary classical theatre are also participants in the culture of television, where we have all learned to process a "flow" of multiple and seemingly incongruous images. It does not seem that far a leap to expect that same audience, when in a theatre, to have little trouble coping when Don Giovanni sings a Mozart aria in Italian while chomping on a Big Mac – or when Harpagon's matchmaker wears a miniskirt and fishnet stockings while parading through a neoclassical mansion, or Oedipus describes his surroundings as "fair Colonus" while standing at a pulpit in preacher's robes. This comparison is not meant to equate revisionist classical production with typical television fare, but rather to point out that they are both manifestations of a particular historical sensibility.

Simultaneity, contradiction, and a nonlinear sense of history are, in various guises, at the core of many cultural critics' attempts to define postmodernism. They are surely implicated in Fredric Jameson's contention that the postmodern era is characterized by a "schizophrenic" relationship to time and history that leaves us "condemned to live a perpetual present with which the various moments of [our] past have little connection and for which there is no conceivable future on the horizon."[5] We have easy access through computer, audio, and video technologies to bits and pieces of the past, words, images, and sounds that can be recalled at the touch of a button and made to seem contiguous in any arrangement. The facile presentation of far-flung anachronisms, especially in the work of Akalaitis, Pintilié, Breuer, and Sellars, can be seen to embody this condition. Our sense of place in history, as reflected in these productions, is, in Jameson's words, "isolated, disconnected, discontinuous." We seem to float in an ever-present limbo, vivid, fluid, but ultimately rootless, and are unable to imagine a relationship to our own history. We celebrate the ingenuity, novelty, and vision it takes to uproot classic dramas from their temporal trappings and transplant them in a mottled contemporary soil. Need we also mourn a mind-set so obsessed by the present that it can neither fathom, seek inspiration, nor find solace in enduring images from the past?

Jameson also points out that postmodern art recalls and recycles historical styles without any sense of attachment or relationship to them. They are choices on the postmodern palette, available to be used, mixed, and juxtaposed at will. This blank quotation Jameson calls "pastiche,"[6] and it, too, is evident in many of the works cited in this study: *Lear*'s Georgia, the props in Pintilié's *Tartuffe,* and the bathroom-door markers in Sellars's *Così* are examples. Todd Gitlin also includes pastiche in his description of the postmodern and adds to it a list of other characteristics that can be helpful in determining just how far out on the postmodern limb each of the classical reinventions sit. After pastiche, Gitlin mentions "blankness; a sense of exhaustion; a mixture of levels, forms, styles; a relish for copies and repetition; a knowingness that dissolves commitment into irony; acute self-consciousness about the formal, constructed nature of the work; pleasure in the play of surfaces; a rejection of history."[7] Some of the items on his list are easily recognizable features of the productions with which I have been concerned, but others suggest that the individual works occupy different positions on a wide critical continuum.

Gitlin defines postmodernism by distinguishing it from its immediate predecessors: realism, which he calls the "premodern," and modernism itself. His analysis cuts to the core of the central critical problem posed by directorial rewrightings; namely, the question of coherence. As Sellars reminds us, the classical concept of coherence, as reported by Aristotle, was that "one-thing-happens-at-a-time" thing. The neoclassicists revived that notion after the medieval and Elizabethan worlds had established other, noisier models that incorporated anachronism, double plotting, and episodic structure. The exuberant Romantics reversed the neoclassical ideal and were themselves overturned by the realists toward the end of the nineteenth century. Today, the modernist "isms" having shattered realism's smooth surface, the question of coherence is again a matter of considerable critical angst. The persistent gnashing of teeth over the "incoherence" of classical rewrightings belongs within that larger aesthetic debate.

That many directorial essays on classic plays echo the cacophony of contemporary life and capitalize on our practiced ability to absorb multiple, simultaneous stimuli partly explains the lack of strict surface unity in these productions. Gitlin's three categories trace the hundred-year devolution of aesthetic unity that provides the backdrop for these works. The premodern (realistic) work of art, Gitlin writes, "aspires to a unity of vision. It cherishes continuity, speaking with a single narrative voice or addressing a single visual center. It honors sequence and causality in time or space." Its momentum is "consecutive" and "linear"; its intentions are elevated; it exists in the stratosphere of "high culture."[8] These seemingly seamless works, reminiscent of classical models, play out a pretense of organic synthesis as they strive to present universal truths and reflect a constant, natural order.

The modernist work, Gitlin contrasts, "still aspires to unity, but this unity, . . . has been . . . constructed, assembled from fragments, or shocks, or juxtapositions of difference." As on a Picasso canvas, multiple "perspectives" and "materials" are brought to bear, but they are ultimately reconciled into a heavily textured unified composition. Serban's *Fragments,* it seems to me, falls within this category, as do Schechner's two classical forays: All three of these attempted, with varying degrees of success, to conjure uniquely theatrical milieus out of old and new stylistic elements. Likewise Garland Wright's productions of Molière, smooth on the surface, contradictory just below, are the pointed, well-kneaded products of a focused and precise directorial hand.

Arriving at the latest phase of cultural evolution, Gitlin announces that

In the postmodern sensibility, the search for unity has apparently been abandoned altogether. Instead we have textuality, a cultivation of surfaces endlessly referring to, ricocheting from, reverberating onto other surfaces. The work calls attention to its arbitrariness, constructedness; it interrupts itself. . . . Everything takes place in the present, "here," that is, nowhere in particular. . . . The work labors under no illusions: we are all deliberately playing, pretending here – get the point?[9]

In postmodern performance, as in postmodern art, the constructed nature of the work is fully exposed, no sleight of hand being applied to conceal its pieced-together component parts: thus the patchwork of *The Gospel at Colonus,* Akalaitis's *Cymbeline,* and the blatantly artificial realisms of Breuer's *Lear* and Sellars's Mozart–da Ponte trilogy. Where previous forms of coherence synthesized, consolidated, and reconciled tensions and oppositions, any predigested unity now seems contrived.

I recently came across the following excerpt from Plutarch, in which he extols the virtues of Menander's unity of effect over the troublesome inconsistencies in Aristophanes' style:

> In [Aristophanes'] diction there are tragic, comic, pompous, and prosaic elements, obscurity, vagueness, dignity, and elevation, loquacity and sickening nonsense . . . but Menander's diction is so polished and its ingredients mingled into so consistent a whole that, although it is employed in connection with many emotions and many types of character and adapts itself to persons of every kind, it nevertheless appears as one and preserves its uniformity in common and familiar words in general use.[10]

I prefer, with the postmodernists, to hedge my bets with Aristophanes.

On another front, Natalie Crohn-Schmidt has demonstrated a kinship between postmodern performance and contemporary scientific thought. Just as deconstruction asks us to challenge the closure and completeness of texts, physicists no longer believe in objective physical reality. Since Niels Bohr, Crohn-Schmidt reminds us, the prevailing belief is that "'there is no quantum world, only an abstract physical description.'"[11] Unified theory posits that human knowledge of the physical world is limited to our powers of observation, that the act of observing constitutes reality, and that phenomena themselves are changed in the act of observation. The only thing directors can stage, then, are the results of their encounters with dramatic texts from the past. What makes these productions uniquely postmodern is the fact that the text and the manifestations of the director's encounter cohabit the performance without necessarily fusing or being reconciled to one another. Yet my satisfying encounters with so many of these productions convinces me that they amount to something more than jumbles or junk piles of scattered ideas and images. The current challenge is to articulate a new model of coherence, a coherence of tensions, oppositions, and flux.

Gitlin is onto something when he sees the elements of postmodern works of art "ricocheting" and "reverberating" off one another. The image that comes to mind, again from science, is of subatomic particles: separate, charged, energized, each retaining its own form and structure while participating in the active process that constitutes the atom. Perhaps it is possible to see the new coherence as a kind of electromagnetic field. The physical and temporal elements of the production, once metaphorically described as the limbs growing out of a spine or tree trunk, may now be compared to those semiautonomous bits of matter that orbit around the nucleus, which is itself comprised of distinct and contradictory particles. If the nucleus is the play-text, then the force that keeps the attracting and repulsing parts in orbit is the director's encounter. The performance coheres through the dynamic of attraction and repulsion among the various particles in the complex play of their intertextuality.

Jameson and Gitlin interpret postmodernism's "cultural recombination" as an exhausted response to the rapid pace of stylistic turnover in the past hundred years and a capitalist culture that values "packaging" over "beauty."[12] The furious, frenetic cramming together of seemingly contradictory elements within postmodern works of art may in fact be symptoms of a millennial anxiety that is part ennui, part race to the finish line; but I cannot agree that lack of "passion," "blankness," "a collapse of feeling" are at the heart of the postmodern reconstitutions of classic plays examined in this study. I hope that my discussions of individual productions have conveyed the palpable sense of seriousness, commitment, and energy that went into their creation and presentation to the public. The ecstasy of Breuer's *Gospel,* the depth of Sellars's trilogy, and the twinkling wink of the Karamazov's *The Comedy of Errors* refute such a supposition.

It is true that a retrospective view of the lot suggests that a certain stylistic and methodological sameness may ultimately signal the end of rewrighting as a means of advancing the theatrical agenda. Its spreading popularity, as evidenced by the likes of Mark Morris's *The Hard Nut,* a 1960s retrofantasy ballet based on Tchaikovsky's *Nutcracker,* suggests that, like any avant-garde approach, it will eventually run its course. At this writing, rumor has it that Peter Sellars is planning to direct a straight, traditional staging of *The Merchant of Venice* sometime in 1994. How else can a renegade artist buck the tide of convention when, for the last decade, prominent classical reinventions were underwritten by such corporate conglomerates as Pepsico, AT&T, and Philip Morris? Are not the politics of opposition diffused once an artistic movement has been embraced, if not co-opted, into the mainstream?

The text-based and director-driven nature of these productions also reveals that they are neither politically nor aesthetically as radical as the critical hoopla surrounding them may have implied. Other contemporary models of production, such as the Wooster Group's appropriations of scripts by Wilder, Miller, and Chekhov, are far more aggressive about deconstructing, displaying, and embedding familiar texts within their performance pieces. The classical reinventions I have looked at are timid by comparison in their wholesale adaptation of text. In terms of the politics of deconstruction, classical rewrighting falls short because the "playwright-god" is displaced in the rehearsal studio by the "director-guru";[13] the collaborative work evolves within a hierarchy headed by an individual authority figure. Jonathan Kalb has denounced "the entire avant-garde enterprise of depriviledging the dramatic text" as "nothing more than a coup d'etat of directors looking to systematize their already considerable dominance in theatrical production."[14] His dismissal is too flip in this context. Too many rich examples support my contention that the exercise of directorial muscle in adapting and reimagining texts has resulted in a revitalized classical theatre that speaks eloquently, if sometimes offhandedly, to a new audience.

The composition of that audience is still another important consideration in a final appraisal of postmodern classical reinventions. Welles in the 1930s and Houseman and Papp a couple of decades later all initiated projects intended to showcase minority talent and draw what would now be called a multicultural audience. They innovated by infusing their classical productions with forms taken from popular and folk culture while others were still prancing around the stage imitating British accents. The prevailing classical norms were remnants, leftovers from the cultural elitism that historian Lawrence Levine explicates in *Highbrow/Lowbrow: The Emergence of Cultural Hierarchy in America.*

Using Shakespeare as his major case study, Levine traces what he calls the "bifurcation" of American culture over the course of the nineteenth century. At the beginning of the century, Shakespeare was played in American theatres to a polyglot clientele of poor, middle-class, and wealthy patrons. Audiences were mostly white, although Levine presents evidence that a sizable "Negro" population attended as well. In other words, the mixture of English, Irish, German, and African-American attendees could be considered culturally pluralistic for its time. The Shakespeare they saw was tailored to the talents of specific leading players; it often featured elaborate, moving scenery, and played to the melodramatic tastes of a young and idealistic populace. Musical numbers were interpolated and farcical afterpieces tacked on to please the crowd. "Shakespeare *was* popular entertainment in 19th-century America," asserts Levine, "a kaleidoscopic, democratic institution presenting a widely varying bill of fare to all classes and socioeconomic groups."[15]

179

Levine goes on to demonstrate how, over the course of the century, assorted social, economic, and political pressures forced a breach in a hitherto heterogeneous American culture. Shakespeare became the province of the wealthy, who seized and retreated with him from the tide of freed slaves and unwashed immigrants that flooded America's cities. Shakespeare took up residence in the bastions of high cult. His plays became "the possession of the educated portions of society who disseminated them for the enlightenment of the the average folk, who were to swallow him not for their entertainment, but for their education."[16] Little wonder it has taken so long for classical theatre to reach beyond the coterie.

Fortunately, Levine reports, "we have in recent decades begun to move gradually but decisively away from the rigid, class-bound definitions of culture forged at the close of the 19th century."[17] The reimagined classics covered here are, I believe, manifestations of that hopeful trend, incorporating, as they do, fusions of high and popular culture and multicultural casts. They assert that gospel, convertibles, TV, and the suburban diner are valid idioms for classical production, and so imply that the folks whose lives are concerned with these things are welcome to join in. Even if JoAnne Akalaitis's utopian colorblind casting policy is more an idealization than a reflection of the racial tensions played out daily on America's streets, the inclusiveness of contemporary classical casting bodes well.

It would be naive, however, to conclude that these productions have in fact brought large numbers of otherwise alienated audience members into the classical theatre. That wide-reaching, truly diverse audience is still more wish than reality. To some extent, appreciation of classical rewrightings presumes prior familiarity with the text and its performance tradition. Thus, while some portion of the audiences for reinterpreted classics might not otherwise be interested in Shakespeare, or Molière, or the opera, it is more likely that many of those who attend these performances are already among the cognoscenti.

So, what implications does all this have for the future of directing and of classical theatre in this country? It is getting harder and harder to find a "straight" production of a classic play, except in the movies. Directorial reinvention has become its own tradition and will, inevitably, form the backdrop to a new rebellion. If the revival of classical texts has been one of the movement's achievements, the speaking and acting of those texts has often been neglected in favor of directorial concept. Because theatre is, ultimately, about human beings acting, feeling, and speaking, it seems inevitable that a renewed emphasis on language will exert itself in future classical experiments. The enormous response to the American tour of Ariane Mnouchkine's Asian-influenced *Les Atrides* in 1992 augurs a simpler, less technologically oriented approach, one that settles in for more protracted focus on the actor and thorough explorations of other models and modes of performance.

On the other hand, the What You Will Theatre Company in London is now performing Shakespeare's plays without benefit of any director at all: They hand out sides and perform after a minimum of technical rehearsal. In Paris, Peter Brook says he's given up on classical theatre for the time being. After his 1990 *The Tempest*, he announced that he had reached "the absolute saturation point with the classics and with classic imagery."[18]

It is impossible to know just what will happen to the classical house Sellars says his and his colleagues' work inhabits. I hope it will keep its windows open to fresh currents and its doors to more new house guests. Its director-hosts will probably be forced to relinquish some degree of control over its destiny, as have its playwright-ghosts. History has shown us that the only constant in life and art is change. The new tenants will probably include more women and people of diverse ethnic and cultural backgrounds who, following this phase, should feel welcome to bring their own concerns, questions, and sensibilities into the house and so transform it again and again. They will inherit a legacy of imaginative classical reinvention from a generation of American directors who will have ushered the classics, alive and kicking, into the twenty-first century.

NOTES

■ ◉ ■

1. REINVENTING CLASSIC THEATRE

1 Ezra Pound, quoted by Rolf Fjelde in the introduction to his translation of Ibsen's *Peer Gynt,* p. iii.

2 Charles Marowitz, *Prospero's Staff: Acting and Directing in the Contemporary Theatre,* p. 33.

3 Peter Sellars, quoted in Arthur Bartow, *The Director's Voice,* p. 279.

4 Jonathan Miller, *Subsequent Performances,* p. 57.

5 Tyrone Guthrie, *A New Theatre,* pp. 103–4.

6 Tyrone Guthrie, in Toby Cole and Helen Krich Chinoy, eds., *Directors on Directing,* p. 246.

7 Tyrone Guthrie, "Directing a Play," in J. Robert Wills, ed., *The Director in a Changing Theatre,* p. 96.

8 Pintilié quoted in Mike Steele, "The Romanian Connection," p. 11.

9 Jonathan Miller, quoted in Richard Gilman, "Directors vs. Playwrights," p. 33.

10 Jonathan Miller, in Ralph Berry, *On Directing Shakespeare,* p. 57.

11 Garland Wright, interview by Mark Bly, *Theater* 15 (Spring 1984): 69.

12 Andrei Serban, interview by the author, March 15, 1989.

13 Tyrone Guthrie, *In Various Directions* (reprint), p. 177.

14 Herbert Blau, *Blooded Thought: Occasions of Theatre,* p. 30.

15 Eric Bentley, "Maiming the Bard," in *The Dramatic Event: An American Chronicle,* pp. 34–5.

16 Stanley Kauffmann, *Persons of the Drama,* p. 131.

17 Gordon Rogoff, "Liviu Ciulei: Murder by Concept," review of *Hamlet* directed by Liviu Ciulei, in *Theatre Is Not Safe,* p. 153.

18 Moira Hodgson, review of *Cosí fan Tutte,* p. 153.

183

19 Allan Wallach, review of *Don Juan,* p. 35.

20 Gilman, "Directors vs. Playwrights," p. 35.

21 Jacques Copeau, "Dramatic Economy," in Cole and Chinoy, eds., *Directors on Directing*, p. 225. The full sentence reads: "Let us hope for a dramatist who replaces or eliminates the director, and personally takes over the directing; rather than for professional directors who pretend to be dramatists."

22 Louis Jouvet, "The Profession of the Director," in Cole and Chinoy, eds., *Directors on Directing*, p. 231. The full sentence reads: "The profession of the director suffers from the disease of immodesty, and even the most sincere do not escape it."

23 Gilman, "Directors vs. Playwrights," p. 34.

24 Ibid., p. 35.

25 Stratos E. Constantinidis, *Theatre Under Deconstruction?: A Question of Approach*, p. 14.

26 Ibid., p. 24.

27 Francis Hodge, "The Director as Critic," p. 284.

28 In fact, design is essential to classical reinventions. Because my primary interest is in the work of directors, however, the all-important contributions of designers are regrettably neglected here. Dennis Kennedy's *Looking at Shakespeare* (Cambridge, England: Cambridge University Press, 1993) is a welcome addition to the overlooked field of contemporary classical design for the stage.

29 Berry, *On Directing Shakespeare*, p. 17.

30 Ibid., p. 22.

31 Robert Brustein, review of *Uncle Vanya* directed by Andrei Serban, *New Republic*, October 24, 1983, p. 34.

32 Gerald Rabkin, "The Play of Misreading: Theatre/Text/Deconstruction," p. 56.

33 Ibid., p. 58.

34 Ibid., pp. 51–2.

35 Blau, *Blooded Thought*, p. 28.

36 Charles Marowitz, *The Marowitz Shakespeare*, p. 11.

37 Robert Brustein, "No More Masterpieces," in *The Third Theatre*, pp. 21–2.

38 Ibid., p. 33.

39 Charles Marowitz, *Prospero's Staff: Acting and Directing in the Contemporary Theatre*, p. 37.

40 Robert Brustein, "Reworking the Classics: Homage or Ego Trip?" pp. H5, H16.

41 Ibid., p. H5.

42 Marowitz, *Marowitz Shakespeare*, p. 24.

43 Jan Kott, "I Can't Get No Satisfaction," pp. 145–6.

44 Miller, *Subsequent Performances*, p. 49.

45 Ibid., p. 35.

46 Ibid., p. 37.
47 Rabkin, "Play of Misreading," p. 59.
48 Ibid., pp. 59–60.
49 Michael Vanden Heuvel, *Performing Drama/Dramatizing Performance: Alternative Theater and the Dramatic Text*, p. 7. The Carlson citation refers to Marvin Carlson, "Theatrical Performance: Illustration, Translation, Fulfillment, or Supplement?"
50 Brustein, "America and the Classics," p. 35.

2. HISTORICAL PRECEDENTS IN EUROPE AND AMERICA

1 Anton Chekhov, *The Seagull*, in *Chekhov: The Major Plays*, translated by Ann Dunnigan (New York & Toronto: Signet Classics, 1964), p. 109.
2 Gordon Craig, in Toby Cole and Helen Krich Chinoy, eds., *Directors on Directing*, p. 149.
3 Jonathan Miller, *Subsequent Performances*, p. 57.
4 Ibid., p. 58.
5 Ibid., p. 57.
6 Dennis Kennedy, *Granville Barker and the Dream of Theatre*, p. 42. This is a valuable source for thorough reconstructions and production histories of both the Euripides and Shakespeare plays.
7 Ibid., p. 123.
8 Ibid.
9 Martin Esslin, "Max Reinhardt: High Priest of Theatricality," p. 15.
10 Max Reinhardt, "Regiebuch for *The Miracle*," in Cole and Chinoy, eds., *Directors on Directing*, pp. 296–7.
11 Reinhardt quoted in Edward Braun, *The Director and the Stage: From Naturalism to Grotowski*, p. 97.
12 Robert Edmond Jones, *The Dramatic Imagination*, p. 73.
13 Alexander Woollcott, review of *Macbeth* directed by Arthur Hopkins, reprinted in Bernard Beckerman and Howard Siegman, eds., *On Stage: Reviews from The New York Times, 1920–1970* , p. 19.
14 Ibid.
15 Arthur Hopkins, "Capturing the Audience," in Cole and Chinoy, eds., *Directors on Directing*, p. 207.
16 Ibid., p. 213.
17 Meyerhold quoted in Braun, *Director and the Stage*, p. 138.
18 Vsevelod Meyerhold, *Meyerhold on Theatre*, Edward Braun, ed., pp. 169–70.
19 Marjorie Hoover, *Meyerhold: The Art of Conscious Theatre*, p. 110.
20 Paul Schmidt, ed., Introduction to *Meyerhold at Work*, p. xvi.

21 Richard Gilman, "Directors vs. Playwrights," p. 34.

22 Gordon Rogoff, "The Meyerhold Train," review of Schmidt, ed., *Meyerhold at Work*, in *Theatre Is Not Safe*, p. 195.

23 Bertolt Brecht, quoted in Braun, *Director and the Stage*, p. 163.

24 Bertolt Brecht, "Theatre for Learning," p. 24.

25 Ibid., p. 23.

26 Werner Hecht, "The Development of Brecht's Theory of the Epic Theatre, 1918–1933," p. 81.

27 Antonin Artaud, "No More Masterpieces," in *Theater and Its Double*, p. 74.

28 Ibid., pp. 75, 76.

29 Ibid., p. 78.

30 Artaud, "The Theatre of Cruelty (First Manifesto)," in *Theater and Its Double*, p. 89.

31 Ibid., p. 94.

32 Artaud, "The Theatre of Cruelty (Second Manifesto)," in *Theater and Its Double*, p. 124.

33 Jerzy Grotowski, interview by Richard Schechner, p. 31.

34 Ibid., p. 34.

35 Ibid., p. 44.

36 Ibid., p. 42.

37 Christopher Innes, *Holy Theatre: Ritual and the Avant-Garde*, p. 165.

38 Grotowski, interview by Schechner, p. 44.

39 Miller, *Subsequent Performances*, p. 60.

40 Peter Brook, *The Empty Space*, p. 99.

41 Ibid., p. 103.

42 Peter Brook, *The Shifting Point*, p. 6.

43 Ibid., p. 3.

44 Ibid., p. 4.

45 Ibid.

46 Ibid., p. 5.

47 See, for example: Roberta Cooper, *The American Shakespeare Theatre: Stratford, 1955–1985*; Hallie Flanagan, *Arena: The History of the Federal Theatre*; Richard France, *The Theatre of Orson Welles*; Tyrone Guthrie, *A New Theatre* and *In Various Directions*; Errol Hill, *Shakespeare in Sable*; John Houseman, *Final Dress* and *Run Through*; Stuart Little, *Enter Joseph Papp: In Search of a New American Theatre*; John O'Connor and Lorraine Brown, *The Federal Theatre Project: Free, Adult, Uncensored*; and books of collected reviews by Eric Bentley, Robert Brustein, Richard Gilman, Stanley Kauffmann, Gordon Rogoff, and John Simon.

48 Brooks Atkinson, review of *The Taming of the Shrew* directed by A. K. Ayliff, reprinted in Beckerman and Siegman, eds., *On Stage*, p. 83.

49 W. O. Trapp, quoted in Alice Margarida, "Two *Shrews*: Productions by Lunt/Fontanne (1935) and A. K. Ayliff (1927)," p. 94.

50 Orville Larson's *Scene Design in the American Theatre from 1915 to 1960* (Fay-etteville: University of Arkansas Press, 1989) provides a thorough overview of their work.

51 Kenneth Macgowan, *The Theatre of Tomorrow,* p. 62.

52 Lee Simonson, *The Stage Is Set,* p. 99.

53 Paul M. Bailey, "Norman Bel Geddes' *Hamlet,*" p. 53.

54 Note the fate of *The Gospel at Colonus,* almost universally admired in the press until its brief Broadway run. See Chapter 3.

55 For a complete description, including the complete text, see France, *Orson Welles on Shakespeare.*

56 Houseman's anecdotal backstage account of this remarkable production in *Run Through* (pp. 190–8) is amusing.

57 Brooks Atkinson, quoted in O'Connor and Brown, *Federal Theatre Project,* p. 8.

58 Lewis Nichols, review reprinted in Beckerman and Siegman, eds., *On Stage,* p. 254.

59 See Hill, *Shakespeare in Sable,* for a more thorough inventory.

60 Joshua Logan, *Josh: My Upside Down, In and Out Life* (New York: Delacorte Press, 1976), p. 318.

61 George Bogusch, review of *A Midsummer Night's Dream* directed by Tyrone Guthrie, *Educational Theatre Journal* 24 (December 1972): 449.

62 Harold Clurman, quoted in Ervin Beck, "Tamburlaine for the Modern Stage," p. 72.

63 Ibid., p. 73.

64 Eric Bentley, "A Director's Theatre," in *The Dramatic Event,* p. 271.

65 Richard Gilman, *Common and Uncommon Masks: Writings on the Theatre, 1961–1971,* p. 274.

66 Walter Kerr, review of *Hamlet* directed by Tyrone Guthrie, p. 17.

67 Ibid.

68 John Gassner, "Broadway in Review" (1955).

69 Houseman, *Final Dress,* p. 28.

70 Ibid., p. 67.

71 John Gassner, review of *Much Ado About Nothing,* p. 216.

72 Ibid., p. 217.

73 Ibid.

74 John Gassner, "Broadway in Review" (1958), p. 240.

75 Houseman, *Final Dress,* p. 166.

76 Glenn Loney, review of *The Taming of the Shrew,* p. 264.

77 Michael Kahn, quoted in Ralph Berry, *On Directing Shakespeare,* p. 21.

78 Michael Kahn, quoted in Cooper, *American Shakespeare Theatre,* p. 172.

79 Michael Kahn, quoted in Berry, *On Directing Shakespeare,* p. 81.

80 Stanley Kauffmann, *Persons of the Drama,* p. 6.

81 Joseph Papp, *Theatre Arts* interview, reprinted in Cole and Chinoy, eds., *Directors on Directing,* p. 432.

82 Joseph Papp, quoted in Hill, *Shakespeare in Sable*, p. 145.
83 Robert Brustein, *Seasons of Discontent: Dramatic Opinions, 1959–6*, p. 226.
84 Ibid.
85 Kauffmann, *Persons of the Drama*, p. 10.
86 A. J. Antoon, quoted in Mervyn Rothstein, "Taking Shakespeare's Shrew to the Old West of the Late 1800s," p. C13.

3. GREEK AND ROMAN PLAYS

1 Antonin Artaud, "The Theatre of Cruelty (First Manifesto)," in *Theatre and Its Double*, p. 99.
2 Marianne McDonald, *Ancient Sun, Modern Light: Greek Drama on the Modern Stage*, p. 6.
3 John Fuegi, *Bertolt Brecht: Chaos According to Plan*, pp. 101–2.
4 Bertolt Brecht, quoted in Werner Hecht, "The Development of Brecht's Theory of Epic Theatre, 1918–1933," p. 77.
5 Gordon Rogoff, *Theatre Is Not Safe*, p. 124.
6 Margaret Croyden, *Lunatics, Lovers, and Poets*, p. 113.
7 Richard Schechner, review of *The House of Atreus*, p. 101.
8 Jonathan Miller, quoted in Jonathan Price, "Jonathan Miller Directs Robert Lowell's *Prometheus*," p. 40.
9 Ibid., p. 43.
10 Jonathan Miller, quoted in Robert Brustein, "No More Masterpieces," in *The Third Theatre*, p. 31.
11 The Performance Group, *Dionysus in '69*, Richard Schechner, ed., n.p.
12 Richard Schechner, interview by the author, November 22, 1993.
13 Julius Novick, review of *Dionysus in '69*, p. 29.
14 Rustom Bharucha, "Directing the Greeks," p. 66.
15 See Mike Steele, "The Romanian Connection," pp. 4–11.
16 Stanley Kauffmann, *Persons of the Drama*, p. 111.
17 Artaud, "First Manifesto," p. 90.
18 Andrei Serban, interview by Eileen Blumenthal, p. 68.
19 Andrei Serban, "The Life in a Sound," pp. 25–6.
20 Andrei Serban, interview re Artaud, p. 28.
21 Elizabeth Swados, interview for TV documentary on Ellen Stewart, broadcast over WNYC-TV, September 21, 1990.
22 Serban, interview by Blumenthal, p. 68.
23 Steele, "The Romanian Connection," p. 11.
24 Serban, interview re Artaud, p. 26.
25 Jan Kott, "Where are *Ajax* and *Philoctetes* Now That We Need Them?" p. 18.
26 Serban, interview by Blumenthal, p. 76.
27 Kauffmann, *Persons of the Drama*, p. 110.

28 Elizabeth Swados, quoted in Margaret Croyden, "Seeking the Emotions That Stirred the Ancient Greeks," p. H1.
29 Andrei Serban, quoted in ibid.
30 Clive Barnes, review of *Agamemnon*, p. C20.
31 Schechner, interview by the author, November 22, 1993.
32 Martin Esslin, review of *Oedipus*, p. 22.
33 Colin Blakely, "Exploration of the Ugly: Brook's Work on *Oedipus*," p. 121.
34 Ibid., p. 122.
35 Esslin, review of *Oedipus*, p. 23.
36 Schechner, interview by the author, November 22, 1993. Subsequent unattributed quotes also derive from this conversation.
37 Arnold Aronson, "A Space for *Oedipus*," p. 28.
38 Rabkin, review of *Oedipus*.
39 Richard Eder, review of *Oedipus*, p. III: 19.
40 Clive Barnes, review of *Oedipus*, p. 59.
41 Lee Breuer, "On *The Gospel at Colonus*," p. 50.
42 Lee Breuer, quoted in William Harris, "Mabou Mines Sets *Lear* on a Hot Tin Roof," p. H5.
43 Ibid., p. H33.
44 Breuer told Gerald Rabkin ("On *The Gospel at Colonus*," p. 49) that *The Gospel* would be his last in a "tripartite scheme" to find "a way into an American classicism," but *Lear*, set in the Deep South in the 1950s, with Ruth Malecczech as matriarch, is clearly a continuation of that search. See Chapter 4.
45 Robert Brustein, review of *The Tempest*, p. 23.
46 Shelley Berc, "Lee Breuer's *Lulu*," p. 70.
47 Breuer, "On *The Gospel at Colonus*," p. 48.
48 Ibid.
49 Ibid.
50 Ibid., p. 49.
51 Alan Rich, "Oedipus Jones," p. 105.
52 Sophocles, *Oedipus Rex*, translated by William Butler Yeats, in Dudley Fitts, ed., *Greek Plays in Modern Translation* (New York: Dial Press, 1947), p. 380.
53 Ibid., p. 382.
54 Sophocles, *Antigone*, translated by Dudley Fitts and Robert Fitzgerald, in ibid., pp. 469–70.
55 Michael Feingold, "Gospel Truth," p. 109.
56 Elinor Fuchs, "Is There Life After Irony?" p. 77.
57 Frank Rich, review of *The Gospel at Colonus*, p. III: 5.
58 Linda Winer, "Gospel That's a Long Way from Home," *New York Newsday*, p. III/11. The hostility of the later critics may be explained by more conservative tastes, but it is also possible that their response had more to do with a recent flood of conceptual classics, which were becoming tedious, rather than

with any loss of inherent value in *The Gospel at Colonus* since its premiere five years earlier. Good theatrical ideas dissipate in a can-you-top-this environment. Another factor might have been the way *The Gospel* was marketed on Broadway. No longer a Next Wave, avant-garde experiment, but a risky commercial venture, the show was touted in television ads as another black musical along the lines of *Dream Girls*. Theatre parties were bussed in from Harlem, and the original spirit of the piece was distorted.

59 Gerald Rabkin, "Lee Breuer and His Double," *Next Wave Festival Souvenir Program* (Brooklyn Academy of Music, 1983), p. 10.
60 Charles Marowitz, *Prospero's Staff: Acting and Directing in the Contemporary Theatre*, p. 115.
61 Richard Corliss, review of *The Gospel at Colonus*, p. 90.
62 "*PAJ* Casebook: Robert Wilson's *Alcestis*," pp. 86–7.
63 Robert Wilson, quoted in David J. Derose, review of *Alcestis*, p. 90.
64 Richard Beacham, "John Barton Directs *The Greeks*," p. 37.

4. THE PLAYS OF SHAKESPEARE

1 Charles Marowitz, *Recycling Shakespeare*, pp. 118–19. These "misconceptions" are actually numbers 4 and 5. The complete, amusing list reads: "(1) Shakespearian production is no different from any other kind of theatre. (2) Shakespeare is entirely different from any other kind of theatre. (3) Only the British can properly perform the works of Shakespeare. (4) The only way to approach Shakespeare is to contemporise him. (5) The only correct way to stage Shakespeare is to adopt the traditional approach. (6) The way to show our appreciation for Shakespeare is to stage him as often as possible. (7) Shakespeare will never die."
2 Ibid., p. 118.
3 Ibid., p. 119.
4 Ibid., p. 120.
5 Jan Kott, "I Can't Get No Satisfaction," pp. 145–6.
6 Susan Sontag, *Against Interpretation*, p. 7.
7 Ibid., p. 13.
8 Ibid., p. 6.
9 Joseph Papp, interview by the author, May 4, 1989.
10 Joseph Papp with Ted Cornell, *William Shakespeare's "Naked" Hamlet*, pp. 20–1.
11 Charles Marowitz, introduction to *The Marowitz Shakespeare*, p. 11.
12 Ibid., p. 13.
13 Ibid., p. 14.
14 Jan Kott, "Hamlet of the Mid-century," in *Shakespeare Our Contemporary*, p. 58.
15 Papp and Cornell, *William Shakespeare's "Naked" Hamlet*, p. 29.

16 Joseph Papp, program notes to *Hamlet* (New York: The Public Theatre, 1967–8).

17 Papp and Cornell, p. 19.

18 Kott, p. 64.

19 Ibid., p. 67.

20 Papp and Cornell, *William Shakespeare's "Naked" Hamlet*, pp. 25–6.

21 Ibid., p. 26.

22 Kott, "Hamlet of the Mid-Century," p. 64.

23 Michael Smith, review of *Hamlet*, p. 29.

24 Peter Sellars updated the self-conscious recording of a stage ceremony in the wedding scene of *Figaro*. See Chapter 6.

25 Clive Barnes, "Slings and Arrows of Outrageous Papp," p. 45.

26 Martin Gottfried, review of *Hamlet*, p. 21.

27 Papp and Cornell, *William Shakespeare's "Naked" Hamlet*, p. 10.

28 Ibid., pp. 12, 13.

29 Richard Schechner, Letter to the Editor, *New York Times*, January 28, 1969, p. 9.

30 Ibid., p. 24.

31 Robert Brustein, review of *Hamlet*, p. 47.

32 Papp and Cornell, *William Shakespeare's "Naked" Hamlet*, p. 26.

33 Ibid., p. 27.

34 Schechner, Letter to the Editor, p. 24.

35 Albert Bermel, "Hamlet in Modern Undress," p. 26.

36 Kott, "Hamlet of the Mid-Century," p. 59.

37 Schechner, Letter to the Editor, p. 9.

38 Brustein, review of *Hamlet*, p. 47.

39 Smith, review of *Hamlet*, pp. 29, 31.

40 Bermel, "Hamlet in Modern Undress," p. 26.

41 Sam Zolotow, "School Aids Object to Papp's Mod *Hamlet*," p. 33.

42 Ibid.

43 Richard Severo, "Papp Gives *Hamlet* to Catch Conscience of School Board," p. 43. The depth and sincerity of Papp's intractable resistance to censorship again became evident in his battles in the early 1990s over restrictions on grants from the National Endowment for the Arts.

44 Vincent Canby, review of touring production of *Hamlet*, p. 15.

45 Gregory Mosher, interview by the author, April 30, 1990. Further unattributed quotes also derive from this interview.

46 Robert Woodruff, interview by Arthur Bartow, in *The Director's Voice*, p. 314.

47 *The Comedy of Errors* was slightly altered when it was revived at the 1984 Olympic Arts Festival in Los Angeles and again at the Lincoln Center Theatre in New York in 1987. I saw the Lincoln Center version.

48 Woodruff in Bartow, *Director's Voice*, p. 319.

49 Ibid.

50 Margaret Webster, *Shakespeare Today*, 1957; quoted in Stanley Wells's intro-
    duction to the Penguin edition of *The Comedy of Errors*, p. 7.

51 Michael Feingold, review of *The Comedy of Errors*, p. 93.

52 Joel Fink, review of *Comedy of Errors*, pp. 415–16.

53 Mel Gussow, review of *Comedy of Errors*, p. III: 11.

54 Fink, review of *Comedy of Errors*, p. 415.

55 Woodruff in Bartow, *Director's Voice*, p. 313.

56 John Simon, review of *The Comedy of Errors*, p. 91.

57 Gussow, review of *Comedy of Errors*, p. III: 11.

58 Edith Oliver, review of *The Comedy of Errors*, p. 72.

59 Gregory Mosher, interview by Arthur Bartow, in *The Director's Voice*, p.
    233.

60 Mosher, interview by the author, April 30, 1990.

61 Samuel Beckett, insert to American Repertory Theatre playbill for *Endgame*,
    1984–5.

62 Robert Brustein, rebuttal in ibid.

63 JoAnne Akalaitis, interview by the author, January 3, 1990. Subsequent unat-
    tributed quotes also derive from this interview.

64 Quoted in Colette Brooks, "'The folly of the fiction': *Cymbeline* Reconsid-
    ered," unpublished MS, p. 1.

65 Harley Granville-Barker, *Prefaces to Shakespeare: Volume 2*, p. 84.

66 Brooks, "'The folly of the fiction'," p. 3.

67 Before Tsypin's designs for *Cymbeline*, movable scenery was a rarity in the
    American nonmusical theatre. It has since made a comeback in productions of
    new plays with cinematic structures, such as Richard Greenberg's *The Extra
    Man* (Manhattan Theatre Club, 1992, set design by Loy Arcenas), Larry Kra-
    mer's *The Destiny of Me* (Lucille Lortel Theatre, 1993, set design by John Lee
    Beatty), and Tony Kushner's *Angels in America* (Walter Kerr Theatre, 1993,
    set design by Robin Wagner).

68 There is no need to reiterate their summaries here. Interested readers are en-
    couraged to consult Elinor Fuchs, "*Cymbeline* and Its Critics: Misunderstand-
    ing Postmodernism," pp. 24–31, and James Leverett, "*Cymbeline* and Its Crit-
    ics: Why the Critics Turned So Savage," pp. 25, 63–5.

69 Arthur Holmberg, "The Liberation of Lear," p. 12.

70 John Rockwell, "Robert Wilson Wins a Faithful Following, but It's in Eu-
    rope," p. C11.

71 Ruth Maleczech, quoted in Ross Wetzsteon, "Queen Lear: Ruth Maleczech
    Gender Bends Shakespeare," p. 40.

72 Ibid.

73 Lee Breuer, quoted in William Harris, "Mabou Mines Sets *Lear* on a Hot Tin
    Roof," p. H5.

74 Michael Feingold, "A Mythic Immediacy," p. 98.

75 Alisa Solomon, interview by the author, June 19, 1990. Subsequent unattrib-

uted quotations from Solomon also derive from this conversation. (Lee Breuer did not respond to repeated invitations to be interviewed.)

76 Maynard Mack, *King Lear in Our Time*, pp. 57–8. One such detail cited by Mack: "Somewhere in the deep background of the causes that call him to this trial may still lurk the notion of the Summons of Death, which sometimes precipitates the psychomachia in the early Morality plays – now lingering on only in the hint Lear gives that he has divided his kingdom, in order that he may 'unburthen'd crawl toward death'" (p. 57).

77 Breuer, quoted in Harris, "Mabou Mines Sets *Lear*," p. H5.

78 Erika Munk, "Subversion by Concept," p. 95.

79 Feingold, "A Mythic Immediacy," pp. 98, 95.

80 A retrospective comparison of *The Gospel at Colonus* and *Lear* reinforces the idea that Breuer's success with the first may have depended to a considerable extent on the working structures provided by Sophocles' text, the Pentacostal service, and Telson's score.

5. THE PLAYS OF MOLIÈRE

1 Peter Sellars, interview by Arthur Bartow, in *The Director's Voice*, p. 285. See Chapter 5.

2 Quoted in David Bradby and David Williams, *Director's Theatre*, p. 69. Planchon has called *Schweyk* the production with which he stopped "copying" Brecht; from then on, he says he merely incorporated into his work Brecht's *Historisierung*, the historical double focus that allows us to view the present through the guise of the past.

3 Roger Planchon, "I Am a Museum Guard," p. 100.

4 Roger Planchon, quoted in Bradby and Williams, *Director's Theatre*, p. 70.

5 Planchon, "I Am a Museum Guard," p. 104.

6 Planchon, quoted in Bradby and Williams, *Director's Theatre*, p. 65.

7 Planchon's 1973 restaging was designed by Henri Monloup. Monloup retained Allio's basic format and his paintings, but pushed the renovation further along to emphasize the sense of destruction. In homage to the first designer, Planchon incorporated poses and gestures from Allio's murals into the acting.

8 Planchon , quoted in Bradby and Williams, *Director's Theatre*, pp. 81–2.

9 Ibid., p. 83.

10 Judith Graves Miller, "Vitez's Molière," p. 74.

11 Ibid., p. 79.

12 Ibid., p. 76.

13 Rosette Lamont, "Lyubimov's *Tartuffe*," p. 84.

14 Yuri Lyubimov, interview by Margaret Croyden; quoted in ibid.

15 Ibid., p. 88.

16 *The Miser* was presented at the American Repertory Theatre in Cambridge, Mass., during May–June 1989.

17 Albert Bermel, *Moliére's Theatrical Bounty: A New View of the Plays*, p. 148.

18 Andrei Serban, "Andrei Serban Introduces *The Miser*," *American Repertory Theatre News*, April 1989, p. 3.

19 Molière, *The Miser and George Dandin*, p. 48.

20 Serban, "Andrei Serban Introduces *The Miser*," p. 3.

21 Molière, *Theatre 1668–1669*, p. 140.

22 Molière, *The Miser and George Dandin*, p. 78.

23 Andrei Serban, interview by the author, Somerville, Mass., April 1989.

24 Molière, *The Miser and George Dandin*, p. 67.

25 Bermel, *Moliére's Theatrical Bounty*, pp. 152–3.

26 Serban, "Andrei Serban Introduces *The Miser*," p. 3.

27 Bermel, *Moliére's Theatrical Bounty*, p. 13.

28 Serban, interview by the author, April 1989.

29 Kevin Kelly, "ART's *Miser* Grasps for a Style," pp. 45, 51.

30 Ibid., p. 51. Kelly was wrong: Pintilié's *Tartuffe* and Wright's *Misanthrope* contained far steamier sex scenes, to cite just two examples.

31 David Hawley, review of *The Misanthrope*.

32 Randall Findlay, review of *The Misanthrope*.

33 One could almost smell them from the audience in a hyperrealistic scene that conjured simultaneous memories of David Belasco and the butcher shop in Kroetz's *Through the Leaves*.

34 Everett Jones, "Mixed Emotions About Molière's *Don Juan*," p. A-7.

35 It is interesting to consider that Shaw rewrote and set the Don Juan legend during the same period in which Ciulei set his *Don Juan*, but *Man and Superman* does not suffer the same lack of vitality.

36 Judith Martin, review of *Don Juan*, p. 22.

37 Novick went so far as to print a disclaimer in the May 14, 1979, *Village Voice* – the issue following the one that ran his review – to correct the wrong impression created by the omission of his original final sentence (i.e., "a way for American actors . . ."), and the addition of the headline "*Don Juan* Half-Met."

38 Richard Foreman, quoted in Gerald Rabkin, "Styles in Production: *Don Juan*, directed by Richard Foreman," p. 69.

39 Ibid.

40 Ibid., pp. 67–8.

41 Allan Wallach, "Letting the Play Speak for Itself," p. II/15.

42 Frank Rich, review of *Don Juan*, p. C5.

43 Julius Novick, "Don Wan," p. 83.

44 Rabkin, "Styles in Production," p. 70.

45 Mel Gussow, "A New Vision of *Tartuffe*," p. III: 11.

46 Hap Erstein, "*Tartuffe* Puts a Chill in Its Farce," p. 2B.

47 William Henry III, "A Schooling in Surveillance," p. 65.

48 Julius Novick, "*Don Juan* Half-Met," p. 104.

6. PETER SELLARS'S MOZART–
DA PONTE TRILOGY

1 I do not pretend to be a music critic and so will limit my comments on the
musical merits of these performances to those of an interested layman. My discussion of Peter Sellars's Mozart–da Ponte trilogy will focus on the same theatrical issues I have discussed in the other chapters; namely, how well the director's conceptual framework reflected and illuminated the original text and,
here, the musical score. Without exception, the singing seemed to me more
than adequate and often quite extraordinary, but I will accept the general con-
sensus of music critics that the voices ranged from mediocre to quite good,
with few raves for any but Sanford Sylvan (Figaro and Alfonso) and James
Maddalena (Guglielmo and Count Almaviva).

Craig Smith's conducting evoked widely disparate responses, from non-
descript and aimless to competent and lively. Andrew Porter, the music critic
for the *New Yorker* and a staunch supporter of Sellars's innovations, accused
Smith of dragging the orchestra through the tragic sections. In *The Nation*,
Edward Said consistently complained Smith's tempi were much too fast, as if
he were trying to avoid the intricacies of the score by rushing over them. *Opera News* praised Smith's work with the music for "clarity, grace and bouyan-
cy" (C. J. Luten, review of *Don Giovanni*, p. 53).

Leaving the musicological tasks to a more appropriately qualified writer, I
analyze these productions in their full dimensions as theatrical events. As Andrew Porter put it, "the performance was exceptional – electrifying – not for
the singing but for the way that everything about it conspired" (review of *Don
Giovanni*, p. 69). And Edward Said wrote in *The Nation*, "Sellars treats the
work as a full-scale intellectual social, and aesthetic project and *not* mainly a
musical one" (review of *Don Giovanni*, p. 318).

2 See Daniel Quinn, "Re-visioning Opera," pp. 87–95.
3 A. M. Nagler, *Misdirection: Opera Production in the Twentieth Century*, p. 11.
4 Said, review of *Don Giovanni*, p. 318.
5 Thomas Disch, review of *Le Nozze di Figaro*, p. 177.
6 Said, review of *Don Giovanni*, p. 318.
7 Donal Henahan, "Wanted: Singing Not Acting," p. H21
8 Donal Henahan, "Labeling This Era May Be Easy After All," p. H29. Henahan barely manages to repress his sneer at the word "legitimate," as if he might
have preferred, like Edmund in *King Lear*, to have used a less polite synonym
for "illegitimate."
9 Ibid.
10 Peter Sellars, interview by the author, November 5, 1989. Subsequent unattributed quotations also derive from this conversation.
11 Peter Sellars, quoted in Arthur Bartow, *The Director's Voice*, p. 279.

12 Peter Sellars, quoted in Will Crutchfield, "Modern Twists Spice a Mozart Opera," p. H1.

13 Peter Sellars, interview by Ron Jenkins, p. 48.

14 He told me: "As you can see, I really do believe in show business. I love show business and spend a lot of my time trying to get it right, and I think, God knows, the Mozart Act I finales are just dazzling from a sheer show biz point of view."

15 Will Crutchfield, "Mozart in the Style of Sellars or Vice Versa," p. C13.

16 The director's remarks in the program notes are considered a production element here because Sellars expected his audiences, like those in the eighteenth century, to refer to the notes during the performances. They are part of his overall concept, serving dual functions: first, helping the audience interpret the action on stage; and second, creating a performance experience redolent of both the past and the present. "Usually I keep the house lights on during the show," he explained, because in the eighteenth century, "the house lights were on and people did have books. You picked them up a couple of days before the performance, and you did read beforehand. It was recreating that that I started with."

The use of such slang expressions as "got down with his bad self" to describe the Count dancing at Figaro's wedding, and "snacking between meals" to describe his extramarital philandering, reveal dangerous tendencies in Sellars's writing that underscore the wisdom of his decision not to attempt original translations of the libretti.

17 Introduction to Sellars's program notes for the trilogy, 1989 Summerfare, p. 3.

18 Ibid., p. 2.

19 Ibid.

20 Sellars, quoted in Arthur Bartow, *The Director's Voice*, p. 277.

21 Peter Sellars, quoted in Michael Kimmelman, "Summerfare Offers a Home for the Leading Edge," p. H21.

22 Peter Sellars, program notes to *Don Giovanni*, 1989 Summerfare, p. 11.

23 Scandals involving Jim Bakker, Gary Hart, Bess Meyerson, and the unseating of a Japanese prime minister confirmed the relevance of that theme to the 1980s.

24 Introduction to program notes, 1989 Summerfare, p. 2.

25 Sellars, interview by the author, November 5, 1989.

26 Richard Wagner, quoted in Andrew Porter, review of *Così fan Tutte*, p. 81.

27 Crutchfield, "Mozart in the Style," p. C13.

28 John Rockwell, review of *Così fan Tutte*, p. C26.

29 Porter, review of *Così fan Tutte*, p. 82.

30 Said, review of *Così fan Tutte*, p. 289.

31 Luten, review of *Don Giovanni*, pp. 52–3.

32 Thomas Disch, review of *Don Giovanni*, p. 254.

33 Said, review of *Così fan Tutte*, p. 289.

34 Porter, review of *Don Giovanni*, p. 66.
35 Introduction to program notes, 1989 Summerfare, p. 2.
36 Ibid.
37 Rockwell, review of *Così fan Tutte*, p. C26.
38 Ibid.
39 Crutchfield, "Mozart in the Style," p. C17.
40 Peter Davis, "A *Così* to Fan Controversy," p. 64.
41 Moira Hodgson, review of *Così fan Tutte*, p. 153.
42 Porter, review of *Così fan Tutte*, p. 82.
43 See Richard Trousdell, "Peter Sellars Rehearses *Figaro*," 66–89.
44 Introduction to program notes, 1989 Summerfare, p. 2.
45 Ibid.
46 Trousdell, "Peter Sellars Rehearses *Figaro*," p. 82.
47 C. J. Luten, review of *La Nozze di Figaro*, p. 50.
48 Crutchfield, "Mozart in the Style," p. C13.
49 Trousdell, "Peter Sellars Rehearses *Figaro*," p. 83.
50 Donal Henahan, "But Why Call it *Don Giovanni*?" p. H25.

7. THE CLASSICS, POSTMODERNISM, AND THE QUESTION OF COHERENCE

1 Peter Sellars, quoted in John Lahr, "Inventing the Enemy," p. 103.
2 Peter Sellars, quoted in Richard Trousdell, "Peter Sellars Rehearses *Figaro*," p. 83.
3 Raymond Williams, *Television: Technology and Cultural Form*, p. 87.
4 Ibid., p. 89.
5 Fredric Jameson, "Postmodernism and Consumer Society," in Hal Foster, ed., *The Anti-Aesthetic: Essays on Postmodern Culture*, p. 119.
6 Ibid., p. 114.
7 Todd Gitlin, "Postmodernism: Roots and Politics," in Ian Angus and Sut Jhally, eds., *Cultural Politics in Contemporary America*, p. 347.
8 Ibid., p. 349.
9 Ibid., p. 350.
10 Quoted by Norma Miller from the Loeb edition of Plutarch (vol. X, H. N. Fowler, ed.; Heinemann, 1936), in her Introduction to *Menander: Plays and Fragments* (London: Penguin Books, 1987), pp. 8–9.
11 Neils Bohr, quoted in Natalie Crohn-Schmidt, *Actors and Onlookers*, p. 8.
12 Gitlin, "Postmodernism: Roots and Politics," p. 350.
13 Stratos E. Constantinidis, *Theatre Under Deconstruction?: A Question of Approach*, p. 24.
14 Jonathan Kalb, quoted in Michael Vanden Heuval, *Performing Drama/Dramatizing Performance: Alternative Theater and the Dramatic Text*, p. 39.

15 Lawrence Levine, *Highbrow/Lowbrow: The Emergence of Cultural Hierarchy in America*, p. 21.
16 Ibid., p. 31.
17 Ibid., p. 255.
18 Peter Brook, quoted in Gerry Raymond, "Peter Brook as Prospero," p. 21.

BIBLIOGRAPHY
≡ ✦ ≡

I. BOOKS

Angus, Ian, and Jhally, Sut, eds. *Cultural Politics in Contemporary America*. New York: Routlege, 1989.

Appia, Adolpho. *The Work of Living Art and Man Is the Measure of All Things*. Miami: University of Miami Press, 1962.

Artaud, Antonin. *The Theatre and Its Double*. Translated by Mary Caroline Richards. New York: Grove Press, 1958.

Auslander, Philip. *Presence and Resistance: Postmodernism and Cultural Politics in American Performance*. Ann Arbor: University of Michigan Press, 1992.

Barthes, Roland. *Image-Music-Text*. New York: Hill & Wang, 1977.

Bartow, Arthur. *The Director's Voice*. New York: Theatre Communications Group, 1988.

Beckerman, Bernard, and Siegman, Howard. *On Stage: Reviews from* The New York Times, *1920–1970*. New York: Arno Press, 1973.

Bentley, Eric. *The Dramatic Event: An American Chronicle*. Boston: Beacon Press, 1956.

Bermel, Albert. *Artaud's Theatre of Cruelty*. New York: Taplinger Publ., 1977.

    Moliére's Theatrical Bounty: A New View of the Plays. Carbondale & Edwardsville: Southern Illinois University Press, 1990.

Berry, Ralph. *On Directing Shakespeare*. New York: Barnes & Noble, 1977.

Blau, Herbert. *Blooded Thought: Occasions of Theatre*. New York: PAJ Press, 1982.

    Take Up the Bodies: Theatre at the Vanishing Point. Champaign: University of Illinois Press, 1982.

Blumenthal, Eileen. *Joseph Chaikin: Exploring Beyond the Boundaries of Theatre*, Directors in Perspective series. New York: Cambridge University Press, 1984.

Bibliography

Bradby, David, and Williams, David. *Director's Theatre*. New York: St. Martin's Press, 1988.

Braun, Edward. *The Director and the Stage:From Naturalism to Grotowski*. New York: Holmes & Meier, 1982.

　The Theatre of Meyerhold: Revolution on the Modern Stage. 1979. Reprint, Portsmouth, N. H.: Heinemann Educational Books, 1988.

Brecht, Bertolt. *Brecht on Theatre*. Translated by John Willett. New York: Hill & Wang, 1964.

Brecht, Stefan. *The Theatre of Visions: Robert Wilson*. New York: Routledge, Chapman & Hall, 1985.

Breuer, Lee. *The Gospel at Colonus*. New York: Theatre Communications Group, 1989.

Brook, Peter. *The Empty Space*. New York: Atheneum, 1968.

　The Shifting Point: Theatre, Film, Opera, 1946–1987. New York: Harper & Row, 1987.

Brustein, Robert. *Critical Moments: Reflections on Theatre and Society, 1973–79*. New York: Random House, 1980.

　Seasons of Discontent: Dramatic Opinions, 1959–65. New York: Simon & Schuster, 1965.

　The Third Theatre. New York: Alfred A. Knopf, 1969.

　Who Needs Theatre? New York: Atlantic Monthly Press, 1987.

Carlson, Marvin. *Theories of the Theatre*. Ithaca, N.Y.: Cornell University Press, 1984.

Cheney, Sheldon. *The New Movement in the Theatre*. 1914. Reprint, Westport, Conn.: Greenwood Press, 1971.

Cole, David. *The Theatrical Event: A Myth, a Vocabulary, a Perspective*. Middletown, Conn.: Wesleyan University Press, 1975.

Cole, Susan Letzler. *Directors in Rehearsal: A Hidden World*. New York: Routledge, 1992.

Cole, Toby, and Chinoy, Helen Krich. *Directors on Directing*. New York: Bobbs Merrill Company, 1963.

Constantinidis, Stratos E. *Theater Under Deconstruction?: A Question of Approach*. New York & London: Garland Press, 1993.

Cooper, Roberta K. *The American Shakespeare Theatre: Stratford, 1955–1985*. Cranbury, N.J.: Folger Books, 1986.

Craig, Gordon. *On the Art of the Theatre*. New York: Theatre Arts Books, 1925.

　Towards a New Theatre: Forty Designs. New York: Theatre Arts Books, 1925.

　Craig on Theatre. Edited by J. Michael Walton. London: Methuen, 1983.

Crohn-Schmidt, Natalie. *Actors and Onlookers*. Evanston, Ill.: Northwestern University Press, 1990.

Croyden, Margaret. *Lunatics, Lovers, and Poets*. New York: McGraw-Hill, 1974.

Eagleton, Terry. *Literary Theory: An Introduction*. Minneapolis: University of Minnesota Press, 1983.

Eaton, Katherine Bliss. *The Theatre of Meyerhold and Brecht*. Westport, Conn.: Greenwood Press, 1985.

Fitts, Dudley, ed. *Greek Plays in Modern Translation*. New York: Dial Press, 1947.

Flanagan, Hallie. *Arena: The History of the Federal Theatre*. 1940. Reprint, New York: Arno Press, 1980.

Foster, Hal. *The Anti-Aesthetic: Essays on Postmodern Culture*. Port Townsend, Wash.: Bay Press, 1983.

France, Richard. *Orson Welles on Shakespeare*. Westport, Conn.: Greenwood Press: 1990.

    The Theatre of Orson Welles. Lewisburg, Penn.: Bucknell University Press, 1977.

Fuegi, John. *Bertolt Brecht: Chaos According to Plan*. Directors in Perspective series. New York: Cambridge University Press, 1987.

    The Essential Brecht. Los Angeles: Hennessey & Ingalls, 1972.

Gilman, Richard. *Common and Uncommon Masks: Writings on the Theatre, 1961–1971*. New York: Random House, 1971.

Gorelik, Mordecai, *New Theatres for Old*. 1940. Reprint, New York: E. P. Dutton, 1962.

Granville-Barker, Harley. *Prefaces to Shakespeare: Volume 2*. Princeton, N.J.: Princeton University Press, 1946. Reprint, 1965.

Grotowski, Jerzy. *Towards a Poor Theatre*. New York: Simon & Schuster, 1968.

Guernsey, Otis L., Jr. *Curtain Times: The New York Theatre, 1965–1987*. New York: Applause Theatre Book Publ., 1987.

Guthrie, Tyrone. *A New Theatre*. New York: McGraw-Hill, 1964.

    In Various Directions. 1965. Reprint, Westport, Conn.: Greenwood Press, 1979.

Hill, Errol. *Shakespeare in Sable*. Amherst: University of Massachusetts Press, 1984.

Hoover, Marjorie L. *Meyerhold: The Art of Conscious Theatre*. Amherst: University of Massachusetts Press, 1974.

Houseman, John. *Final Dress*. New York: Simon & Schuster, 1983.

    Run Through. New York: Simon & Schuster, 1972.

Hughes, Ted. *Seneca's Oedipus*. Garden City N.Y.: Doubleday, 1972.

Ibsen, Henrik. *Peer Gynt*. Translated with an Introduction by Rolf Fjelde. Minneapolis: University of Minnesota Press, 1980.

Innes, Christopher. *Edward Gordon Craig*. Directors in Perspective series. New York: Cambridge University Press, 1983.

    Holy Theatre: Ritual and the Avant Garde. New York: Cambridge University Press, 1981.

Jones, David Richard. *Great Directors at Work: Stanislavsky, Brecht, Kazan, Brook*. Berkeley: University of California Press, 1986.

Jones, Edward T. *Following Directions: A Study of Peter Brook*. New York: Peter Lang Publ., 1985.

Bibliography

Jones, Robert Edmond. *The Dramatic Imagination*. New York: Theatre Arts Books, 1941.

  The Theatre of Robert Edmond Jones. Edited by Ralph Pendleton. Middletown, Conn.: Wesleyan University Press, 1958.

Kauffmann, Stanley. *Persons of the Drama*. New York: Harper & Row, 1976.

  Theatre Criticisms. New York: Performing Arts Journal Publ., 1984.

Kennedy, Dennis. *Granville Barker and The Dream of Theatre*. Cambridge, U.K.: Cambridge University Press, 1985.

King, Bruce, ed. *Contemporary American Theatre*. New York: St. Martin's Press, 1991.

Kott, Jan. *Shakespeare Our Contemporary*. Translated by Boleslaw Taborski. Garden City, N.Y.: Doubleday, 1964.

  The Theatre of Essence. Evanston, Ill.: Northwestern University Press, 1984.

Kumiega, Jennifer. *The Theatre of Grotowski*. Portsmouth, N.H.: Heinemann Educational Books, 1987.

Levine, Lawrence. *Highbrow/Lowbrow: The Emergence of Cultural Hierarchy in America*. Cambridge, Mass.: Harvard University Press, 1988.

Little, Stuart. *Enter Joseph Papp: In Search of a New American Theatre*. New York: Coward Books, 1974.

McDonald, Marianne. *Ancient Sun, Modern Light: Greek Drama on the Modern Stage*. New York: Columbia University Press, 1992.

Macgowan, Kenneth. *The Theatre of Tomorrow*. London: T. Fischer Unwin, 1923.

Macgowan, Kenneth, and Jones, Robert Edmond. *Continental Stagecraft*. 1922. Reprint, New York: Benjamin Blom, 1964.

Mack, Maynard. *King Lear in Our Time*. Berkeley & Los Angeles: University of California Press, 1965.

Marowitz, Charles. *The Marowitz Shakespeare*. New York: Drama Book Specialists, 1978.

  Prospero's Staff: Acting and Directing in the Contemporary Theatre. Bloomington & Indianapolis: Indiana University Press, 1986.

  Recycling Shakespeare. New York: Applause Theatre Book Publ., 1991.

Meyerhold, Vsevelod, *Meyerhold on Theatre*. Edited by Edward Braun. New York: Hill & Wang, 1969.

Miller, Jonathan. *Subsequent Performances*. New York: Viking Press, 1986.

Molière, Jean Baptiste Poquelin de. *Four Comedies*. Translated by Richard Wilbur. New York: Harcourt Brace Jovanovich, 1982.

  The Misanthrope and Tartuffe. Translated by Richard Wilbur. New York: Harcourt Brace & World, 1965.

  The Miser and George Dandin. Translated by Albert Bermel. The Actor's Molière series. New York: Applause Theatre Book Publ., 1987.

  Theatre 1668–1669. Edited by René Bray. Paris: Société des Belles Lettres, 1947.

Bibliography

Nagler, A. M. *Misdirection: Opera Production in the Twentieth Century.* Hamden, Conn.: Archon Books, 1981.

Novick, Julius. *Beyond Broadway: The Quest for Permanent Theatres.* New York: Hill & Wang, 1968. Second edition, 1969.

O'Connor, John, and Brown, Lorraine. *The Federal Theatre Project: Free, Adult, Uncensored.* London: Eyre Methuen, 1980.

Oenslager, Donald. *Scenery Then and Now.* New York: W. W. Norton, 1936.

O'Neill, R. H., and Boretz, N. M. *The Director as Artist.* New York: Holt, Rinehart & Winston, 1987.

Osinski, Zbigniew. *Grotowski and His Laboratory.* Translated and abridged by Lillian Vallee and Robert Findlay. New York: Performing Arts Journal Publ., 1986.

Papp, Joseph, with Cornell, Ted. *William Shakespeare's "Naked" Hamlet.* New York: Macmillan, 1969.

Performance Group, The. *Dionysus in '69.* Edited by Richard Schechner. New York: Farrar, Straus & Giroux, 1970.

Purdom, C. B. *Granville-Barker.* Cambridge: Harvard University Press, 1956.

Reinelt, Janelle, and Roach, Joseph. *Critical Theory and Performance.* Ann Arbor: University of Michigan Press, 1992.

Rogoff, Gordon. *Theatre Is Not Safe: 1962–1986.* Evanston, Ill.: Northwestern University Press, 1987.

Roose-Evans, James. *Experimental Theatre from Stanislavsky to Today.* New York: Universe Books, 1973.

Salenius, Elmer W. *Harley Granville Barker.* Boston: Twayne Publ., 1982.

Savran, David. *Breaking the Rules: The Wooster Group.* New York: Theatre Communications Group, 1986.

Sayler, Oliver M., ed. *Max Reinhardt and His Theatre.* 1924. Reprint, Salem, N.H.: Ayer Company Publ., 1968.

Schechner, Richard. *Environmental Theatre.* New York: Hawthorne Books, 1973.

Schevill, James. *Break Out! In Search of New Theatrical Environments.* Chicago: Swallow Press, 1973.

Schmidt, Paul, ed. *Meyerhold at Work.* Austin: University of Texas Press, 1980.

Scolnicov, Hanna, and Holland, Peter, eds. *The Play Out of Context: Transferring Plays from Culture to Culture.* New York: Cambridge University Press, 1989.

Selbourne, David. *The Making of* A Midsummer Night's Dream: *An Eye-Witness Account of Peter Brook's Production from First Rehearsal to First Night.* Portsmouth, N.H.: Heinemann Educational Books, 1984.

Shakespeare, William. *The Comedy of Errors.* Edited with an introduction by Stanley Wells. Middlesex, U.K.: Penguin Books, 1972. Reprint, 1984.

Shank, Theodore. *American Alternative Theatre.* New York: Grove Press, 1982.

Simon, John. *Uneasy Stages: A Chronicle of the New York Theatre, 1963–1973.* New York: Random House, 1973.

Simonson, Lee. *The Stage Is Set.* New York: Theatre Arts Books, 1963.

Sontag, Susan. *Against Interpretation*. New York: Dell, 1966.

Speaight, Robert. *Shakespeare on the Stage*. Boston: Little, Brown, 1973.

Styan, J. L. *Max Reinhardt*. Directors in Perspective series. New York: Cambridge University Press, 1982.

Taylor, John Russell. *Orson Welles: A Celebration of a Life*. Boston: Little, Brown, 1986.

Vanden Heuvel, Michael. *Performing Drama/Dramatizing Performance: Alternative Theater and the Dramatic Text*. Ann Arbor: University of Michigan Press, 1991.

Williams, David. *Peter Brook: A Theatrical Casebook*. Portsmouth, N.H.: Heinemann Educational Books, 1988.

Williams, Raymond. *Television: Technology and Cultural Form*. New York: Schocken Books, 1975.

Wills, J. Robert, ed. *The Director in a Changing Theatre*. Palo Alto: Mayfield Publ., 1976.

II. ARTICLES

"American Directors on Directing: The Second Generation," special issue, *Theater* 15 (Spring 1984). Includes interviews with JoAnne Akalaitis, Adrian Hall, Mark Lamos, Peter Sellars, Robert Woodruff, and Garland Wright.

"American Experimental Theatre Then and Now," special section, *Performing Arts Journal* 5 (Fall 1977): 13–24.

Amitin, Mark. "The Living Theatre Abroad: Radicalizing the Classics. An Interview with Julian Beck and Judith Malina," *Performing Arts Journal* 14 (1981): 26–40.

Arnold, Paul. "The Artaud Experiment," *Tulane Drama Review* 22 (Winter 1963): 15–29.

Aronson, Arnold. "A Space for *Oedipus*," *U.S. Institute for Theatre Technology Bulletin* (Summer 1978): 26–30.

Artaud, Antonin. "States of Mind: 1921–45," translated by Ruby Cohn, *Tulane Drama Review* 22 (Winter 1963): 30–73.

Bailey, Paul M. "Norman Bel Geddes' *Hamlet*," *The Drama Review* 91 (Fall 1981): 39–54.

Barton, John. "Notes on *The Greeks*," *Theater* 11 (1980): 33–6.

Beacham, Richard. "John Barton Directs *The Greeks*," *Theater* 11 (1980): 37–42.

Beck, Ervin. "Tamburlaine for the Modern Stage," *Educational Theatre Journal* 23 (March 1971): 62–74.

Berc, Shelley. "Lee Breuer's *Lulu*," *The Drama Review* 90 (Summer 1981): 63–86.

Bharucha, Rustom. "Directing the Greeks," *Theater* 11(Summer 1980): 65–71.

Blakely, Colin. "Exploration of the Ugly: Brook's Work on *Oedipus*," interview by Margaret Croyden, *The Drama Review* 43 (Spring 1969): 120–4.

Bly, Mark. "Notes on Robert Wilson's *Medea*," *Theater* 12 (Summer 1981): 65–8.

Bibliography

Bogart, Anne. "Making It New," *American Theatre* 6 (September 1989): 5.

Brecht, Bertolt. "On Chinese Acting," translated by Eric Bentley, *Tulane Drama Review* 6 (September 1961): 130–6.

"Theatre for Learning," translated by Edith Anderson, *Tulane Drama Review* 6 (Autumn 1961): 18–25.

Brecht, Stefan. "Theatre Report: *Dionysus in '69*," *The Drama Review* 43 (Spring 1969): 156–68.

Breuer, Lee. "Mabou Mines: How We Work," *Performing Arts Journal* 1 (Spring 1976): 29–32.

"On *The Gospel at Colonus*," interview by Gerald Rabkin, *Performing Arts Journal* 22 (1984): 48–51.

Brustein, Robert. "America and the Classics," *Theatre Profiles* 7 (Theatre Communications Group, 1986): 35–40.

"No More Masterpieces," *Yale Theatre* 1 (Spring 1968): 10–19; also in *The Third Theatre*, pp. 18–34.

"Reworking the Classics: Homage or Ego Trip?" *New York Times*, November 6, 1988, pp. H5, H16.

Carlson, Marvin. "Theatrical Performance: Illustration, Translation, Fulfillment, or Supplement?" *Theatre Journal* 37 (March 1985): 5–11.

Cartwright, Diane. "Priscilla Smith of the Great Jones Repertory Project," *The Drama Review* 71 (Fall 1976): 75–82.

Case, Sue-Ellen. "Peter Stein Directs *The Oresteia*," *Theater* 11 (Summer 1980): 23–8.

Cohn, Ruby. "Old Myths in the New Theatre," *Educational Theatre Journal* 23 (December 1971): 398–408.

Copeland, Roger. "Avant-Garde Stage: From Primal Dreams to Split Images," *New York Times*, January 11, 1987, p. H4.

Coppenger, Royston. "Lee Breuer's *Gospel*," *Theater* 15 (Fall 1984): 71–80.

Croyden, Margaret. "Brook's *Tempest* Experiment," *The Drama Review* 43 (Spring 1969): 125–8.

"Seeking the Emotions That Stirred the Ancient Greeks," *New York Times*, May 8, 1977, pp. H1, H14.

Crutchfield, Will. "Modern Twists Spice a Mozart Opera," *New York Times*, July 13, 1986, p. H1.

Curchack, Fred. Interview by Rosette Lamont, *Stages* (December 1989): 6, 43.

Davis, Rick. Review of *The Seagull* directed by Lucian Pintilié. *Performing Arts Journal* 22 (Spring 1984): 83–6.

"Three American Designers: An Interview with Jane Greenwood, Ming Cho Lee, and Michael Yeargan," *Theater* 13 (Winter 1981–2): 76–82.

"Dramaturgy in America, 1986," special issue, *Theater* 17(Summer–Fall 1986): 5–62.

Eco, Umberto. "Semiotics of Theatrical Performance," *The Drama Review* 73 (March 1977): 107–17.

Bibliography

Eddy, Bill. "Theatre Report: *The Trojan Women* at La Mama," *The Drama Review* 64 (Winter 1974): 11.

Esslin, Martin. "Max Reinhardt: High Priest of Theatricality," *The Drama Review* 74 (June 1977): 3–24.

France, Richard. "The 'Voodoo' *Macbeth* of Orson Welles," *Yale Theatre* 5 (1974): 66–78.

Fuchs, Elinor. "*Cymbeline* and Its Critics: Misunderstanding Postmodernism," *American Theatre* 6 (December 1989): 24–31.

Gershman, Judith. "The Molière Cycle of Antoine Vitez," *Performing Arts Journal* 13 (1980): 75–80.

Gilman, Richard. "Directors vs. Playwrights," *Saturday Review* (April 1982): 32–3.

"Greeks at CCNY," *Theatre Magazine* (June 1915).

Greene, Alexis. "Mabou Mines Turns Twenty," *Theater Week* (January 29, 1990): 10–15.

　　　"A One Man *Tempest:* Fred Curchack Tackles Shakespeare's Play," *Theater Week* (November 6, 1989): 36–9.

Grotowski, Jerzy. "Faustus in Poland," *The Drama Review* 24 (Summer 1964): 120–33.

　　　Interview by Richard Schechner. *The Drama Review* 41 (Fall 1968): 29–45.

Harris, William. "It's a Wrap for the Adventurous Summerfare," *New York Times*, July 30, 1989, pp. H1, H38.

　　　"Mabou Mines Sets *Lear* on a Hot Tin Roof," *New York Times*, January 21, 1990, pp. H5, H33.

Hecht, Werner. "The Development of Brecht's Theory of Epic Theatre, 1918–1933," *Tulane Drama Review* 6 (September 1961): 40–97.

Henahan, Donal. "Labeling This Era May Be Easy After All," *New York Times*, September 7, 1986, p. H29.

　　　"A Tale of Two Operas: Or When Not to Interfere," *New York Times*, October 25, 1987, p. H27.

　　　"Wanted: Singing Not Acting," *New York Times*, June 27, 1987, p. H21.

Hodge, Francis. "The Director as Critic," *Educational Theatre Journal* 11 (December 1959): 280–4.

Holmberg, Arthur. "Greek Tragedy in a New Mask Speaks to Today's Audiences," *New York Times*, March 1, 1987, pp. H1, H25.

　　　"The Liberation of Lear," *American Theatre* 5 (July–August 1988): 12–17.

Kalb, Jonathan. "The Underground *Endgame*," *Theater* 16 (Spring 1985): 88–91.

　　　"Whose Text Is It Anyway: *The Balcony* at A.R.T.," *Theater* 17 (Summer–Fall 1986): 97–9.

Kauffmann, Stanley. "A Life in the Theatre: How a Great Actor and Director Gave Shakespeare to the Twentieth Century," *Horizon* (August 1975): 80–5.

Kellman, Alice. "Actors and Acting: Joseph Chaikin," *The Drama Review* 71 (Fall 1976): 17–26.

Kimmelman, Michael. "Summerfare Offers a Home for the Leading Edge," *New York Times*, June 21, 1987, p. H21.

Kirby, Michael. "Introduction to Reinterpretation Issue," *The Drama Review* 90 (Summer 1981): 1–2.

"Richard Foreman's Ontological-Hysteric Theatre," *The Drama Review* 58 (Summer 1973): 5–32.

Kott, Jan. "I Can't Get No Satisfaction," *The Drama Review* 41 (Fall 1968): 143–9.

"Molière Our Contemporary," *Tulane Drama Review* 11 (Spring 1967): 163–70.

"Where Are *Ajax* and *Philoctetes* Now That We Need Them?" interview with Joel Schecter, *Theater* 11 (Summer 1980): 18–22.

Kuhlke, William. "Vakhtangov and the American Theatre of the 1960s," *Educational Theatre Journal* 19 (May 1967): 179–87.

"La Mama Celebrates Twenty Years," *Performing Arts Journal* 17 (1982): 6–28.

Lamont, Rosette. "Lyubimov's *Tartuffe*," *Theater* 11 (Summer 1980): 82–8.

Leverett, James. "*Cymbeline* and Its Critics: Why the Critics Turned So Savage," *American Theatre* 6 (December 1989): 25, 63–5.

Living Theatre, The. "The Living Theatre in *Prometheus*: A Collective Creation," *Performing Arts Journal* 14 (1981): 41–7.

McKloskey, Susan. "Shakespeare, Orson Welles, and the 'Voodoo' *Macbeth*," *Shakespeare Quarterly* 36 (Winter 1985): 406–16.

Maleczech, Ruth. Interview by David Berreby, *New York Newsday* (December 7, 1988): 69.

Margarida, Alice. "Two *Shrews*: Productions by Lunt/Fontanne (1935) and A. K. Ayliff (1927)," *The Drama Review* 90 (Summer 1981): 87–100.

Marowitz, Charles. Interview by Don Shewey, *Theater* 9 (Summer 1978): 30–3.

"LEAR Log," *The Drama Review* 22 (Winter 1963): 103–21.

Marx, Robert. "Grand Finale," *Opera News* (July 1989): 14–16, 33.

Mazer, Cary M. "Actors or Gramophones: The Paradox of Granville Barker," *Theatre Journal* 36 (March 1984): 5–24.

Miller, Judith Graves. "Vitez's Molière," *Theater* 11 (Summer 1980): 74–81.

Nahshon, Edna. "With Foreman on Broadway: Five Actors' Views," *The Drama Review* 71 (Fall 1976): 84–100.

O'Connor, John S. "But Was It 'Shakespeare'?: Welles' *Macbeth* and *Julius Caesar*," *Theatre Journal* 32 (October 1980): 337–40.

"The *PAJ* Casebook: Robert Wilson's *Alcestis*," *Performing Arts Journal* 28 (1986): 78–115.

Pavis, Patrice. "The Interplay Between Avant-Garde Theatre and Semiology," *Performing Arts Journal* 15 (1981): 75–86.

Planchon, Roger. "I Am a Museum Guard," interview by Rosette Lamont, *Performing Arts Journal*, 16 (1981): 97–109.

Price, Jonathan. "Jonathan Miller Directs Robert Lowell's *Prometheus*," *Yale Theatre* 1 (Spring 1968): 40–4.

Quinn, Daniel. "Re-visioning Opera," *Performing Arts Journal* 13 (1980): 87–95.

Rabkin, Gerald. "Is There a Text on This Stage?: Theatre/Authorship/Interpretation," *Performing Arts Journal* 26 (1985): 142–59.

"The Play of Misreading: Text/Theatre/Deconstruction," *Performing Arts Journal* 19 (1983): 44–60.

"Styles in Production: *Don Juan,* directed by Richard Foreman," *Performing Arts Journal* 18 (1982): 67–70.

Raymond, Gerry. "Peter Brook as Prospero," *Theatre Week* (January 21–27, 1991): 14–21.

Raynor, Vivien. "The Conceptualists," *New York Times*, July 12, 1985, p. III: 24.

Rich, Frank. "Audacious Gambles with High Comedy," *New York Times*, July 25, 1982): H3, H16.

Richie, Donald. "Peter Brook's *A Midsummer Night's Dream,*" *The Drama Review* 50 (Spring 1971): 330–3.

Rockwell, John. "Robert Wilson Wins a Faithful Following but It's in Europe," *New York Times*, June 20, 1990, p. C11.

Rogoff, Gordon. "Shakespeare with Tears," *The Drama Review* 23 (Spring 1964): 163–79.

Rojo, Jerry. "Interview: Environmental Theatre," *Performing Arts Journal* 1 (Spring 1976): 20–8.

Romero, Laurence. "Dramaturgs and the Classics," *Theater* 11 (Summer 1980): 59–63.

Rothstein, Mervyn. "Taking Shakespeare's *Shrew* to the Old West of the Late 1800s," *New York Times,* June 19, 1990, pp. C13, C18.

Rouse, John. "Structuring Stories: Robert Wilson's *Alcestis,*" *Theater* 18 (Winter 1986–7): 56–9.

Schechner, Richard. "*The Bacchae:* A City Sacrificed to a Jealous God," *Tulane Drama Review* 12 (Summer 1961): 124–34.

"In Warm Blood: *The Bacchae,*" *Educational Theatre Journal* 20 (October 1968): 415–24.

"Radicalism, Sexuality, and Performance," *The Drama Review* 44 (Summer 1969): 89–110.

"Six Axioms," *The Drama Review* 39 (Spring 1968): 41–64.

Sellars, Peter. Interview by Ron Jenkins, *Theater* 15 (Fall 1984): 46–52.

Serban, Andrei. Interview by Eileen Blumenthal. *Yale Theatre* 8 (Summer 1977): 66–77.

Interview re Artaud, by Colette Brooks and Joel Schecter. *Theater* 9 (Summer 1978): 25–9.

"The Life in a Sound," translated from French by Eileen Blumenthal, *The Drama Review* 72 (Winter 1976): 25–6.

Severo, Richard. "Papp Gives *Hamlet* to Catch Conscience of School Board," *New York Times*, January 31, 1968, p. 43.

Spillane, Margaret. "Gender-Bending *Lear*," *Theater Week* (January 29, 1990): 16–19.

Steele, Mike. "Peer Today," *American Theatre* 6 (July–August 1989): 22–9.

"The Romanian Connection," *American Theatre* 2 (July–August 1985): 4–11.

Sullivan, Dan. "Playwright vs. Director: Who Has the Last Word?" *Los Angeles Times Magazine*, February 10, 1985, p. 41.

Trousdell, Richard, "Peter Sellars Rehearses *Figaro*," *The Drama Review* 129 (Spring 1991): 66–89.

Wallach, Allan, "Letting the Play Speak for Itself," *Newsday*, July 25, 1982, p. II/15.

Weber, Carl. "Brecht as Director," in J. Robert Wills, ed., *The Director in a Changing Theatre*, pp. 69–77.

Wesker, Arnold. "Interpretation: To Impose or Explain," *Performing Arts Journal* 32 (1988): 62–76.

Wetzsteon, Ross. "Queen Lear: Ruth Maleczech Gender Bends Shakespeare," *Village Voice*, January 30, 1990, pp. 39–42.

Williams, Gary Jay. "From the *Dream* to *The Mahabharata*: Or, Draupadi in the Deli," *Theater* 19 (Spring 1988): 28–31.

Zolotow, Sam. "School Aids Object to Papp's Mod *Hamlet*," *New York Times*, January 22, 1968, p. 33.

III. REVIEWS

N.B.: This section lists only reviews that are not reprinted in books already listed.

Barnes, Clive. Review of *Agamemnon* directed by Andrei Serban, *New York Times*, May 20, 1977, p. C20.

Review of *Don Juan* directed by Richard Foreman, *New York Post*, July 2, 1982, p. 32.

Review of *Oedipus* directed by Richard Schechner, *New York Post*, December 8, 1977, p. 59.

"Slings and Arrows of Outrageous Papp," review of *Hamlet* directed by Joseph Papp, *New York Times*, December 27, 1967, p. 45.

"Travesty of Shakespeare," Review of *Cymbeline* directed by JoAnne Akalaitis, *New York Post*, June 1, 1989, p. 31.

Beaufort, John. "Update of Bard's *Cymbeline* Is Riddled with Incongruities," review of *Cymbeline* directed by JoAnne Akalaitis, *Christian Science Monitor*, June 16, 1989.

Bermel, Albert. "Hamlet in Modern Undress," review of *Hamlet* directed by Joseph Papp, *New Leader*, January 15, 1968, p. 26.

Brustein, Robert. Review of *Hamlet* directed by Joseph Papp, *Plays and Players*, March 1968, p. 47.

Review of *The Tempest* directed by Lee Breuer, *New Republic*, August 22, 1981, pp. 23–5.

Canby, Vincent. Review of touring production of *Hamlet* directed by Joseph Papp, with Cleavon Little as Hamlet, *New York Times*, July 4, 1968, p. 15.

Corliss, Richard. Review of *The Gospel at Colonus*, *Time Magazine*, January 2, 1984, p. 90.

Crutchfield, Will. "Mozart in the Style of Sellars or Vice Versa," *New York Times*, July 25, 1989, pp. C13, C17.

Davis, Peter. "A *Così* to Fan Controversy," review of *Così fan Tutte* directed by Peter Sellars, *New York Magazine*, August 4, 1986, pp. 64–5.

Review of *Don Giovanni* directed by Peter Sellars, *New York Magazine*, August 3, 1987, pp. 48–9.

Review of Mozart–da Ponte trilogy directed by Peter Sellars, *New York Magazine*, August 7, 1989, pp. 48–9.

Derose, David J. Review of *Alcestis* directed by Robert Wilson, *Theatre Journal* 39 (March 1987): 89–90.

Disch, Thomas. Review of *Don Giovanni* directed by Peter Sellars, *Nation*, September 4, 1989, pp. 254–6.

Review of *Le Nozze di Figaro* directed by Peter Sellars, *Nation*, August 27, 1988, p. 177.

Eder, Richard. "Ciulei Transfers *Don Juan* to Pre–World War I Era," *New York Times*, April 7, 1979, p. 13.

Review of *Oedipus* directed by Richard Schechner, *New York Times*, December 8, 1977, p. III: 19.

Erstein, Hap. "*Tartuffe* Puts a Chill in Its Farce," review of *Tartuffe* directed by Lucian Pintilié, *Washington Times*, March 15, 1985, pp. 1B–2B.

Esserman, Lauren. Review of *Stuff As Dreams Are Made On* by Fred Curchack, *Phoenix* (Brooklyn), November 9, 1989.

Esslin, Martin. Review of *Oedipus* directed by Peter Brook, *Plays and Players*, May 1968, p. 22.

Feingold, Michael. "A Mythic Immediacy," review of *Lear*, *Village Voice*, February 6, 1990, pp. 95, 98.

"Camp Followers," review of *Cymbeline* directed by JoAnne Akalaitis (with *The Lisbon Traviata*), *Village Voice*, June 13, 1989, p. 97.

"Gospel Truth," *Village Voice*, November 22, 1983, p. 109.

Review of *The Comedy of Errors* directed by Robert Woodruff, *Village Voice*, June 16, 1987, p. 93.

Findlay, Randall. Review of *The Misanthrope* directed by Garland Wright, *Minnesota Daily*, June 19, 1987.

Fink, Joel. Review of *The Comedy of Errors* directed by Robert Woodruff, *Theatre Journal* 35 (October 1983): 415–16.

Friedrich, Otto. Review of *Don Giovanni* directed by Peter Sellars, *Time Magazine*, August 7, 1989, p. 63.

Fuchs, Elinor. "Contra Molière," review of *Tartuffe* directed by Lucian Pintilié, *Village Voice*, April 16, 1985, pp. 102, 104.

"Is There Life After Irony?" *Village Voice,* January 3, 1984, p. 77.

Gassner, John. "Broadway in Review" review of 1955 season at American Shakespeare Festival, Stratford, Conn., *Educational Theatre Journal* 7 (October 1955): 219.

——— "Broadway in Review," review of 1958 season at American Shakespeare Festival, Stratford, Conn., *Educational Theatre Journal* 10 (October 1958): 240–1.

——— Review of *Much Ado About Nothing* directed by John Houseman and Jack Landau, *Educational Theatre Journal* 9 (October 1957): 216–17.

Gold, Sylviane. "Molière Minus the Bathtub," review of *The Misanthrope* directed by Garland Wright, *Wall Street Journal,* June 17, 1987, p. 24.

Gottfried, Martin. Review of *Hamlet* directed by Joseph Papp, *Women's Wear Daily,* December 27, 1967, p. 21.

Gussow, Mel. "A New Vision of *Tartuffe,*" review of *Tartuffe* directed by Lucian Pintilié, *New York Times,* April 2, 1985, p. III: 11.

——— Review of *The Gospel at Colonus, New York Times,* April 3, 1988, p. H5.

——— Review of *The Comedy of Errors* directed by Robert Woodruff, *New York Times,* June 1, 1987, p. III: 12.

Hawley, David. Review of *The Misanthrope* directed by Garland Wright, *St. Paul Pioneer Press and Dispatch,* June 12, 1987.

Henahan, Donal. "But Why Call It *Don Giovanni?*" *New York Times,* August 2, 1987, p. H25.

——— "Did Mozart Order a Side of Fries?" Review of *Così fan Tutte* directed by Peter Sellars, *New York Times,* July 17, 1988, p. H25.

Henry, William, III. "A Schooling in Surveillance," review of *Tartuffe* directed by Lucian Pintilié, *Time,* August 24, 1984, p. 65.

Hodgson, Moira. Review of *Così fan Tutte* directed by Peter Sellars, *Nation,* August 30, 1986, pp. 153–4.

——— Review of *Don Giovanni* directed by Peter Sellars, *Nation,* September 5, 1987, pp. 208–9.

Jacobson, Aileen. "For Mabou Mines, It's Queen Lear," *New York Newsday,* January 26, 1990, p. III: 3.

Jones, Everett. "Mixed Emotions About Molière's *Don Juan,*" Review of *Don Juan* directed by Liviu Ciulei, *Potomac News,* April 16, 1979, p. A-7.

Kelly, Kevin. "ART's *Miser* Grasps for a Style," review of *The Miser* directed by Andrei Serban, *Boston Globe,* May 19, 1989, pp. 45, 51.

Kerner, Leighton. "Mozart Told True," review of Peter Sellars's Mozart–da Ponte Trilogy, *Village Voice,* August 6, 1989, p. 80.

Kerr, Walter. Review of *Hamlet* directed by Joseph Papp, *New York Times,* January 7, 1968, pp. II: 1, 13.

——— Review of *Hamlet* directed by Tyrone Guthrie, *New York Herald Tribune,* May 9, 1963, p. 17.

Kissel, Howard. "Shakespeare as Victorian Sideshow," review of *Cymbeline* directed by JoAnne Akalaitis, *Daily News,* June 1, 1989, p. 51.

"Steer Clear of this *Lear*," *Daily News*, January 29, 1990, p. 37.

"This *Stuff* Is Too Hip for Its Own Good," *Daily News*, November 3, 1989, p. 66.

Lahr, John. "Inventing the Enemy," review of *The Persians* directed by Peter Sellars, *New Yorker*, October 18, 1993, pp. 103–6.

Lardner, James. "*Don Juan* Woos and Wins," review of *Don Juan* directed by Liviu Ciulei, *Washington Post*, April 5, 1979, pp. D1, 17.

Loney, Glenn. Review of *The Taming of The Shrew* at the American Shakespeare Festival, *Educational Theatre Journal* 17 (October 1965): 264.

Luten, C. J. Review of *Don Giovanni* directed by Peter Sellars, *Opera News*, November, 1987, pp. 52–3.

Review of *Le Nozze di Figaro* directed by Peter Sellars, *Opera News*, December 10, 1988, pp. 48–50.

Martin, Judith. Review of *Don Juan* directed by Liviu Ciulei, *Washington Post*, April 6, 1979, p. 22.

Meersman, Roger. Review of *Don Juan* directed by Liviu Ciulei, *Sentinel* (Baltimore), April 1, 1979.

Munk, Erika. "Subversion by Concept," review of *Lear*, *Village Voice*, February 6, 1990, pp. 95, 98.

Novick, Julius. "Akalaitis's Shakespeare Mixes Good Faith and Cheap Laughs," *New York Observer*, June 12, 1989, p. 15.

Disclaimer to editing of May 7 review of *Don Juan*, *Village Voice*, May 14, 1979.

"*Don Juan* Half-Met," review of *Don Juan* directed by Liviu Ciulei, *Village Voice*, May 7, 1979, pp. 103–4.

"Don Wan," review of *Don Juan* directed by Richard Foreman, *Village Voice*, July 13, 1982, pp. 82–3.

Review of *Dionysus in '69*, *Nation*, July 8, 1968, p. 29.

Oliver, Edith. Review of *The Comedy of Errors* directed by Robert Woodruff, *New Yorker*, June 15, 1987, p. 72.

Review of *Oedipus* directed by Richard Schechner, *New Yorker*, December 19, 1977, p. 114.

Porter, Andrew. Review of *Così fan Tutte* directed by Peter Sellars, *New Yorker*, August 11, 1986, pp. 81–2.

Review of *Don Giovanni* directed by Peter Sellars, *New Yorker*, August 10, 1987, pp. 66–9.

Review of *Le Nozze di Figaro* directed by Peter Sellars, *New Yorker*, August 15, 1988, pp. 63–4.

Review of Peter Sellars's Mozart–da Ponte Trilogy, *New Yorker*, August 21, 1989, pp. 74–5.

Rabkin, Gerald. Review of *Oedipus* directed by Richard Schechner, *Soho Weekly News*, December 8, 1977.

Bibliography

Rich, Alan. "Oedipus Jones," review of *The Gospel at Colonus*, *Newsweek*, 21 November 1983, p. 105.

Rich, Frank. "Fantasy *Cymbeline* Set Long After Shakespeare," *New York Times*, June 1, 1989.

"Mabou Mines Creates a *King Lear* All Its Own," *New York Times*, January 20, 1990, p. C5.

Review of *Don Juan* directed by Richard Foreman, *New York Times*, July 2, 1982, p. C3.

Review of *The Gospel at Colonus*, *New York Times*, March 25, 1988, p. III: 5.

Rockwell, John. Review of *Cosí fan Tutte* directed by Peter Sellars, *New York Times*, July 18, 1986, p. C26.

"A Sellarized *Figaro* in First Performance," *New York Times*, July 15, 1988, p. C3.

Rousuck, J. Wynn. "*Tartuffe* Is Brilliant, but Borders on Crazy," review of *Tartuffe* directed by Lucian Pintilié, *Washington Sun*, March 15, 1985, pp. 1B, 12B.

Said, Edward. Review of *Cosí fan Tutte* directed by Peter Sellars, *Nation*, September 18, 1989, pp. 289–91.

Review of *Don Giovanni* directed by Peter Sellars, *Nation*, September 26, 1987, pp. 318–20.

Saville, Jonathan. "The Wright Interpretation," review of *The Misanthrope* directed by Garland Wright, *San Diego Reader*, June 25, 1987.

Schechner, Richard. Review of *The House of Atreus*, *Educational Theatre Journal* 21 (March 1969): 101.

Simon, John. Review of *The Comedy of Errors* directed by Robert Woodruff, *New York Magazine*, June 15, 1987, p. 91.

Smith, Michael. Review of *Hamlet* directed by Joseph Papp, *Village Voice*, January 4, 1968, pp. 29, 31, 39.

Sorgenfrei, Carol Fisher. Review of *King Lear* directed by Robert Wilson, workshop production in Los Angeles, May 1985. *Theatre Journal* 37 (December 1985): 496–8.

Steele, Mike. Review of *The Misanthrope* directed by Garland Wright, *Minneapolis Star and Tribune*, June 12, 1987, pp. 1C–2C.

"Theatre Review," *Theatre Journal* 1–40 (1949–88), inclusive.

Waldemar, Carla. "The Glorious Guiding Light," review of *The Misanthrope* directed by Garland Wright, *Twin Cities Reader*, June 17, 1987.

Wallach, Allan. Review of *Don Juan* directed by Richard Foreman, *Newsday*, July 2, 1982, p. II/15.

Watt, Douglas. Review of *Don Juan* directed by Richard Foreman, *Daily News*, July 2, 1982, p. F5.

Wilson, Edwin, "Tiresome Molière," review of *Don Juan* directed by Richard Foreman, *Wall Street Journal*, July 9, 1982, p. 17.

Winer, Laurie. "McNally and Shakespeare," review of *Cymbeline* directed by Jo-

Anne Akalaitis (with *The Lisbon Traviata*), *Wall Street Journal*, June 9, 1989, p. A9.

Winer, Linda. "Gospel That's a Long Way from Home," *New York Newsday*, March 25, 1988, p. III/11.

"The Whys Have It in *Cymbeline*," review of *Cymbeline* directed by JoAnne Akalaitis, *Newsday*, June 1, 1989, pp. II: 5, 11.

Zarilli, Phillip. "Theatre Report: Richard Schechner's *Richard's Lear*," *The Drama Review* 92 (Winter 1981): 92–6.

IV. UNPUBLISHED MANUSCRIPTS

Brooks, Colette. "'The folly of the fiction': *Cymbeline* Reconsidered," Graduate School Paper. New Haven: Yale University School of Drama, [1977–8]. Photocopy.

Green, Amy. Rehearsal log for *The Miser* directed by Andrei Serban. American Repertory Theatre, Cambridge, Mass., March-May 1989. Notebook.

V. ORIGINAL INTERVIEWS

Akalaitis, JoAnne. Interview by the author, January 3, 1990, by telephone. Tape recording.

Mosher, Gregory. Interview by the author, April 30, 1990, by telephone. Tape recording.

Papp, Joseph. Conversation with the author, May 4, 1989. City University Graduate Center, New York.

Rabkin, Gerald. Conversations with the author, throughout 1989–90, by telephone.

Schechner, Richard. Interview by the author, November 22, 1993, New York City. Tape recording.

Sellars, Peter. Interview by the author, November 5, 1989, by telephone. Tape recording.

Serban, Andrei. Interviews by the author during rehearsals for *The Miser*, March–May 1989. American Repertory Theatre, Cambridge & Somerville, Mass.

Solomon, Alisa. Interview by the author, June 19, 1990. New York, New York. Tape recording.

VI. LIVE PERFORMANCES

Akalaitis, JoAnne. Director. *Cymbeline* by William Shakespeare. New York Shakespeare Festival. Public Theatre, New York, June 1989.

Antoon, A. J. Director. *The Taming of the Shrew* by William Shakespeare. New York Shakespeare Festival. Delacorte Theatre, Central Park, New York, July 1990.

Breuer, Lee. Director. *The Gospel at Colonus* adapted from Sophocles by Lee Breuer and Bob Telson. Brooklyn Academy of Music. The James Doolittle Theatre, Los Angeles, June 1984.

    Director. *Lear*, based on *King Lear* by William Shakespeare. Mabou Mines. Triplex Theatre, New York, January 1990.

    Director. Scenes from *Lear:* A Work in Progress. Mabou Mines. Storm King, New York, July 1988.

Curchak, Fred. *Stuff As Dreams Are Made On*. Brooklyn Academy of Music, Brooklyn, New York, November 1989.

Sellars, Peter. Director. *Cosí fan Tutte* by Wolfgang Amadeus Mozart and Lorenzo da Ponte. Pepsico Summerfare, Purchase, New York, July–August 1989.

    Director. *Don Giovanni* by Wolfgang Amadeus Mozart and Lorenzo da Ponte. Pepsico Summerfare, Purchase, New York, July–August 1989.

    Director. *Le Nozze di Figaro* by Wolfgang Amadeus Mozart and Lorenzo da Ponte. Pepsico Summerfare, Purchase, New York, July–August 1989.

Serban, Andrei. Director. *Fragments of a Trilogy: Electra, Medea, and The Trojan Women*. New York: La Mama ETC, 1977, and revival; 1987.

    Director. *The Miser* by Molière. American Repertory Theatre, Cambridge, Mass., May 1989.

Wajda, Andrzej. Director. *Hamlet IV*. The Stary Theatre of Cracow. Pepsico Summerfare, Purchase, New York, August 1989.

Woodruff, Robert. Director. *The Comedy of Errors*. Lincoln Center Theatre. Vivian Beaumont Theater, Lincoln Center, New York, June 1987.

VII.   VIDEORECORDINGS

Akalaitis, JoAnne. Director. *Cymbeline* by William Shakespeare. New York Shakespeare Festival, Public Theatre, New York, 1989. Archival videorecording. Theatre on Film and Tape, Billy Rose Theatre Collection, New York Public Library Performing Arts Research Center at Lincoln Center. Videocassette.

    Director. *Endgame* by Samuel Beckett. American Repertory Theatre, Cambridge, Mass. Archival videorecording, 1984. Theatre on Film and Tape, Billy Rose Theatre Collection, New York Public Library Performing Arts Research Center at Lincoln Center. Videocassette.

Breuer, Lee. Director. *The Gospel at Colonus,* adapted from Sophocles by Lee Breuer and Bob Telson. Brooklyn Academy of Music. Archival videorecording, 1980. Jerome Robbins Archives of the Recorded Moving Image, Dance Research Collection, New York Public Library Performing Arts Research Center at Lincoln Center, New York. Videocassette.

Grotowski, Jerzy. Director. *Akropolis*. Polish Laboratory Theatre [as shown on "Camera Three," CBS], 1969. Theatre on Film and Tape, Billy Rose Theatre Collection, New York Public Library Performing Arts Research Center at Lincoln Center. Videocassette.

Serban, Andrei. Director. *Fragments of a Trilogy*. La Mama ETC. Archival video-recording, 1976. Segments also shown on "Camera Three" [CBS], 1974. Theatre on Film and Tape, Billy Rose Theatre Collection, New York Public Library Performing Arts Research Center at Lincoln Center. Videocassette.

Woodruff, Robert. Director. *The Comedy of Errors* by William Shakespeare. Lincoln Center Theatre. Broadcast on "Live from Lincoln Center," PBS, 1987. Video-recording. Theatre Resource Collection, Department of Speech and Theatre, Kingsborough Community College, City University of New York. Videocassette.

Wright, Garland. Director. *Don Juan* by Molière. Denver Center Theatre Company. Archival videorecording, 1985. Theatre on Film and Tape, Billy Rose Theatre Collection, New York Public Library Performing Arts Research Center at Lincoln Center. Videocassette.

Director. *The Misanthrope* by Molière. The Guthrie Theatre, Minneapolis. Archival videorecording, 1987. Theatre on Film and Tape, Billy Rose Theatre Collection, New York Public Library Performing Arts Research Center at Lincoln Center. Videocassette.

INDEX

Photographs are indicated by page numbers in italics.

217

Index

218

Index

219

Index

225